NEOCLASSICAL
POLITICAL ECONOMY

NEOCLASSICAL POLITICAL ECONOMY

The Analysis of Rent-Seeking
and DUP Activities

Edited by
DAVID C. COLANDER

BALLINGER PUBLISHING COMPANY
Cambridge, Massachusetts
A Subsidiary of Harper & Row, Publishers, Inc.

International Standard Book Number: 0-88410-999-2

Library of Congress Catalog Card Number: 84-11124

Printed in the United States of America

Library of Congress Cataloging in Publication Data

Main entry under title:

Neoclassical political economy.

Based on papers originally presented at the Christian A. Johnson
Conference on Economic Affairs held in Middlebury, Vermont, in
April 1983.
   Includes index.
   1. Neoclassical school of economics—Congresses. 2. Rent—
Congresses. 3. Monopolies—Congresses. 4. Competition—
Congresses. I. Colander, David C. II. Christian A. Johnson
Conference on Economic Affairs (1983 ; Middlebury, Vt.)
III. Title: Rent-seeking and DUP activities.
HB98.2.N46 1984   330.15'5   84-11124
ISBN 0-88410-999-2

To the memory of
Christian A. Johnson
whose generosity made possible
the conference upon which this volume is based.

CONTENTS

LIST OF FIGURES

LIST OF TABLES

ACKNOWLEDGMENTS

This book, more than most, is a group effort. The papers in this volume were originally presented at the Christian A. Johnson Conference on Economic Affairs held in Middlebury, Vermont, in April 1983. Without that conference there would have been no book, and special thanks must go to all those who attended and supported the conference. Mrs. Wilmont Kidd, President of the Christian A. Johnson Endeavor Foundation, goes high on the list. The Foundation not only made the conference possible; it also made my being at Middlebury possible. The former, I can say, has greatly benefited Middlebury College; I hope the latter has, also. Mrs. Kidd and the Foundation have done more than provide financial backing. They have also maintained a strong interest in the welfare of Middlebury and in the success of the conference. For that, I, the Economics Department, and the entire Middlebury community heartily thank her.

Running a conference is not an easy task and without the tremendous support of many individuals, it would not have run at all. Two people stand out: Sheila Cassin, the Economics Department secretary, and Janet Flory, the director of the Conference Center. Without them there would have been only confusion.

As will quickly become evident, this volume does not represent a mere re-printing of conference papers. The publisher would not have allowed it and I would not have wanted to do so. Most papers went through extensive revisions in order to make the papers fit together and complement one another. To all those involved I offer a special thank you.

When you are giving authors as much grief as I gave them, you need co-conspirators, and I had a number of them. These include members of my senior seminar at Middlebury, who critiqued the papers extensively. I learned much from them and I thank them.

After the class got through with the papers, other people had their go, including two anonymous referees who provided many useful suggestions; Carol Franco, senior editor of Ballinger; Cynthia Insolio Benn, the copy editor; and Dave Barber. Besides the Ballinger contingent I also had a secret weapon—Helen Reiff, who helped edit and organize the volume. There are, of course, many others to thank but the publisher tells me the preface cannot be a book.

David Colander
Middlebury, Vermont
April 1984

INTRODUCTION

"RENT-SEEKING" AND NEOCLASSICAL POLITICAL ECONOMY

Man has almost constant occasion for the help of his brethren, and it is in vain for him to expect it from their benevolence only. He will be more likely to prevail, if he can interest their self-love in his favour, and show them that it is for their own advantage to do for him what he requires of them. Whoever offers to another a bargain of any kind proposes to do this. Give me that which I want, and you shall have this which you want, is the meaning of every such offer; and it is in this manner that we obtain from one another the far greater part of those good offices which we stand in need of. It is not from the benevolence of the butcher, the brewer, or the baker, that we expect our dinner, but from their regard to their own interest. We address ourselves, not to their humanity but to their self-love, and never talk to them of our own necessities but of their advantages.

This quotation from Adam Smith is probably the most famous in economics; it is the basis of the *invisible hand* theorem that underlies many, if not most, economic policy prescriptions. Leave the economy alone; competition among self-seeking individuals guides it in the desired direction. But Adam Smith also wrote:

People of the same trade seldom meet together, even for amusement and diversion, but that the conversation ends in a conspiracy against the public, or in some contrivance to raise price.

1

This quotation shows another side of the economic process, one in which the invisible hand does not seem to be working. Individuals left to their own devices continually try to escape competition in a process that has been called *rent-seeking* but that also goes by a variety of other names—cartelization, monopolization, or DUP (directly unproductive profit-seeking) activities. Not only does the invisible hand guide people toward activities beneficial to society, it also has an underside; individuals following their own self-interest continually attempt to see that the invisible hand does not work. Stephen Magee aptly calls this aspect of human behavior the *invisible foot*. If one follows that analogy, competition might be described as a game in which invisible feet are stomping on invisible hands.

Traditional neoclassical general equilibrium theory has focused on the invisible hand aspect of competition and has elegantly explained the conditions under which self-seeking individuals unwittingly serve society's goals. Frank Hahn (1980: p. 123), in assessing general equilibrium theory, stated the following:

> [We are] near the end of that road. Now that we have got there we find it less enlightening than we had expected. The reason is partly that the world has moved on and is no longer as decentralized as it used to be, and partly that the road we pursued is excessively narrow and made—we now feel—with too little allowance for the wild and varied terrain it had to traverse. We have certainly arrived at an orderly destination, but it looks increasingly likely that we cannot rest there.

In response to such assessments, the research program of economists has evolved into one exploring broader implications—not only studying when the invisible hand works, but also studying when and why it does not. The chapters of this book are part of a broader research program that might be appropriately called *neoclassical political economy.*

This new research program involves the analysis of individuals' attempts to escape the invisible hand of the market and to redirect policy proposals for their own advantage. Whereas traditional neoclassical welfare economics assumes government an exogenous force, trying to do good, new neoclassical political economists argue that government is at least partially endogenous and the policies it institutes will reflect vested interests in society.

The difference between the old and new analysis can be seen by considering the likely effects of market disequilibrium. Traditional neoclassical analysis tells us that whenever there is excess supply, price will fall; whenever there is excess demand, price will rise. That is the invisible hand at work. The new neoclassical political economists argue that simultaneously, and just as predictably, individuals will organize to prevent price from rising or falling in order to secure or maintain rents. That is the invisible foot at work. One can understand how the economy really works only by simultaneously considering both of these activities.

Traditional neoclassical economic analysis assumes a specific set of perfectly competitive institutions. The new political economy theorists challenge whether the "perfectly competitive equilibrium" is stable. For it to be so, all individuals would need to accept passively the institutions and government policies upon which it is based. If, however, the marginal gain from changing the institution is less than the marginal gain from maintaining it, that competitive equilibrium will not be stable, even if it existed at some point in history.

The new neoclassical political economists argue that under reasonable assumptions about organizational costs, we would expect the competitive equilibrium in a variety of markets to evolve into an imperfectly competitive form. At the perfectly competitive margin, the incentive to protect the competitive equilibrium is often small and the potential rent from cartelization is large. Thus, even though the competitive equilibrium is Pareto optimal, it will not be freely chosen by most societies. For this reason perfect competition cannot serve as the paradigm for economics.

The foregoing arguments are hardly novel. That makes it all the more amazing that the logical next question—What type of equilibrium will be attained?—has never been formally considered. It is that question that this book addresses.

HISTORY OF RENT-SEEKING ANALYSIS

Economists' informal concern with rent-seeking activities has existed for a long time. Classical economists' conception of competition had a rent-seeking flavor. In their view, individuals were continually trying to build up monopolies and as they did so they created quasi-rents or monopolistic profits. The desire to share in those rents led others to enter the industry, pushing the price down, if not to the perfectly competitive level, at least to a level close to the competitive level. For classical economists, the competitive equilibrium was a dynamic one in which there was an equal building up and breaking down of monoplies.

Despite their view that monopolization was inevitable, classical economists generally advocated a *laissez faire* policy. That policy did not follow directly from their theoretical analysis; it was based in part on an empirical judgment about the goals and effectiveness of government. They saw government primarily as a tool by which individuals established and protected monopolies, and they believed that without government intervention the competitive process would work reasonably well. If the government stayed out of the competitive process, eventually competition would work. In their view government intervention generally made things worse.

Pierro Sraffa's 1926 article "The Laws of Returns under Competitive Conditions" challenged the classical economists' view that monopolies were self-limiting and laid the groundwork for a variety of important innovations in economic theory. Sraffa argued that with decreasing costs, the tendency was toward monopoly or a single firm's domination of an industry. Once established, the firm could effectively protect its monopoly on the basis of lower costs. New entry, even without government protection, would be difficult, and the competitive process, while it might eventually work, would not work quickly enough. Sraffa's view was clearly not the form of dynamic competition that classical theorists had in mind.

In response to Sraffa's article, Jacob Viner (1931) reformulated cost curve analysis making the distinction between short-run cost curves subject to diminishing returns and long-run cost curves governed by economies of scale. Thereafter, mainstream economic analysis focused on the short-run analysis, which was designed to avoid Sraffa's criticisms, leaving the long run to fend for itself. Simultaneously, the concept of competition evolved from the *competitive process* view to a more formalistic view of perfect competition.[1] With this transformation economists stopped asking the messy question of whether the "eventually" in the competitive process was fast enough and moved on to refining the analysis of the perfectly competitive model.

Attempts by Robinson (1933) and Chamberlain (1933) to integrate the concepts of monopoly and competition did not become part of the theoretical core of economic theory, and further development of the perfectly competitive model led to the refinement of concepts of efficiency, welfare, and general equilibrium. Those refinements elegantly showed how perfectly competitive markets led to "optimal results." The result was what Kenneth Boulding called "the celestial mechanics of a non-existent world."

Despite a general acceptance of the limited applicability of the perfectly competitive model, it remained central to the mainstream economic model and served both as a reference point for welfare considerations and as a framework for analysis. There were, of course, critics. Austrians criticized the neoclassical model's failure to consider the competitive process and to take account of the role of the entrepreneur. Post-Keynesians criticized the model's failure to incorporate an analysis of time and to make reasonable assumptions about corporate practices; institutionalists criticized the model's failure to recognize explicitly the institutional structure within which individuals operated; game theorists criticized the model's limited concept of equilibrium; while public choice theorists criticized the model's failure to incorporate the economic human being's political behavior.

Despite the myriad complaints the traditional neoclassical model survived and even flourished. Even when estimates of welfare losses from deviations from competition proved to be so small (0.5 percent or 1 percent of total GNP) that a cynic might ask: Why go through all that analysis for such a little loss?, most economists merely shrugged their shoulders and said: It might be irrelevant, but it is beautiful. Actually, a cynic did not ask the question; Robert Mundell did when he wrote: "Unless there is a thorough theoretical examination of the validity of the tools upon which these studies (of losses from monopoly) are founded ... someone will inevitably draw the conclusion that economics has ceased to be important" (1962: p. 622).

Gordon Tullock (1967) responded to this question, answering somewhat vaguely but nonetheless provocatively, that the loss from monopoly, tariffs, and taxes is much larger than is conventionally measured. It includes not only the Harberger triangle, but also the entire amount of the tax, tariff, or monopoly profit. His reasoning was as follows: Individuals would compete for the rents or lobby for the revenues, and (assuming competition in rent-seeking) it is worthwhile for each person to spend up to the amount times the probability that he will receive the profit or tax. He argued that combined, individuals will compete the entire rents or profits away. With this article, Tullock began what might be called the public choice branch of rent-seeking analysis, with many of the relevant articles included in a 1980 book, *Toward a Theory of the Rent-Seeking Society*, edited by James Buchanan, Robert Tollison, and Gordon Tullock.[2]

Two central ideas run through most of this public choice literature: First, that rent-seeking occurs primarily through the political process and, second, that the best way to limit rent-seeking is to limit government. Thus, it shares many of the same views of government with the classical economists, and the analysis was a natural extension of the public choice analysis of regulation.

The public choice literature was not alone in its interest in rent-seeking ideas. In 1974 Anne Krueger considered why developing countries seemed not to grow. Her argument was similar to Tullock's, but she developed it in a much more formal model and added the first empirical estimates of the losses from quotas. She argued that individuals compete for the rights to import in order to win the monopoly rents that derived from them and that such activities are a loss to society that must be considered in the analysis.

In many ways it was natural that much of the new literature in neoclassical political economy developed in reference to international trade issues. Economists have long recognized that groups lobby for tariffs and quotas. Moreover, probably more than in any other area, economists are united in their support of free trade. What is surprising is that economists had not previously integrated that analysis into their formal model.

With the article in which she coined the phrase *rent-seeking* Krueger prompted a considerable literature on rent-seeking in international trade, and in 1982 Bhagwati wrote that "in the area of international trade-theoretic analysis in particular, it would hardly be an exaggeration to say that this has been among the few leading topics of research recently" (1982c, p. 988).

Perhaps more than any other economist, Jagdish Bhagwati has extended that analysis and recognized its potential. He pointed out that while Krueger's model was limited to the rents resulting from quotas (hence the name *rent-seeking*), the issue was far more general. There could also be tariff seeking, revenue seeking, and a variety of other restriction-seeking activities, all of which he classified under the general heading *directly unproductive profit-seeking* (DUP) *activities*.

To model all these activities formally and simultaneously is a formidable job that is still in its infancy. In a seminal paper Brock and Magee (1978) began the general analysis of the political economy of tariffs when they studied the issue in a game-theoretic framework. They argued that the tariff is endogenously determined, with the costs of the endogenous tariff shifting the production possibility frontier inward. Bhagwati and Srinivasan (1980) approached the issue differently and assumed that the tariff was independently set up but that the revenues were not divided according to an initially specified rule, rather resource-using revenue-seeking activity occurred in the distribution of the revenue. Findlay and Wellisz (Chapter 6) have further refined the model and developed a general equilibrium model with endogenous political activity. In Chapter 1 Bhagwati, Brecher and Srinivasan reiterate a suggestion of Magee and Brock (1983) that eventually the international trade model will become a $2 \times 2 \times 2 \times 2$ model (which Findlay appropriately labeled the 2×4 model) with completely endogenous rent-, revenue-, and tariff-seeking. (If it does, as it surely should, I am sure that students will rue the day Anne Krueger thought up the term.)

The public choice and international trade fields are not the only ones evolving into the new neoclassical political economy. Although not explicitly formulated within a rent-seeking framework, Mancur Olson's analysis exemplifies the new political economy. In his classic 1965 book, *The Logic of Collective Choice*, Olson extended neoclassical economic ideas to politics. His recent book, *The Rise and Decline of Nations* (1982), extends his earlier analysis and considers the implications of rent-seeking on economic institutions. Olson argues that collective action is as natural as individual action, and once the "public goods" aspect is overcome, special interest groups will develop.

Using this simple analysis, he extends his theory of collective choice to explain why growth rates differ among societies. His key explanation is that the process of rent-seeking (individuals forming into groups to lobby for their specific interests) places restrictions and constraints on society and, as it does so, reduces the society's growth rate. He argues that unless a country experiences a sudden institutional change such as a war (some have called such changes "Olson shocks") that breaks up these groups, "institutional sclerosis" will set in: the economy's growth will become more and more sluggish and will eventually stop.

Another field that has been important in the development of neoclassical political economy is economic history. By considering the motivations of rent-seeking individuals, economic historians have provided new insights and interpretations of important historical events. For example, in Chapter 13 Gary Anderson and Robert Tollison argue that the child labor laws were not the result of well-meaning individuals' good intentions but were a reflection of skilled workers' attempts to prevent competition and to maintain their own rents. Besides providing such insights, economic historians such as Douglass North have considered the evolution of institutions in response to political pressures, providing explanations why particular institutions developed at certain times. Those institutions, in turn, fostered or hindered economic growth. Rent-seeking entered in because it was individuals' economic needs and desires that determined which institutions would be set up. Their analysis has become so important that it has acquired the name, *the new economic history.*

THE ROLE OF THIS BOOK

Obviously, there is much more to be said about the new neoclassical political economy. Important works have been left out, such as the work of Gary Becker (1983) and Assar Lindbeck (1976). However, the preceding section should be sufficient to give the reader a feel for this new literature. It should fill in some gaps in the excellent summaries of Tollison (1983), Bhagwati (1982c), and Magee (Chapter 3) and serve as an introduction to the chapters of this book, which are both an extension of the previous analysis and a cross-fertilization of ideas of the various schools and approaches.

The role of this book and the conference upon which it is based is to place the rent-seeking arguments in broader perspective and to consider their policy implications. The book includes leading advocates of the various groups and provides some insight into the differences and similarities of the various schools of thought.

The differences between the international trade approach and the public choice approach are in large part methodological as opposed to substantive. Trade theorists are formalists; they think in terms of Rybczynski lines, Metzler paradoxes, and x-by-x general equilibrium models. Public choice theorists are nonformalists and integrate far more ideas into their implicit model, but sometimes it is difficult to ascertain precisely what their model is. As Stephen Magee has remarked, these differences offer significant potential gains from trade.

Of the substantive issues differentiating the two approaches, probably the most basic question (but also a somewhat irrelevant one) is what to call the subject. Everyone agreed that the name *rent-seeking* was not ideal, but there was no agreement on an alternative. Most public choice theorists were willing to continue to use *rent-seeking* for lack of a better alternative. Many of the international trade theorists preferred the term *directly unproductive profit-seeking* (or DUP) *activities.* This split in usage was a bit ironic, since the term *rent-seeking* comes from the international trade literature.

One of the problems with the term *rent-seeking* is that Krueger's seminal paper limited its concern to the rents accruing from quotas. If rents were only returns to quotas, then other political behavior would require other nomenclature. Following this logic, the international trade approach has an analysis of such activities as monopoly-seeking, tariff-seeking, and revenue-seeking, all of which fall under the umbrella *DUP activities.*

The public choice branch of economics adopted the term *rent-seeking* primarily because it was catchy, but they used it in a broader context, in which *rents* refer to all income obtained from trade restrictions. That usage seems reasonable on the surface but leaves numerous more substantive problems. For example, as Mancur Olson has pointed out, rents can accrue not only to unproductive trade restrictions; they can also accrue to productive or profit-seeking activities, such as when a firm lowers its costs. Such cost-reducing activities create rents but do not make society worse off. A second problem was pointed out by Bhagwati and Srinivasan (1982); even seemingly unproductive activities can be "output-enhancing" when one considers rent-seeking in a second-best context. Where some trade restrictions exist, the addition of others can actually improve society's welfare.

Bhagwati and Srinivasan's point raises even more fundamental issues. Whatever we call these activities, how do we know which ones are unproductive or rent-seeking, and how do we differentiate these activities from productive activities? In answering this question, some clarification of terminology is helpful. While most of the literature discusses waste, output, productive and unproductive activities in terms of physical output, these concepts are merely proxies for social welfare. Social welfare, not physical output, is the relevant concept and people must judge activities according to their own social welfare functions. Because each individual has his or her own social welfare function, what is rent-seeking to one person might not be rent-seeking to another. The only activities unambiguously under the rent-seeking umbrella are those activities all possible social welfare functions classify as welfare reducing, a set of activities that is likely to be rather small.

What prevents this restriction from reducing the set of rent-seeking activities to the null set is an implicit assumption of the form of the allowable social welfare function. Only Kantian social welfare functions are allowed, in which one must judge distributional effects by their general rather than their specific distributional consequences. Thus, one could easily call one's own attempt to lobby for a tariff *rent-seeking* and hence social welfare reducing, even though the tariff's introduction would increase one's private utility.

Two additional points extend the range of rent-seeking activities. Since most individuals favor income equality, activities with no proegalitarian result can be classified as rent-seeking without violating most social welfare functions. Second, many activities have ambiguous distributional consequences and, for these, output is a reasonably good proxy for social welfare. These limitations expand the set of activities that can reasonably be called rent-seeking into a relatively large set. These include most attempts of trade groups to achieve monopolies, quotas, tariffs, and many, but not all, regulatory restrictions.

A third substantive point that is nicely brought out in this book is the role of ideology and morality in the new neoclassical political economy. Whereas traditional neoclassical economics has enormous difficulty even formulating the problem of ideology, the new neoclassical political economics recognizes its importance, although how to include it in the analysis remains in dispute.

Such disputes are signs of progress. The substantive problems are problems with all normative or policy prescriptive economics. Rent-seeking analysis merely brings the issues into the open and requires economists to specify precisely why they consider certain activities bad.

THE MEASUREMENT OF RENT-SEEKING LOSSES

Once the term is defined, the logical next question is: How large are the welfare losses from rent-seeking? Anne Krueger (1974) and Richard Posner (1975) both estimated these losses; Krueger estimating a loss of 7.3 percent of national income for India and 15 percent of national income attributable to the rents of import licenses alone for Turkey, while Posner estimated total welfare losses in the United States from regulatory actions at 3 percent of gross national product and argued that these constitute the primary losses in the economy.

These early measurements of rents have been subject to a variety of both theoretical and empirical attacks. The assumption that the welfare loss equals the profit was challenged by Tullock (1980), and he demonstrated why there is no simple relationship between rents and the welfare loss from rent-seeking.

A second criticism of these early welfare loss measurements is that the analysis only considers certain aspects of rent-seeking. Rent-seeking activities are likely to occur in all transactions and bargaining. For example, in tax collection, individuals would find it worthwhile to spend up to the amount of the tax to avoid paying; once the revenue is collected, individuals are likely to spend up to the amount of government revenues to gain a share of that spending. Numerous other examples of rent-seeking exist. One need merely look at the myriad private restrictions in the economy, such as tenure for professors, corporate managers' appropriations of rents, and private enforcement of monopoly positions, to get a sense of the importance of private rent-seeking.

Ezra Mishan (1981), approaching the issue from a different perspective, has estimated the losses from "non-productive activities" in society at 50 percent of our total GNP, and there seems little doubt that with a bit of hand waving (which necessarily accompanies such estimates) the estimated welfare loss from rent-seeking could be increased to well over that and could approach 100 percent of total income.[3]

SUMMARY OF THE CHAPTERS

The preceding discussion loses much of the electricity and dissension that was evident at the Middlebury Conference on Economic Issues where these chapters were presented as papers. However, some of that electricity can be detected in the chapters, many of which have been substantially revised to reflect the conference discussion. The chapters fit neatly into five separate sections. Part I of this book provides an introduction to the subject and demonstrates both the diversity and similarity of approach of the various groups. Bhagwati, Brecher and Srinivasan's opening chapter, "DUP activities and Economic Theory," summarizes the state of development of the approach, asking the question, "How serious for economic theory as conventionally practiced is the systematic integration of DUP phenomena into our analysis?" They provide an excellent taxonomy of DUP categories and consider implications for both positive and normative analysis. Their conclusion that "the integration of DUP activities into theoretic analysis is a serious business" is representative of how important many of the participants believe the subject is.

Chapter 2, by Douglass North, relates the rent-seeking approach with the new economic history approach and Mancur Olson's approach. Besides providing an excellent overview of the three approaches, North also nicely captures the need to integrate the role of ideology into neoclassical political economy.[4] The final chapter in the introductory part, by Stephen Magee, surveys the endogenous tariff theory literature and provides an excellent background for the development of thought within the pure theory of international trade.

Not all economists are rent-seeking advocates (although they may all be rent-seekers). Part II includes the chapters of two critics of rent-seeking. Warren Samuels and Nicholas Mercuro's chapter, "A Critique of Rent-Seeking Theory," provides a scathing attack on what they find to be the "hidden biases" in some previous public choice rent-seeking literature. They argue that rent-seeking analysis is merely a mask for political ideology and that it "cannot properly and conclusively sustain many of the principal uses to which it has been put," or can do so only "on the basis of selective and . . . dubious, unrealistic and question begging assumptions." Their critique is representative of many institutionalists' reaction to rent-seeking. Rather than seeing it as a positive advance in which neoclassical economics is broadening its horizons by moving back to political economy, some institutionalists go beyond Samuels and Mecuro's position and see rent-seeking as an illicit intrusion of their turf, which in its simplicity loses almost all insight into the problem.

Michael McPherson's chapter, "Limits on Self-Seeking: The Role of Morality in Economic Life," similarly cautions rent-seekers not to become too enamored of their approach. He argues that society depends upon cooperation and self-imposed limits on self-seeking behavior, something with which neither traditional neoclassical economics nor rent-seeking analysis has adequately come to grips.

Given the proclivities of the profession, neoclassical political economy will only supplant traditional neoclassical economics if its insights can be captured in formal models. Part III considers the problems of modeling rent-seeking behavior. Chapter 6, by Ronald Findlay and Stanislaw Wellisz, "Toward a Model of Endogenous Rent-Seeking," formally sets up a two-sector small open general equilibrium model with a tariff formation function and determines a Cournot–Nash equilibrium. They neatly sidestep the issue of ideology with their tariff formation function, which includes various sectors' ideological preferences. This Cournot–Nash equilibrium incorporating political behavior provides an alternative to the competitive equilibrium of traditional neoclassical economics. Using their model they demonstrate how outcomes will vary given different political regimes, thereby highlighting the importance of including politics in the analysis. As Magee states in his summary to Chapter 3, this is an important contribution to the formal modeling of rent-seeking activities.

In Chapter 7, "Purchasing Monopoly," Harold Demsetz considers how the problem of monopolization or rent-seeking changes the normal analysis of competition and monopoly. He argues that traditional neoclassical theory has no theory of monopoly; it merely assumes it. By including an analysis of the process of monopolization in the normal partial equilibrium model, Demsetz shows how the results are changed and offers the beginning of a theory of market structure. In "Coalitions and Macroeconomics," Olson and I focus on the implications of his theory for macroeconomics, arguing that macroeconomic theory has failed to come to grips with the institutional constraints placed upon the economy by such collective action. We argue that there is a bias in the costs of lobbying, a bias that contributes to the inflationary pressures in the economy. We conclude our chapter by suggesting that tax-based incomes policies theoretically might offset such rent-seeking behavior. In Chapter 9, Elias Dinopoulos modifies the assumptions of full revenue-seeking that Bhagwati and Srinivasan (1980) used in their model of the optimal tariff in the presence of lobbying, demonstrating how the Bhagwati and Srinivasan result is thereby changed. He demonsrates that the optimum tariff depends on the fraction of the tariff lobbied for and on the elasticity of foreign reciprocal demand.

Part IV considers some applications and empirical tests of rent-seeking theory. In Chapter 10, Stanislaw Wellisz and Ronald Findlay use the theory to explain why protection is so high in most less developed countries. They argue that because of a bias in the costs of lobbying, protectionist forces generally win out over free trade forces.

In "Rent-Seeking and the Growth and Fluctuations of Nations," Frederic Pryor empirically tests Olson's thesis in what he calls "the great growth rate" and "the great growth retardation" contests. According to Pryor, the tests raise some disturbing questions about the theory, and while Olson's thesis "appears to obtain some verification . . . the results do not seem very impressive." Chapter 12, by William Brock and Stephen Magee, provides a possible explanation why Pryor's results were not especially supportive of Olson's theory. They present a model in which initially growth would be slower in the invisible hand (competitive) economy than it would be in the invisible foot (rent-seeking) economy. In general, they find no necessary relationship between growth rates and redistribution. They do, however, find that the propensity to redistribute increases with income and wealth, a finding that supplements Olson's arguments. Besides providing that explanation, their models demonstrate the complexity of drawing any empirical conclusions from the rent-seeking analysis.

The final chapter in Part IV, "A Rent-Seeking Explanation of the British Factory Acts," demonstrates another aspect of the rent-seeking approach. Looking at the development of the labor laws in England, Gary Anderson and Robert Tollison show how rent-seeking analysis can provide new ways of looking at history. They argue that contrary to conventional wisdom the Factory Acts were not "enlightened intervention" of the state; "they actually represented the mechanism by which skilled male operatives attempted to limit competition from alternative labor supplies."

A number of implications from rent-seeking analysis have been drawn about policy, especially by the public choice branch. Those implications are closely tied to the property rights and new economic history schools of thought and focus on the need to place restrictions on government activities to prevent rent-seeking. Other branches of rent-seeking analysis such as Mancur Olson's theory of collective choice, the international trade DUP analysis, and Lindbeck's endogenous politicians analysis take a much broader view of policy implications. Part V considers these issues.

Both sides are represented in this book. Chapter 14, by Kenneth Koford and me, "Taming the Rent-Seeker," presents a broad range of policy options, options that include both more and less government involvement. James Bennett and Thomas DiLorenzo's chapter, "Political Entrepreneurship and Reform of the Rent-Seeking Society," presents the public choice view in an analysis of how ingenious politicians have figured out ways around the balanced budget limitations. They end on a rather pessimistic note—even constitutional restrictions are evaded. Gordon Tullock offers a slightly more optimistic view in the next chapter, arguing that, while the gains to stopping rent-seeking are not very high for individual economists, neither are the costs, and that if all economists spend some time providing information to the general public, not only can we do well, we can also do a little good.

Precisely why self-seeking economists should care about doing good was an issue considered in Chapter 5, by McPherson. He argues that morality and a sense of commitment are a necessary part of any well-functioning society. If the basic rent-seeking model does not include the gains a society receives from cooperative actions, its policy recommendations might make society worse off. The problem that McPherson does not address is how a greater measure of this morality can be achieved.

As you read this book, it should be apparent that the conclusions that follow from the rent-seeking model are likely to be the subject of debate for some time to come. It is the hypothesis of many (but not all of the contributors to this book) that the neoclassical political economic paradigm is a dynamic new approach that is likely to improve both the way we teach economics and our understanding of economic policies. It is an area from which all the contribuors hope to derive significant rent in the future.

NOTES TO INTRODUCTION

1.   For a discussion of this development, see George Stigler (1957).
2.   An excellent review of the public choice rent-seeking literature was written by Robert Tollison (1982).
3.   Obviously, such estimates would go too far; there are a few productive activities left in today's society, but most would agree that rent-seeking is both a large and a major growth industry. In examining these losses, one must remember that, once widespread rent-seeking is considered, care must be taken to avoid double counting; if there are rents in rent-seeking, the actual loss is reduced.
4.   These criticisms of rent-seeking analysis are reiterated in Chapter 6, where Findlay and Wellisz argue that in order to arrive at a Cournot–Nash equilibrium, the ideology must be made explicit; they are reiterated also, in a different way, in both Chapter 4, by Samuels and Mercuro, and in Chapter 5, by McPherson.

RENT-SEEKING
The New Political Economy

1 DUP ACTIVITIES AND ECONOMIC THEORY

Jagdish N. Bhagwati, Richard A. Brecher, and T. N. Srinivasan

Recently, several economists have directed their talents to examining the impact of what have been termed *directly-unproductive profit-seeking* (DUP) activities (Bhagwati 1982c). Among the more prominent such contributors, distinguished by different schools of thought, are (1) Buchanan, Tullock, and other important members of the public choice school, with their major work now conveniently collected in Buchanan, Tollison, and Tullock (1980) and reviewed well in Tollison (1982); (2) Bhagwati, Findlay, Hansen, Krueger, Magee, Srinivasan, Wellisz, and other international economists, whose work is reviewed and systematized in Bhagwati (1982c) and Magee (Chapter 3); (3) Becker (1983), Peltzman, Posner, Stigler, and other members of the Chicago school, whose notable work is variously available; and (4) Lindbeck (1976), whose influential work on "endogenous politicians" is widely known.

The quantity and variety of this work suggest its importance but, to date, no one has examined just how important it is. Thus, this chapter examines the ambitious question: How serious for economic theory, as conventionally practiced, is the systematic integration of DUP phenomena into our analysis?

The first section defines DUP activities and offers a taxonomy of DUP categories or types that will serve our later analysis. The subsequent sections consider the implications of different DUP categories for positive analysis and address welfare or normative implications.

DUP ACTIVITIES: CONCEPT AND TAXONOMY

The phenomena addressed in this book share one essential characteristic. They all represent ways of seeking profits (income) by undertaking directly unproductive activities. That is, they yield pecuniary returns but produce no goods or services that enter a conventional utility function directly or indirectly. Insofar as such activities use real resources, they result in a contraction of the availability set open to the economy. Tariff-seeking lobbying, tariff evasion, and premium seeking for given import licenses, for example, are all privately profitable activities. However, their direct output is zero in terms of the flow of goods and services entering a conventional utility function. Tariff seeking yields pecuniary income by changing the tariff and hence factor rewards; evasion of a tariff yields pecuniary income by exploiting the differential price between legal (tariff-bearing) imports and illegal (tariff-evading) imports; and premium seeking yields pecuniary income from the premiums on import licenses. (Krueger's (1974) analysis of what she termed *rent-seeking* activities relates to a subset of the broad class of these DUP activities; she is concerned with the lobbying activities triggered by different licensing practices of governments.[1])

From the viewpoint of the analysis presented below, DUP activities can be categorized as endogenous or exogenous.[2] Endogenous DUP activity results from the interplay of the DUP acitvity with the otherwise orthodox economic specification of the "pure" economic system. Exogenous DUP activity is embodied in a model where the policy can be *exogenously* specified while the DUP activity is endogenous to that policy. Examples of the former, using tariff theory, are models where the tariff is endogenously determined; examples of the latter are models where a tariff, exogenously specified to be in place, leads to seeking for the revenues resulting from the tariff, and models where the tariff is evaded. The former class of DUP activities raise deeper questions for economic analysis than the latter, as we will contend.

DUP ACTIVITIES AND POSITIVE ANALYSIS

Exogenous Policy

When the policy that induces DUP activity is exogenously specified, the implications of such DUP activity for positive analysis are tantamount to introducing an essentially nontraded sector with zero output but positive inputs into the formal model. Depending on the problem and the model, such a specification alters the analytical conclusions and the policy intuitions derived therefrom. We illustrate this by briefly considering two recent DUP-theoretic analyses in tariff and transfer theory: one on revenue seeking, by Bhagwati and Srinivasan (1980), and one on transfer seeking, by Bhagwati, Brecher, and Hatta (forthcoming).

Revenue Seeking and the Metzler Paradox. Conventional trade theory tells us that, provided suitable convexity assumptions are satisfied, a small country will find that a tariff necessarily increases the domestic price and output of the protected good. The Metzler paradox is that, for a large country (one that can influence its terms of trade), the tariff leads to such an improvement in the international terms of trade that the tariff-inclusive domestic price of the importable good falls and hence the importable good is paradoxically deprotected. We thus have the Metzler *price* paradox and hence what we can call, the Metzler *production* paradox, in the conventional 2 × 2 model of trade theory.

The introduction of revenue seeking, as Bhagwati and Srinivasan (1980) have shown, allows us to obtain the Metzler production paradox, even if the Metzler price paradox is eliminated by assuming a small country. To see why, consider Figure 1-1. $F_y F_x$ is the production possibility curve, and the world price is determined by the slope of the line through P^*. With free trade, this small economy would produce at P^*. With a tariff, production shifts to $\hat{P}$, implying that

Figure 1-1. Revenue Seeking and Metzler Production Paradox.

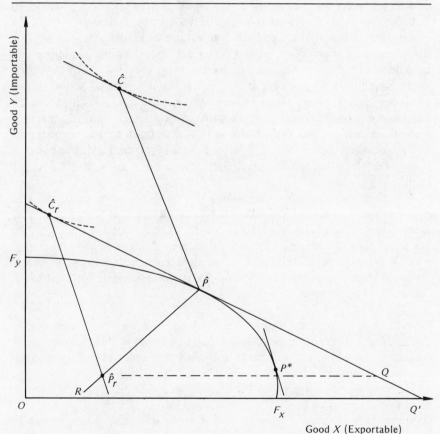

production of the importable good Y has increased, and consumption shifts to $\hat{C}$. However, if the tariff leads to DUP lobbying for the tariff revenues, then the production of one or both, goods must decline as resources are diverted toward revenue seeking. If we make the one-for-one assumption—that competitive revenue seeking leads to diversion of one dollar's worth of resources for every dollar's worth of revenue—then the equilibrium will shift such that consumption is at $\hat{C}_r$ on the national-income-at-market-price budget line $\hat{P}\hat{C}_r$, and production is at $\hat{P}_r$ where the world price line $\hat{C}_r\hat{P}_r$ intersects the generalized Rybczynski line $\hat{P}R$ (which reflects successive withdrawals of resources for revenue seeking, at the given tariff-inclusive prices). Trade is defined by $\hat{C}_r$ and $\hat{P}_r$; tariff revenue therefore is equal to the dashed distance $\hat{P}_r Q$, which in turn exactly equals (given the one-for-one assumption) the value of resources diverted to revenue seeking because it is equal to the value of reduced output of goods as measured by the difference between $\hat{P}$ and $\hat{P}_r$ at domestic prices. Revenue seeking, in this depiction, takes the form analytically of a nontraded activity that pays market-determined wages and rentals to factors (equal to those in goods production) and whose output is simply the revenue that is sought by the lobby.

An alternative analytical approach is to assume that tariff collection involves the use of real resources (for building customs sheds, paying customs inspectors, etc.). In the one-for-one case, each dollar of revenue collected involves a dollar's worth of real resources in its collection. With either depiction, while the value of goods production reduces, thanks to real resource diversion, it is fully offset by the *revenue* in equilibrium, and hence national income/expenditure on goods at domestic market prices is determinate as $\hat{P}\hat{C}_r$, with factor income in goods production being determined at $\hat{P}_r$ and factor income in revenue seeking being equal to the revenue and both adding up to OQ' as the national expenditure or budget line.

Note then that Figure 1-1 shows the production of the imported good Y at $\hat{P}_r$ as less than at P^*; the Metzler production paradox obtains. The conventional *substitution* effect of the tariff does protect, taking production from P^* to $\hat{P}$; but this is more than offset by the *income* effect of the induced revenue seeking, which shifts production again, to $\hat{P}_r$. That the (generalized) Rybczynski line is positively sloped, as in the present example, is a necessary but not a sufficient condition for this outcome.

Transfer Seeking and the Terms-of-Trade-Change Criterion. An application of this analysis to the transfer problem can again be shown to change dramatically the conventional criterion for change in the terms of trade—as in the forthcoming article by Bhagwati, Brecher, and Hatta.

Thus, consider the case where the transfer, instead of being received directly by consumers or given to them as a lump-sum gift as in conventional analysis, goes into the governmental budget and then leads to transfer-seeking lobbying.

Figure 1–2. Transfer-Seeking Equilibrium.

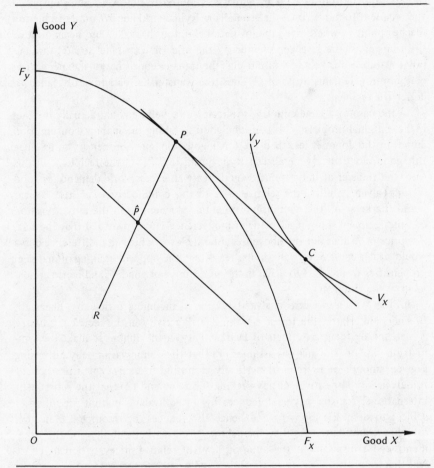

(In principle, we could also assume symmetrically that the donor country experiences reduced lobbying when it makes the transfer, a case we discuss later.) Also consider again the one-for-one assumption such that the transfer-seeking lobbying uses up a value of domestic primary factors *equal* in total to the amount of the transfer. This situation is analyzed in Figure 1–2.

Initially, the recipient country produces on its production-possibility frontier $F_y F_x$ at point P, consumes on its social indifference curve $V_y V_x$ at point C, and trades with the donor country (the rest of the world) along price line PC from point P to point C. Let us now consider the case where the terms of trade cannot change.

In the small-country case, the transfer has of course no impact on the goods-price ratio. The transfer-seeking activity of lobbyists, however, causes output in the recipient to move down the generalized Rybczynski line PR until production reaches point $\hat{P}$, where the value of national output has fallen by the amount of the transfer to the level represented by the price line (parallel to PC) through point $\hat{P}$. Since this value of output plus the transfer equals national expenditure, consumption remains at point C. Thus, the transfer has paradoxically failed to enrich the recipient.

In the case of a large country, the recipient's welfare could actually decline, if the marginal propensity to consume good X (along the income-consumption curve) in the donor is less than the (analogous) marginal propensity to produce this good along the (generalized) Rybczynski line PR in the recipient. In this case, the transfer at initial prices would create an excess world demand for good X, and (given stability) the relative price of this commodity would rise to clear world markets. As the equilibrium price line steepens from the initial position PC, the recipient must reach a lower indifference curve, provided that the relative price of X does not rise above the autarkic level (where an indifference curve would touch curve $F_y F_x$). By similar reasoning, the opposite ranking of marginal propensities would lead to a fall in the world price of good X, and hence enrichment of the recipient.

In the *symmetric case* analyzed in the forthcoming article by Bhagwati, Brecher, and Hatta, the transfer-seeking DUP activity in the recipient country is matched by identical effects of DUP activity in the donor. To make the symmetry complete, the analysis assumes (1) that the donor was initially disbursing a given amount of revenue domestically, resulting in equivalent utilization of resources in competitive subsidy-seeking lobbying and (2) that the subsequent international transfer payment reduces by an equivalent amount the subsidies subject to domestic lobbying and hence also reduces the resource use on such lobbying equivalently. As they then show, given market stability and the aforementioned proviso about the autarkic level of relative prices, national welfare will then improve (worsen) for the donor and worsen (improve) for the recipient *if and only if* the recipient's marginal propensity to produce its own importable is greater (less) than the donor's marginal propensity to produce this good.

Endogenous Policy

The endogenization of policy *via* DUP activity is also subversive of traditional intuitions. Traditionally, economists are trained to think of governments as neutral in positive analysis and of economic agents who compete, perfectly or imperfectly, in alternative types of market environments. Once policy is endogenized, this approach is undermined. With endogenous policy, economic agents attempt to influence policy in their favor; thus, there is a noneconomic marketplace, in which economic agents can simultaneously conduct their profit-making activities.[3] We thus have *two* components of the overall model: the orthodox *economic* specification and the *political* specification. Profit motivation may equally extend to both, but the economic returns accrue through induced-policy changes influencing economic returns in the traditionally economic sphere of the model.

As with the exogenous-policy DUP activities analyzed earlier, the results in positive analysis are extremely sensitive to the change in the way the total economic system is modeled. For example, the customary view is that, given an exogenously specified tariff, an improvement in the terms of trade will reduce the domestic production of the importable good in an economy with given resources, well-behaved technology, and perfect markets. But this conclusion need not follow, or may be seriously weakened, if the effect of the terms of trade change is to trigger tariff-seeking lobbying successfully.

While there is a vast and growing literature on political economy models that endogenize policy through DUP-activity specification in a variety of contexts, several efforts of a general-equilibrium type have emerged recently in trade-theoretic literature in particular.[4] We will give an indication here of the nature of these models by drawing on two of the early papers on tariff seeking: Findlay and Wellisz (1982) and Feenstra and Bhagwati (1982). These papers may be characterized in the following way:

1. Economic *agents* that engage in lobbying are defined. Findlay and Wellisz include two specific factors in two activities in the specific factors model. Their interests are in conflict since goods price changes affect them in an opposite manner. In Feenstra-Bhagwati (1982), there is only one economic agent (that hurt by import competition) who engages in lobbying, in the 2 X 2 Hecksher-Ohlin-Samuelson model.

2. The agents lobby to have a *policy* adopted or to oppose it. If the model is interpreted as a steady state rather than a static one, agents have to continue lobbying in a steady state to retain a policy once it is adopted or to preclude its adoption at any time. In both the Findlay-Wellisz paper and Feenstra-Bhagwati, that policy is uniquely defined to be a tariff, but the model can be generalized to other forms of trade restrictions.

3. The "government," as an economic agent, is not explicit in Findlay-Wellisz. The cost-of-lobbying functions that postulate the tariff as a function of the lobbying resources spent in proposing and opposing a tariff are *implicitly* assuming a government that is subject to these opposing lobbying efforts. In Feenstra-Bhagwati, by contrast, there is a *two-layer* government: the lobbying process interacts with one branch of government (e.g., the legislature) to enact a *lobbying tariff*. Another branch of the government (e.g., the president in the United States) then uses the subsequent tariff revenues to bribe the lobby into accepting a different, welfare-superior *efficient tariff*. The revenue bribe *plus* the

earned income from the market place at the efficient tariff yields the same income for the lobby as does the lobbying tariff.[5]

These papers nicely define how the theoretical analysis of endogenous policy-making can be approached in the conventional manner of economic theory. By taking a simple set of political-cum-economic assumptions they manage to get a neat, simple model working. Through a combination of elements from the Findlay–Wellisz and Feenstra–Bhagwati models, this work will eventually lead to the extension of the traditional 2 × 2 × 2 model of the Hecksher–Ohlin–Samuelson (HOS) type to an augmented 2 × 2 × 2 × 2 model, in which two lobbies and capitalists and workers engage in tariff-seeking lobbying.

These models can also be enriched in different directions. One way is to develop further the role of the government. Recall that the Feenstra–Bhagwati model postulates a two-layer view of the government. It combines the view (taken exclusively in Findlay–Wellisz) that the government is "acted upon" by political lobbies causing the tariff to become a function of the resources expended (presumably in financing reelection) by the respective lobbies, with the view that the government acts so as to maximize a conventional social welfare function. Instead, one could develop the sometimes propounded view that the government acts to maximize its *revenue*, since doing so maximizes its patronage. If so, Harry Johnson's (1950–51) classic analysis of maximum-revenue tariff in a conventional world where other economic agents are not engaged in lobbying yields the politically endogenous tariff.

The analysis can also be extended to include a larger set of *policy instruments* for which the economic agents can lobby in response to import competition. Thus, as a supplement to tariffs, one can consider policy instruments in regard to international factor and technological flows. Without formally incorporating them into a model that endogenously yields the equilibrium choice or policy-mix of instruments in response to import competition, Bhagwati (1982b, c), Sapir (1983), and Dinopoulos (1983) have analyzed the *preferences* that different economic agents could have between these instruments when faced by import competition (i.e., improved terms of trade). Such analyses throw light on the incentives for lobbying for *different* policy adoptions by the government and hence yield the necessary insights into why certain policy options rather than others emerge as actual responses to import competition.

DUP ACTIVITIES AND WELFARE ANALYSIS

Exogenous Policies

The welfare effects of specific policies, and of parametric changes in the presence of exogenously specified policies, can be extremely sensitive to whether induced DUP activities are built into the model or not. We will consider two cases.

Shadow Prices in a Tariff-Distorted, Small Economy in Cost-Benefit Analysis.
Bhagwati and Srinivasan (1982), following on Foster's (1981) work, have shown that shadow prices for primary factors in a small, tariff-distorted open economy are different, depending on whether the tariff has or has not resulted in revenue seeking. In fact, the shadow prices can be shown to be the market prices when revenue seeking obtains.

The shadow factor prices for a small, tariff-distorted economy are known from the cost-benefit literature to be derivable from the world goods prices given the distorted techniques. On the other hand, it is obvious from the fact that if revenue seeking is present, as in Figure 1-1, the economy operates on the national expenditure, social budget line defined at the market, tariff-inclusive prices. Therefore, a marginal withdrawal of factors from the distorted, DUP equilibrium will evidently imply an opportunity cost reflecting the market prices.[6] To put it another way, with the entire revenue sought away, the consumer expenditure on goods equals income at market prices for factors. And these factor prices do not change (as long as incomplete specialization continues), as we vary factor endowments, thanks to the tariff. As such, the value of change in the labor (capital) endowment by a unit is its market reward. Hence, the shadow factor prices in this DUP-activity-inclusive model are the market prices.[7] The invisible hand strikes again!

Policy Rankings with Revenue Seeking. Recall that, for a small economy, a consumption tax on the importable (production tax on the exportable) is welfare superior to a tariff at the same *ad valorem* rate since it avoids the additional production (consumption) loss associated with the tariff. Once full revenue seeking à la Bhagwati and Srinivasan (1980) is consistently taken into account, however, this welfare ranking is reversed. This is seen as follows.

With a tariff at *ad valorem* rate t, let the output vector of the economy be (X^t, Y^t) under no revenue seeking. Let the free-trade (i.e., zero-tariff) output vector be (X^0, Y^0). With full revenue seeking under the tariff, consumers maximize utility given a relative price of $(1 + t)$ of the importable good Y (with the world relative price normalized at unity) and income y equal to $[X^t + (1 + t)Y^t]$. They thus derive utility $v(1 + t, X^t + (1 + t)Y^t)$ expressed in terms of their indirect utility function $v(p, y)$. On the other hand, with a consumption tax at an *ad valorem* rate t and full revenue seeking, they face the same price $(1 + t)$ but an income of $(X^0 + Y^0)$, thus obtaining utility: $v(1 + t, X^0 + Y^0)$. From the fact that (X^t, Y^t) maximizes the value of output given the tariff t, we get

$$\left\{X^t + (1 + t)Y^t\right\} \geq \left\{X^0 + (1 + t)Y^0\right\} \geq \left\{X^0 + Y^0\right\} .$$

Figure 1-3. Tariff *versus* Consumption Tax, Both with Full Revenue Seeking.

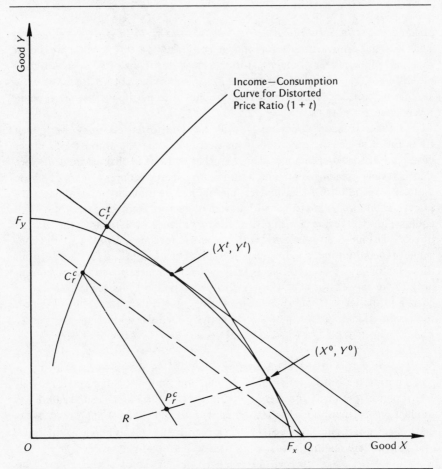

Hence,

$$v(1 + t, X^t + (1 + t)Y^t) > v(1 + t, X^0 + Y^0);$$

that is, a tariff with full revenue seeking is superior to a consumption tax with full revenue seeking.

The foregoing argument is illustrated in Figure 1-3.[8] Without any revenue seeking and free trade, equilibrium production is at (X^0, Y^0). With a tariff, production shifts at relative price ratio $(1 + t)$ to (X^t, Y^t). With tariff-revenue seeking, consumption is at C_r^t, as shown in Figure 1-1 also. Shift, however, to a consumption tax on good Y with attendant revenue seeking. Production then remains at (X^0, Y^0) and the income, measured in terms of good X, is OQ, and is spent at the consumption-tax-inclusive price ratio $(1 + t)$ along line QC_r^c, taking consumption to C_r^c. Figure 1-3 also shows production in the consumption-tax-cum-seeking equilibrium. It is given at P_r^c by the intersection of the world price line from C_r^c and the R-line, which is the Rybczynski line for the world price ratio (unity) at (X^0, Y^0). Evidently, welfare at C_r^t dominates that at C_r^c: the tariff is superior to the consumption tax.

Consider now the comparison between a production tax on good X and a tariff, both yielding identical domestic producer price ratio and with attendant full revenue seeking. Under the tariff, equilibrium consumption is then at C_r^t in Figure 1-4. But shift now to the production tax. Income, in terms of good Y, will then be OQ as with the tariff, but consumers will face the world price ratio (unity) and consumption will be at C_r^p. The production equilibrium will then be at P_r^p, the intersection between the expenditure line QC_r^p and the R-line from (X^t, Y^t) at the tax-distorted price $(1 + t)$. Evidently, C_r^t dominates C_r^p: welfare under the tariff exceeds that under an identical production tax, when full revenue seeking obtains in each case.

The intuitive explanation of these results is that, with no revenue seeking, a consumption (production) tax generates more revenue than a tariff at the same rate,[9] the reason being that the offsetting production (consumption) subsidy effect of a tariff is absent. In effect, what we are getting into is a situation where there are *two* distortions, rather than one, associated with each of the policies being ranked: the direct distortion implied by the policy itself and the indirect distortion implied by the (induced) DUP activity. What is interesting in the specific policy-rankings considered here is that these rankings are still possible, and in fact get reversed, when the indirect DUP effect is considered.

From a welfare-theoretic viewpoint, therefore (policy-induced) DUP activities can play a possibly critical role in determining desirable policy intervention. This conclusion is also dramatically supported by the welfare-theoretic analysis of transfers. Recall from our discussion of the DUP-theoretic transfer problem and from Figure 1-2 that, in the traditional 2×2 (non-DUP) framework, exacting a reparation payment will always be enriching for the recipient of the resulting transfer in a Walras-stable market. Once, however, full transfer seeking is permitted, this is no longer so! Thus, take the case of a "large" recipient country, as illustrated in Figure 1-2. Deterioration in the terms of trade is *sufficient* to immiserize the recipient in a Walras-stable market, whereas such deterioration in the terms of trade cannot ever be large enough to offset the primary gain from the transfer in a Walras-stable market in the orthodox non-DUP-activity 2×2 model.

We therefore need to reexamine a number of policy intuitions if policies do induce DUP activities in the real world, as they indeed do. The world lies somewhere along the continuum defined by two end points: one where no DUP activity is induced and the other where DUP activity is induced fully (on a one-

Figure 1–4. Tariff *versus* Production Tax, Both with Full Revenue Seeking.

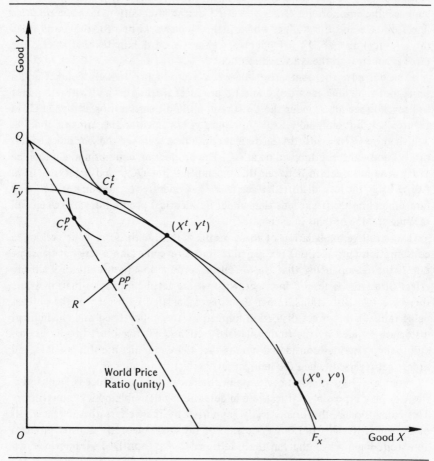

for-one basis).[10] But whereas we have charted reasonably in depth the former end, we are only beginning to understand and sketch the latter end. An agenda for research to map the latter landscape clearly awaits a new generation of researchers in all branches of economic theory.

Endogenous Policy

A far more critical question is raised, however, once you fully endogenize policy in DUP-theoretic models. Take a tariff-seeking model of any species that you

Figure 1-5. Welfare Costs of Endogenous and Exogenous Tariffs.

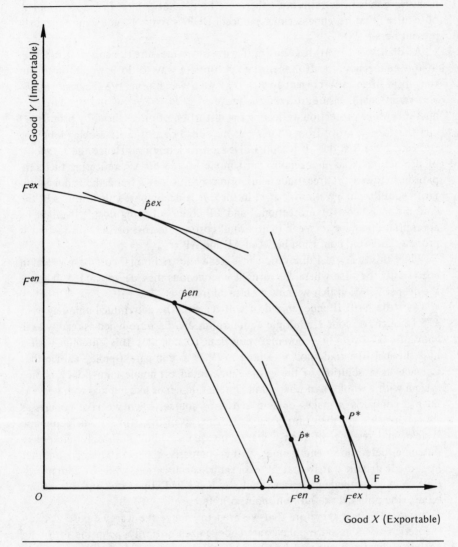

prefer. The endogenous tariff that emerges then in such a model may be illustrated in Figure 1-5. $F^{ex}\ F^{ex}$ is the production possibility curve when all resources are deployed for producing X and Y and an *exogenous* tariff leads this small economy from P^* at given world prices to $\hat{P}^{ex}$ under protection. But now the model is augmented to endogenize the tariff and, in equilibrium, resources are used up in tariff-seeking DUP activity and the tariff-inclusive equilibrium is at $\hat{P}^{en}$. The hypothetical production possibility curve $F^{en}\,F^{en}$ takes the endowment of factors as *net* of those used up in tariff-seeking *equilibrium*: the tariff-inclusive goods price ratio must therefore be tangent to it at P^{en}. It is assumed, of course, that revenue-seeking-induced DUP activity is not simultaneously present here.[11]

As Bhagwati (1980) has shown, if we wish to measure the cost of protection in this endogenous-tariff model, the appropriate way to do it would be to put the world price ratio tangent to $F^{en}\,F^{en}$ at $\hat{P}^*$ and, using the Hicksian equivalent-variational measure, to take the move from $\hat{P}^{en}$ to $\hat{P}^*$ as the standard production cost of protection, reflecting the distortion of prices faced by producers) and the further move from $\hat{P}^*$ to P^* as the added cost of tariff-seeking lobbying (reflecting the loss due to resource diversion to lobbying). Hence the *total* cost of protection in an endogenous-tariff model would be AF, reflecting the comparison between the free-trade-equilibrium position at P^* and the endogenous-tariff-equilibrium position at $\hat{P}^{en}$. In turn, it is decomposed then into AB, the conventional "cost of protection," and BF, the "lobbying cost." It might be appropriate perhaps to speak of the total cost as the cost of the "protectionist process," to avoid confusion between AF and AB.[12]

While this analytical innovation to extend the traditional cost-of-protection analysis to the case where the tariff is endogenous may be applauded, it raises the deeper question that we now wish to address.

Once the tariff is endogenized, it will generally be determined uniquely as at $\hat{P}^{en}$ (though, of course, multiple equilibriums can be introduced as readily as in conventional "strictly economic" models). To compare this outcome with a hypothetical free-trade policy leading to P^* is to compare a policy choice that is made as a solution to the entire, augmented economic-cum-policy-choice system with a wholly hypothetical policy that descends like manna from heaven! Such a comparison makes obvious sense, of course, when we take policies as exogenous: we are then simply varying them, given the conventional economic system, and reading off their welfare consequences. But, with only one policy outcome determined endogenously, the comparison between it and another hypothetical policy arrived at by exogenous specification, while of course possible, is not compelling. It is virtually as if we had wiped out one side of our model (the political side) for our point of reference!

It would appear therefore that we need to *change* the way we pose welfare-theoretic questions once policies are endogenized critically, as in the foregoing analysis. Thus, it is not particularly meaningful to rank-order policies as in traditional analysis, once policies are endogenous. Nor is it appropriate to compare them vis-à-vis a reference point (such as P^* in Figure 1–5) that reflects an exogenously specified policy.

Rather, it would appear that the analysis must now shift focus and concentrate on *variations around the endogenous equilibrium* itself (i.e., around $\hat{P}^{en}$ in Figure 1–5). Thus, it is customary to ask, given a policy, what happens to welfare when accumulation comes about, or when technical know-how changes, etc. We can rephrase those questions as follows, keeping in mind that there are now two parts of the overall economic system, the economic and the political: What will happen to welfare if, on the economic side of the model, changes such as accumulation and technical progress occur; and what happens if changes occur instead on the political side such as an increased cost of lobbying for a tariff if there is an exogenous shift in attitudes against protection?[13] In short, the overall system must be solved for endogenous policy change and for final welfare impact for parametric changes that can occur now *either* in the economic *or* equally in the political side of the overall, augmented system. An interesting way to decompose the overall welfare impact of such parametric changes on either the economic or the political side of the system could be to assume first that policy does remain exogenous and then, in the next stage, to allow it to change to its endogenous value. The first stage might capture the essence of what we have come to think of as the customary impact of a parametric change in the system; the second stage may be taken to correspond to the fact that policy is endogenous.

CONCLUDING REMARKS

Evidently, therefore, the integration of DUP activities into theoretic analysis is a serious business. We hope that we have raised the issues sharply enough to stimulate the response of our fellow economists in the shape of future research on what promises to be an extremely important innovation in economic theorizing.

NOTES TO CHAPTER 1

1. Her focus is on licensing or quantity restrictions and the rents thereon, and her generic set of rent-seeking activities excludes from its scope other DUP activities such as price-distortion-triggered DUP activities or distortion-triggering DUP activities. For a fuller analysis of the relationship, analytical and terminological, between DUP and rent-seeking activities, see Bhagwati 1983.
2. Other classifications, addressed better to other purposes, are also possible, as in the synthesis of the welfare effects of DUP activities Bhagwati 1982c.
3. Of course, this is also true of DUP lobbying and policy-evading models we considered in the case where the policy *causing* the DUP activity was specified exogenously.
4. The earliest, pioneering work is that of Brock and Magee (1978, 1980).
5. Feenstra and Bhagwati note that the efficient tariff may paradoxically exceed the lobbying tariff if the shadow price of lobbying activity is negative.

We might add that some critics have expressed concern that any model should have a multi-layered or multi-polar government, that this amounts to viewing government as "schizophrenic." However, the view that governments must be monolithic seems inconsistent with a reading of even the *New York Times*, not to mention political-science literature. Dinopoulos (Chapter 9 of this book) also considers a two-layer government where the revenue-seeking lobby acts on the legislature and the executive determines the optimal tariff taking this lobbying into account.

6. Thus, as Anam (1982) has shown, Johnson's (1967) type of immiserizing growth in the presence of a tariff is impossible when all tariff revenues are sought.

7. If not all of tariff revenues are subject to seeking, the shadow prices would be differently defined, as noted by Anam (1982).

8. For an important diagrammatic analysis of a consumption tax with revenue seeking, see Anam 1982. Anam showed that such a tax might be welfare-inferior to a tariff in achieving a given level of consumption for one good.

9. See also Anam 1982 on this point.

10. The latter end point may even be more drastic if, as Tullock (1980) has suggested, seeking leads to more resources being spent on chasing a prize than the value of the prize itself, depending on how you model the terms and conditions of such a chase.

11. Tullock (1980) and Bhagwati (1982b) analyze the case where this DUP activity is simultaneously present.

12. Bhagwati (1980) also shows that it is incorrect to argue that the cost of an endogenous tariff at t percent always exceeds the cost of an exogenous tariff at t percent. This proposition involves comparing $\hat{P}^{ex}$ with $\hat{P}^{en}$; and, since this is a second-best comparison, the endogenous tariff can be less harmful than the exogenous one. This is also at the heart of the problem with the Buchanan–Tollison definition of DUP activities, as discussed in Bhagwati (1983).

13. On this point, see Brecher 1982.

2 THREE APPROACHES TO THE STUDY OF INSTITUTIONS

Douglass North

The study of institutions can be approached in a variety of ways. This chapter explores the differences and areas of congruence in three approaches to the study of institutions. I begin by outlining my own approach, a transactions cost approach to institutions. I then compare it to the rent-seeking approach developed by Buchanan, Tollison, and Tullock and others and the distributive coalitions framework embodied in Mancur Olson's new study.[1] Finally, I point up the similarities and the differences in these three approaches.

My theory of institutions in *Structure and Change* focuses on transactions costs, which are defined as the costs of specifying and enforcing contracts. Institutional arrangements are defined as contractual agreements among principals or between principals and agents made to maximize their wealth by realizing the gains from trade as a result of specialization (including specialization in coercion). The approach is complementary to the neoclassical approach in that it explores the *costs* entailed in capturing the gains from trade; consequently, it is the other side—the other half—of economic activity.

This framework rests on three fundamental assumptions: (1) that individuals behave in their own, rather than the collective, interests; (2) that specifying and enforcing the rules that underlie contracts is costly; and (3) that ideology modifies maximizing behavior. Let us explore each assumption in turn.

The behavioral postulate of wealth maximization is the cornerstone of economic theory. It is also the cornerstone of this theory of institutions. The postulate is this: Individuals, in the absence of constraints, maximize at any and all margins. If there were no constraints, we would, indeed, live in a classic Hobbesian jungle in which life would be nasty, brutish, and short. Constraints, in the

33

form of economic institutions, by limiting certain types of behavior, make human organization and civilization possible.

Individual maximization is the key to understanding the forms of organization that develop. Individuals may stand to gain by forming organizations to limit their behavior, both in political terms and within an economic framework, but if it is very costly to be able to detect behavior, then individuals may also gain by disobeying the rules that they themselves agree are important for other people to obey. It follows that the problems and costs of organization mainly involve attempts to define and enforce contractual rules that it is in the individual's interest to disobey.

The second assumption—that it is extremely costly to specify and enforce the contractual rules underlying institutions—severely limits the type of contracts and institutions that develop. The problem of contractual limitation is especially acute in transactions between principals and agents, where measuring valued attributes exchanged is extremely costly. Problems of constraining the agents and the costliness of measuring the output of the agent in terms of the many aspects that are involved in the contract pose the fundamental dilemma of agency and determine the shape of institutions dealing with hierarchy. (See Jensen and Meckling 1976.) In such contracts, the principal attempts to constrain the behavior of the agent in such a way as to fulfill or to carry out the principal's objective of realizing the wealth from the gains of trade. But measuring the agent's output, or even determining the parameters to attempt to measure, is extremely difficult and costly. Thus, inevitably, agents are not perfectly constrained.

The costs of measurement constitute the first part of the total costliness of contractual arrangements. Enforcement is imperfect not only because it is costly to measure what constitutes contract fulfillment and, therefore, parties can argue convincingly that they are, indeed, within the contract, but, more seriously, it is imperfect because the enforcement officials themselves are agents and therefore are themselves not perfectly constrained. Judges, juries, mediators, and arbitrators have their own utility function, which, in turn, influences the way they view the decisionmaking process. Judges, juries, and others who make decisions are influenced by their view of the fairness of the contract. Thus, no matter which party has been injured, if the justice system or the people enforcing justice view the contract as being unfair, they may very well decide that the contractual arrangement itself should be abrogated. This brings us to the third assumption: that ideology influences behavior and the framework of institutions of a society.

It follows from this third assumption that no theory of institutions would be complete if it excluded ideology. The reason is straightforward. Because it is costly to measure performance, people may find it easy to get away with poor performance; but they can be influenced in their behavior by their conviction about the fairness or justice of contracts. Accordingly, we must try to understand how people arrive at views about the fairness of institutional arrangements. We begin by recognizing that ideology is ubiquitous: individuals have a need to rationalize the world around them. In that sense, ideology, as a device by which to deal with the multiple problems of everyday living that confront one, economizes on the amount of information that people must have. But it is more than that—it also involves a judgment about the fairness or legitimacy of the contractual or institutional arrangements within which individuals live and act.

Ideologies are derived from the experiences people have. If all people had the same experiences, we could expect that their perspectives about the world around them would tend to be the same. Consensus ideologies, such as one will find in tribal societies, exist because the members of the society essentially have gone through the same experiences and, therefore, have a common set of beliefs, myths, taboos that guide their views and perceptions. Divergent ideologies grow up because individuals have diverse experiences that lead them to have different views about the world around them. Ideology thus hinges upon the very same theoretical basis that underlies the gains from trade—that is, the gains from trade arise because of specialization and division of labor, but divergent ideologies, conflicting views about the justice and fairness of the system, also emerge from these sources. They may emerge from geographic specialization in that geographically different groups evolve different customs, traditions and languages as they confront different problems. Or they may emerge from occupational specialization, which results in impersonal exchange and a loss of personalized relationship between employer and employee.

There is little new in the preceding discussion, but its implications for modeling institutions are profound. To the degree that the members of a society have the same ideological framework, the formal rules of the society that underlie institutions will not have to be defined very clearly and enforcement mechanisms and procedures may be minimal or even absent altogether. But to the degree that society has diverse ideologies reflecting the growth of specialization and the division of labor, more resources will have to be devoted, first to defining the rules precisely, and second to enforcing those rules. Such definition and enforcement is necessary because, with conflicting ideologies, the individual participants will feel no necessity to constrain individual maximization (cheating, shirking, etc.) at the expense of the other party. Given the costliness of measuring performance, ideological consensus or alienation is a fundamental influence upon the form of institution.

When this contracting approach is extended to apply to political institutions, three specific hypotheses emerge. First, the state trades for revenue a group of services that we call protection and justice. Since there are economies of scale in providing these services, the total cost to society is lower as a result of an organization specializing in these services than it would be if each individual protected his own property. Second, the state attempts to act like a discriminating monopolist, separating each group of constituents and devising property rights for each so as to maximize the revenue of the state and its ruler. Third, the state is constrained by the opportunity cost of its constituents, since there always exist potential rivals to provide the same set of services. The rivals are other states, as well as individuals within the existing political economic unit who are potential rulers. The degree of monopoly power of the ruler, therefore, is a function of the degree of coercive power the ruler has on the one hand, and the closeness of substitutes available to the various groups of constituents, on the other.

The fundamental constitutional framework of such a society will provide a set of property rights (i.e., specify the ownership structure in both factor and product markets) for maximizing the rents accruing to the ruler, but within such a framework the objective will be to reduce transactions costs in order to foster maximum output of the society and, therefore, increase tax revenues accruing to the ruler of the state. This second objective will result in the provision of a set of public (or semipublic) goods and services designed to lower the costs of specifying, negotiating, and enforcing contracts that underlie exchange. In addition, the state will promulgate moral and ethical codes of behavior designed to lower compliance costs.

The key feature of this approach to the study of political institutions is that the two objectives of the ruler of the state are typically inconsistent and result in inefficient property rights. That is, the first objective is aimed at maximizing the rents accruing to the ruler. The second objective is aimed at producing an efficient set of property rights. In effect, the property rights structure that will maximize rents to the ruler is in conflict with those that would produce economic growth. An ownership structure that provides incentives for efficient resource allocation is also one that would produce destabilizing consequences as a result of technological change, the spread of more efficient markets, and in general, continuous alteration in relative prices. Changes in the opportunity costs of constituents, in turn, would change the bargaining power of constituents versus rulers.

In short, the process of growth in this model is inherently destabilizing, but so is no growth when a political economic unit exists in a world of competing political economic units. Relatively inefficient property rights threaten the survival of a state in the context of more efficient neighbors, and the ruler faces the choice of extinction or of modifying the fundamental ownership structure to enable the society to reduce transactions costs and to raise the rate of growth.

The theory of public choice rent-seeking involves the study of how people compete for artificially contrived transfers (Tollison 1982: 28). The resources devoted to such dissipation of contrived rents are wasted. This waste is in contrast to the competitive dissipation of economic rents, which plays a critical role in the dynamics of a market economy. Although institutions in the private sector can create contrived rents, the rent-seeking literature focuses on government as the source of contrived rents and invokes the contrasting principal/agent relationship of the private sector to the public sector to point out the contrast between political and economic institutions. An interest-group modeling of the political process then explores the way rents are contrived and competed for.

On the face of it, the rent-seeking approach and the transactions costs approach are quite similar. Agency theory is a major component of each, although I am not aware that the rent-seeking literature would describe the problem of agency to the specific measurement and enforcement factors advanced in the transactions cost approach. The rent-seeking approach has gone much further in exploring the effects of specific decisionmaking rules upon the efficiency of economic activity; but my model of mercantilism and that developed by Ecklund and Tollison (1980) are consistent. The most striking contrast between the two approaches is that the rent-seeking literature is consistently an interest-group modeling of the political process in which ideological constraints on maximizing at certain margins are not a part of the argument. A second contrast is that the rent-seeking literature invokes Pareto efficiency standards in measuring the performance, whereas the transactions cost approach implies that there is no meaningful standard of Pareto efficiency possible, since one cannot specify a least-cost structure of government for any given economic output. This inappropriate use of the Pareto criteria is true not only of the public choice rent-seeking literature; it is also true of the international trade DUP approach. While this approach allows a possible role for ideology (see, for example, Chapter 6, by Findlay and Wellicz), it still uses the Pareto criteria in ranking alternative policies and in defining unproductive activities.

Mancur Olson's new book, an extension of *The Logic of Collective Action*, explores the consequences of special interest groups for the performance of an economy over time. Olson's contribution has been to show the way such distributive coalitions evolve and affect the specific aspects of an economy's performance. His detailed analysis of the characteristics of these coalitions is a major contribution to understanding institutions. But, as with the rent-seeking and DUP approaches, it leaves little room for ideology because it follows an interest-group modeling approach in which there is no room for nonfree riding. The reality is that people often do things that are not in their pure self-interest. Unless that reality is included, the models, even though they are improvement over the straight neoclassical approach, will be incomplete.

My specific criticism of Olson's approach is that it is not easy to see how he got there. Since his approach is strictly an interest-group modeling of behavior, it would appear to be consistent with the rent-seeking model; but because he does not specify the nature of the state, one is left with the implication that the state is simply a passive reflection of interest groups, whereas the rent-seeking model is explicitly concerned with the impact of decisionmaking rules and agency upon performance. His welfare implications are not explicit and thus it is difficult to fault him directly. But that is not because he has dealt with the problems of ideology, the state, and institutions; it is only because he has left their role so vague. Olson provides no modeling of the inherent nature of institutions.

Indeed, there is no discussion of the positive contribution of institutions in the general framework of economic organization and activity.

CONCLUSION AND IMPLICATIONS FOR FURTHER RESEARCH

While there are differences, the three approaches differ primarily in emphasis. The transaction cost approach attempts to provide a fundamental theoretical framework of the costs of contracting, and to build from that a general theory of political and economic institutions. Its major emphasis is on the way transaction costs, in conjunction with the state, shape the property rights structure and thereby determine the performance of economies. The rent-seeking model focuses on an interest-group modeling of the political system, specifying a certain structure of decision rules and then analyzing the consequences of these decision rules. The Olson model, although it has no explicit modeling of the state, analyzes interest-group interaction and concludes that the institutions that develop reduce efficiency and productivity levels of the system.

In the transaction cost model it is inefficient property rights, a consequence of the state, that increase the costs of contracting and retard growth. In the rent-seeking model, it is particular attributes of government, frequently derived from the agency relationship, that produce inefficiency in the system. In the Olson model, it is the increasing power of distributive coalitions that introduces rigidity into the system and consequent inefficiencies.

These approaches are complementary. Although neither the rent-seeking framework nor the distributive coalition approach explicitly focuses on the structure of property rights as the determinants of performance, they do not contradict such an analysis. The transactions cost model provides an underlying theory of institutions; the rent-seeking models and the distributive-coalition models go much further in providing careful, detailed analyses of exactly what is going on in the system that produces the set of inefficiencies.

Obviously much more can be said. However, my main points can be summarized in the following four assertions:

1. Any theory of institutions must be built upon a structure that specifies why it is costly for individuals to interact. Two kinds of costs are involved. First are the costs that would be incurred even if all the parties to exchange had the same objective function. In such a world shirking, opportunism, and agency would not exist. There would be simply those costs of information involved in discovery and coordination—essentially, the economics of information as developed by Hayek (1937 and 1945) and Stigler (1961). Second, costs exist because of the high costs of measurement and enforcement in a world of individualistic maximizing. Such costs are the consequence of universal moral hazard that arises

because of asymmetrical information. It is the latter that is the most important influence in shaping the structure of institutions.

2. No theory of institutions can be complete without involving ideology as a constraint on maximizing at certain margins, because measurement and enforcement are costly. The strength of ideology is the premium individuals are willing to incur not to free ride; in its absence—that is, in a world of universal maximizing by individuals—the costs of contracting would be so great that economic activity would be limited indeed and the stability of institutions impossible. It is ideological conviction that underlies the stability of institutions, and it is its reverse—alienation—that both raises the costs of contracting and induces individuals to engage in large group action to change institutions. If ideology is not important, then economists must explain the enormous amount of resources that political units and other principals in political and economic activity devote to attempting to convince participants of the justice or injustice of contractual arrangements.

3. A theory of political institutions must explore both the positive role that the state plays in economic organization—in specifying and enforcing contracts—and the negative role that it plays. The rent-seeking model is largely confined to the second but has an implicit concern with the first in its invoking Pareto efficient standards—that is, its concern with artificial rents. The rent-seeking approach has not developed a framework that tells us how to capture the gains from trade in an "efficient" political framework, however. The rent-seeking model measures the waste of rent-seeking as the deviation from the competitive equilibrium—an equilibrium with zero transactions costs, whereas the measure we want is the *deviation* from an efficient level of transactions cost by government.

4. While Olson's analysis gives us an extended look into the way interest groups affect economic performance, it largely ignores the developments in the theory of property rights, transactions costs, and agency that have occurred. The basic contributions of Ronald Coase (1937, 1960), of Armen Alchian (1965) and Harold Demsetz (1964, 1967) on the theory of property rights, and of Jensen and Meckling (1976) on agency theory nowhere play a part in Olson's framework. Olson's work could have been written in good part in 1965 as the second half of *The Logic of Collective Action*. What is missing in Mancur Olson's provocative study is a modeling of institutions. Interest groups or distributive coalitions are only a part of a larger whole; in effect, there is no model of the structure of voluntary organizations of which distributive coalitions are a variant. Indeed, many distributive coalitions got their start as "productive" institutions, or because of ideological conviction that overcame initial free riding. While Olson hints at such issues in his interesting discussion of the length of time it takes distributive coalitions to form and the growing costs of decisionmaking in such coalitions as they mature, he fails to develop it.

Taken together, the three approaches to institutions are, I believe, largely complementary; but there are so many missing parts to the puzzle that we have just begun what must be a long effort to integrate convincingly the theory of institutions with the rest of economic theory.

As suggested by these four assertions, although the new economic theories of institutions are advances, all three have their limitations. None provides for an overall analytical framework of the pluralist state. Thus, we have yet to formulate a general model of modern political economic organization.

NOTE TO CHAPTER 2

1. The Introduction and other chapters of this book explain the rent-seeking and distributive coalitions approaches. Thus, I concentrate on my approach and how it interacts with others. (For further elaboration of the three approaches, see North 1981, Tollison 1982, and Olson 1982.)

3 ENDOGENOUS TARIFF THEORY
A Survey

Stephen P. Magee

There are at least three classes of theories for why tariffs exist: policy theories, terms-of-trade theories, and political theories. In policy theories, tariffs exist to achieve policy goals: e.g., infant industry protection, industry output or employment maintenance, or government revenue. Johnson (1951) showed how to calculate the maximum revenue tariff, and the literature that followed would fit nicely into a Niskanen (1968) bureaucratic model. Policy theories fell out of favor, however, when Bhagwati (1971) and others showed that tariffs are quite inefficient at achieving most policy goals and are usually dominated by other policies (see also Bhagwati 1982a). In terms-of-trade theories, tariffs are a tool of international redistribution: they permit a country to increase its welfare at the expense of other countries. Johnson (1960) pioneered the optimum tariff literature and showed how to calculate explicitly the tariff rate that would increase a country's terms of trade so as to maximize the country's welfare.[1] Bhagwati and Srinivasan (1973) examine both the revenue-maximizing tariff and the optimal tariff in the presence of smuggling. One empirical problem with optimal tariff theory is its implication that small importers would have zero tariffs: this conflicts with the especially high tariffs observable in many small nations.

The third class of tariff theories looks to domestic political considerations. Until about a decade ago, political explanations of tariffs were black box theories. International economists, myself included, would state that tariff rates are

---

I am indebted to Jagdish Bhagwati and David Colander for many helpful comments on this chapter.

exogenously determined by political processes beyond our understanding. While that statement is probably still true, we know somewhat more today. William Brock and I wrote a set of papers (1975, 1978, 1980) making tariffs endogenous and the outcome of domestic conflicts over the distribution of income. We used public choice theory to develop a special interest theory with lobbies and political parties displaying maximizing behavior. According to this view, tariffs are an equilibrating variable in political markets, which balance opposing forces in redistributional battles. This and other work on endogenous tariff theory is summarized in a recently completed book (Magee, Brock, and Young 1983).

The literature on the policy theories and the terms-of-trade theories of tariffs is vast and has been around for some time. However, political theories of tariffs are newer, and nearly half of the work in this area is still unpublished because of recent growth in this literature. For this reason and because of my own rather narrow specialization, this survey will review only domestic political theories of endogenous tariffs. The reader will not be spared the directly unproductive indulgence of my citing my own work. We do not consider here empirical studies of endogenous tariffs. The literature on that subject is large and growing, but it has already been surveyed nicely by Baldwin (1982) and Frey and Schneider (1982). For expositional convenience, the word *tariff* is used throughout this study, although it should be understood that the theories discussed here can be applied with minor variation to protection generally (and perhaps to other redistributive policies).

A SHORT HISTORY OF ENDOGENOUS
TARIFF THEORY

The domestic models of endogenous tariffs have been built on redistributive arguments. These studies typically investigate a small economy in order to eliminate all terms-of-trade motivations and to focus all of the analysis on who gains and who loses domestically from protection. Tariffs are a consequence of a redistributive conflict between a successful protariff group, which seeks them to increase its wealth, and a less successful antitariff group, which wishes to prevent the transfer. Table 3-1 provides a brief history of recent endogenous tariff theory.

Consider first some predecessors of the theory. Kindleberger (1951) had an early paper on interest groups and international trade theory. Tullock (1967) suggested that the economic resources used to obtain the rents from tariffs and monopolies would cause their welfare effects to exceed the traditional deadweight loss measures. Krueger (1974) coined the term *rent-seeking*, which is defined as the use of economic resources to obtain politically created rents. Her contribution to endogenous tariff theory was indirect because rent-seeking resources were devoted to obtaining import licenses under an exogenously deter-

Table 3–1. Endogenous Tariff Theory.

	Partial vs. General Equilibrium	Modeling Approach (Goods, Factors, Lobbies, Parties)	Lobbying	Party Behavior	Voter Behavior
Brock and Magee (1975, 1978, 1980)	P	$0 \times 0 \times 2 \times 2$	Endogenous	Endogenous	Probabilistic
Findlay and Wellisz (1982)	G	$2 \times 3 \times 2 \times 0^a$	Endogenous	Exogenous	Exogenous
Feenstra and Bhagwati (1982)	G	$2 \times 2 \times 1 \times 1^b$	Endogenous	Exogenous	Exogenous
Magee and Brock (1983)	G	$2 \times 2 \times 2 \times 2^b$	Endogenous	Endogenous	Probabilistic
Young and Magee (1982, 1983)	G	$2 \times 2 \times 2 \times 2^b$	Endogenous	Endogenous	Probabilistic
Mayer (1983)	G	$2 \times 2 \times 0 \times 2^b$ and $2 \times n \times 0 \times 2^a$	Exogenous	Exogenous	Endogenous

Note: Behavior is labelled "endogenous" if the actors at the head of the column display explicit maximizing behavior.
a. Jones–Neary model with two fixed factors and one variable factor.
b. HOS (Heckscher–Ohlin–Samuelson) model with two variable factors.

mined quota in a two-good, one-factor general equilibrium model. The term *rent* is used because the policy generating it is assumed to be fixed. Brock and I (1975, 1978, 1980) made both tariffs and lobbying endogenous with two lobbies and two political parties. In our game-theoretic setup, the pro- and anti-tariff lobbies each channeled resources to the political parties to maximize the incomes of their clienteles while the two political parties each chose positions on the tariff to maximize their probabilities of election. We employed a partial equilibrium framework.

Findlay and Wellisz (1982) were the first to employ an apparatus such as Brock and I had suggested to explain tariffs endogenously in general equilibrium. They had two fixed factors of production, one of which wanted a tariff and other of which wanted free trade. Each employed labor optimally to lobby for their preferred policy. This paper was rudimentary because neither parties nor voters were introduced, but it was an important one. I had not been able to place the Brock-Magee framework into a general equilibrium model, but Findlay and Wellisz showed that it was possible. We (Magee and Brock, 1983) followed their work by adding to their analysis two political parties explicitly maximizing their probabilities of election with one sponsoring a tariff and the other an export subsidy (i.e., a negative tariff) in a general equilibrium Heckscher–Ohlin model. We also had voters who picked parties probabilistically. Our two-good, two-factor, two-lobby, two-party apparatus with all actors maximizing has been labeled the $2 \times 2 \times 2 \times 2$ model, or, in the more colorful language of Ronald Findlay, "the 2×4 model," because of its stark emphasis on self-interest. Feenstra and Bhagwati (1982) followed with a very different approach. They had a labor lobby pursuing a tariff, but being opposed by a beneficent government. The government would use the tariff revenue generated to reduce the demands of the tariff lobby via a subsidy and obtain an endogenous "efficient" tariff.

Because of the generality of the functional forms, neither Findlay and Wellisz nor Brock and I were able to do much more than set up the first-order conditions and provide some interesting speculations on potential applications and questions that the framework could address. Young and I (1982) followed with specific functional forms: Leontief production for both goods and a logit probability of election function describing voter behavior. This allowed explicit solutions for the levels of lobbying, the equilibrium policies by both parties and even the equilibrium probabilities of electoral success by the two parties. While we obtained explicit numerical solutions for these variables, the equations were nonlinear and sufficiently complex that explicit comparative statics were not attempted. Young and I (1983) followed with a paper using the same logit function for voters but Cobb–Douglass functions for both production and consumption. Young devised an ingenious and simple solution for the equilibrium levels of lobbying, the policies, and the probabilities of election of both parties which permitted explicit comparative statics.

In Young and Magee, the voters were the only actors whose behavior was not explicitly modeled in an optimizing framework. This omission has been closed very nicely in a paper by Mayer (1983). He follows the median voter literature and assumes that both parties will choose the tariff that is preferred by the median voter. If the median voter has a greater endowment of labor per unit of capital than the economy as a whole, then the political equilibrium will display positive tariffs if the economy imports labor-intensive goods. Second, Mayer introduces a Jones-Neary fixed-factor model, in which he explains how industries with little numerical support in the electorate can receive tariffs because of voting costs. While most of the eligible electorate may lose a small amount because of a tariff, this may be less than their cost of voting. In short, Mayer merges trade theory with the median voting literature and permits explicit maximization by the median voter. In contrast, Brock, Young, and I assume that voters possess imperfect information and that their choice of a party can be described by a probability of election function (e.g., logit) in which they trade off the benefits of information (from lobbying resources) against the costs of the redistributive policy. Mayer's important contribution is not without cost: he assumes that parties do not act strategically; that both parties are equally protectionist; and that special interest lobbies do not exist. An important unsolved problem in endogenous tariff theory is whether the median voter model can be merged with the special-interest lobbying model.

While it does not provide a formal model of endogenous tariffs, a provocative paper by Messerlin (1981) explains European (particularly French) tariffs in a bureaucratic context. Because the size and power of a bureau will be positively associated with the economic size of the industry it oversees (à la Niskanen), import competing bureaus sponsor tariffs while export bureaus sponsor export subsidies (negative tariffs). Messerlin argues that (1) if scope of the protectionist bureau is enlarged, it will become less protectionist and (2) politicians will be less protectionist than bureaus. This contention has causal empirical support in the United States since it appears that protectionist sentiment wanes as the geographical scope increases as we move from the House to the Senate to the presidency. Feenstra and Bhagwati (1982) also describe this case with their assumption that lobbies will pressure the legislative branch of government for a lobbying tariff while general interests will pressure the executive branch for an efficient tariff.

TARIFFS AND ASYMMETRIES

All of the previous studies explain tariffs as an outgrowth of asymmetries in one or more of five variables: lobbying organization costs, the distribution of wealth, redistribution effects, information, or government organization. Olson (1965) investigated at some length the hypothesis that narrowly concentrated and homogenous interest groups would press more vigorously for redistributive policies such as tariffs than large and heterogenous groups would oppose them.

Most of the endogenous tariff writers have some variation on the lobbying cost theme. For example, Brock and I (1975) view cross-sectional tariffs as "prices" that clear political markets. The political system is an institutionalized market in conflict resolution and the endogenous tariffs that emerge are the terms of trade reflecting the lower organizational costs of particularized (protectionist) interests relative to generalized (free trade) interests. Consider a political battle between a few import-competing firms who want higher tariffs and many consumers of the commodity. As we look across industries, the lower the organizational costs for particularized interests relative to generalized interests, the higher the predicted tariff rate (*ceteris paribus*).

Second, Mayer (1983) bases his explanation of tariffs on asymmetric distributions of wealth. He argues that if organization costs were symmetric for all groups, tariffs would still emerge if the median voter held a relatively larger endowment of the scarce factor than the average endowment for the economy as a whole. A symmetric distribution is required for the median and the mean endowment to be equal and hence to yield free trade.

Third, Baldwin (1976) argues that asymmetrical intensities of preferences (asymmetrical effects of tariffs) can lead to logrolling, or vote trading, which might explain tariffs even if the preceding two asymmetries are absent. This could arise if two economic groups each desired protection and neither had a majority of the electorate, but if they combined forces and each voted for the other's tariff, a majority would be obtained. Political scientists note that coalitions of this sort are not unique so that free trade coalitions can emerge as well. Fourth, asymmetrical distributions of information, coupled with one or more of the aforementioned, contribute to positive tariffs. To see the reasoning, consider the positions of voters attempting to choose among one of two parties running for office. The median voter possesses less information than insiders of both parties about the psychological quirks of both—about their moral fiber, hidden propensities to engage in nuclear conflict, and so on. In this situation, voters will be more likely to vote for the candidate with the greatest economic resources and the lowest distortions. The papers by Brock, Findlay, myself, Wellisz, and Young generally model voter behavior in this way. Fifth, asymmetries in the representation of economic interests within government organizations form the basis of Messerlin's (1981) bureaucratic argument for tariffs.

TARIFFS AND WELFARE

The traditional estimates of the welfare costs of distortionary policies had been implausibly low because of their exclusive focus on measuring deadweight losses (see, e.g., Harberger 1962). Tullock suggested that these welfare measures would understate the true cost by the resources expended in the competition over the redistribution effects. He stated verbally the optimality condition for the allocation of lobbying expenditures by a protariff interest group, although he did not have a formal model. Krueger's (1974) paper on rent-seeking was the first in which these costs could have been measured explicitly, lobbying being endogenous in her model. An entire literature has arisen on the theory of rent-seeking, fueled primarily by public choice theorists (see the controversy between Tollison (1982) and Bhagwati (1983) on this issue).

Since Krueger, the major welfare development in the international economic literature has been Bhagwati's (1980) discovery that lobbying could increase rather than decrease welfare. This is an important contribution because it highlights the difference between partial and general equilibrium analysis. Until Bhagwati, several of us were of the incorrect opinion that the devotion of economic resources to redistributive ends was necessarily welfare reducing. Notice that Bhagwati's result is an exception and not a rule. He would be the first to argue that, in most cases, a systemic rule of "no lobbying" would dominate one of "everyone lobbying" in redistributive games. Bhagwati and Srinivasan (1980) extended this work by building a formal general equilibrium model in which economic resources are extracted from an economy by a lobby to obtain revenue that is being collected by an exogenously imposed tariff. In their framework, the tariff itself is the distortion that can generate negative shadow prices, and in some cases the lobbying for the tariff revenue can increase welfare. In both of these studies, the tariffs were exogenous. Feenstra and Bhagwati (1982) build a model in which the tariff is endogenous and in which the same second-best welfare effects of lobbying can still emerge.[2] Bhagwati's important result has been modified subsequently and refined in papers by Bhagwati and Srinivasan (1982), Anam (1982), and Dinopoulos (1983). Fries (1983) has an interesting analysis of the same problem with uncertainty.

Irrespective of what happens to aggregate welfare, the literature to this point generally presumes that at least one of the lobbies gains from lobbying while others in the economy lose; otherwise, the lobbying by that lobby would appear to be foolish. Is it possible that even this assessment is too optimistic and that the process of lobbying could lead everyone in society to be worse off, including the strongest lobby? Using Leontief production and probit probability of election functions, Young and Magee (1982) found that when both capital and labor lobbied over endogenous tariffs in a two-factor economy, both factors were worse off than they would have been with free trade in about 40 percent of the equilibria.

The results need explanation since it appears ridiculous for factors to voluntarily lobby for policies that make them all worse off. Our explanation is a prisoner's dilemma theory of endogenous tariffs: Free trade is not an equilibrium since either lobby could make itself better off at the other's expense with a small lobbying expenditure; if either factor voluntarily desists from lobbying, it can be exploited dramatically by the other factor; thus, the only equilibrium is for both to lobby. Like the two prisoners who confess, in the game theory example, both lobbies can be trapped by their own avarice in lobbying games. The prisoner's dilemma result has been applied in political science and economics extensively: e.g., to arms races. Young and I applied it to endogenous tariff theory, following Messerlin's (1981) lead. Other perversities also emerged in Young and Magee (1982): no equilibrium existed for the political lobbying game in well over half of the cases. This means that not everyone can be happy, no matter what the state of the economic and political situation, which means continual frustration for one or more of the lobbies, political parties, and economic agents. When an equilibrium could be found, there were always two equilibria and frequently three. The multiple equilibrium problem had been noted earlier by Young (1982) in his investigation of the Findlay-Wellisz model and noted also by Fennstra and Bhagwati in their model. The presence of multiple equilibria is suggestive for empirical work because it means that two economies can be identical in every political and economic parameter of apparent significance and yet can display very different equilibrium values of their tariffs, export subsidies, lobbying expenditures, probabilities of election for the procapital and prolabor parties, and welfare.

If everyone can be worse off in redistributive tariff games, what are the limits on the proportion of an economy's resources that can be consumed in lobbying? Young and I (1983) find that lobbying as a proportion of national income will hit an upper limit of 50 percent with risk neutrality. However, with risk aversion, we obtain a "black hole result," wherein lobbying can consume up to 100 percent of national income. In this equilibrium, only a small fraction of the economy will be engaged in productive activity while the rest will be battling over shares of the (nearly nonexistent) pie. Our intuition initially told us that this result might be most likely when one of the factors or parties was especially powerful relative to the other. Ironically, this proved to be incorrect. The black hole outcome was developed in a countervailing power case in which the two factors were of equal size and power and the economic and political system was symmetrical, giving neither factor an inherent advantage. These results were developed with specific functional forms: Cobb–Douglass production and consumption and logit probability of election functions. While the black hole result is a polar case, it may offer insight for some of the redistributional perversities known to exist in developing countries.

Tullock (1967) and Findlay and Wellisz (1982) suggest that the welfare losses from rent-seeking might be high and yet the policies that elicit these losses might be low. Young and I (1983) provide explicit support for this hypothesis. We investigate the effects of economic parameter changes that increase the responsiveness of all factor prices to product prices (the latter are the focus of rent-seeking) and find that each lobby will contribute a larger fraction of its resources to lobbying and yet the equilibrium distortions (tariffs and export subsidies) both fall. In other cases, parametric changes can lead to the more intuitive case of positive association between rent-seeking and the distortions. Thus the source of economic change must be identified before any statement can be made about the relationship between lobbying and policy distortions (since both are endogenous).

Thus far, all of the welfare statements have applied only to the economic actors in the country. What about the political actors? I will not argue here that welfare statements can be made about political parties; I will simply report some comparative statics on changes in the probabilities of election of the parties in an endogenous tariff framework. These results apply only in cases in which the probability of election is unitary elastic with respect to both resources and policies (positive with respect to resources and negative with respect to distortionary policy). Young and I (1982) find that an increase in a country's endowment of capital will increase the probability of election of the party supported by the capital lobby, as might be expected. That model used Leontief production. When Cobb–Douglass production and consumption are present, the electoral probabilities of election are independent of the factor endowment ratios (Young and Magee, 1983). The latter paper also produces another paradox. Make the responsiveness of capital's price to product prices greater than labor's. What happens in the new equilibrium? Not surprisingly, capital devotes a larger fraction of its resources to lobbying. We might also expect two other results: that the procapital party would be better off in the new equilibrium and would quote a lower export subsidy than before since less inducement is needed to attract resources from the capital lobby. However, neither of these speculations is true. The increase in the capital lobby contributions causes the prolabor party to cut the tariff it sponsors to attempt to recoup with a greater appeal to voters; the procapital party's optimal counterresponse is to set a higher export subsidy. It turns out that in the new equilibrium, the negative voter effects of the higher export subsidy more than outweigh the positive voter effects of greater assistance from the capital lobby; consequently, the probability of election of the procapital party drops. In this case, what was good for General Motors is bad for the Republicans. In short, partial equilibrium intuition may be a poor guide to the ultimate effects of parameter changes in general political-economic equilibrium.

GAME-THEORETIC CONSIDERATIONS

The preceding point illustrates the potential danger of using intuitive partial equilibrium reasoning in endogenous tariff models. The pitfalls emanate from two sources. The first is the general equilibrium nature of many of these models, an obvious point. The second is the constant sum nature of the political equilibrium in a democracy. Since every parametric change will usually help one party and hurt the other, the accommodating adjustments by both parties must be carefully reasoned. For example, Brock and I (1975) showed that if the tariff positions of two parties are placed on the axes, the reaction curves of the two parties always have opposite slopes in the neighborhood of equilibrium. The proof is based on the second-order conditions: the first party maximizes its probability of election while the second minimizes the first's probability of election. This "reverse slope theorem" means that any small movement in the neighborhood of equilibrium will show one party desiring to increase and the other party desiring to decrease its tariff.

There is a trick that permits relatively safe use of one's intuition in probabilistic voting models. If the ultimate changes in the ratios of the lobbying resources and in the ratios of the distortionary policies can be forecast, the change in the probability of election is unambiguous if the two ratios move in opposite directions. That is, if the ratio of lobbying resources favoring a party rises and the ratio of its distortionary policy falls, its electoral success rises. When the two ratios move together, a party is always helped by one of the movements and hurt by the other, so that the effects on the parties are ambiguous.

Another game-theory issue in model construction is the choice of the equilibrium concept. While there are many possibilities, most writers to date have employed Cournot–Nash and Stackelberg equilibria. The former takes all of the choice variables of the other actors as parameters, whereas a Stackelberg leader will make his choice only after calculating how the choice variable of another player will vary optimally from the latter's point of view. While the latter would appear to be the most sophisticated ploy to follow, it can be played by only a limited number of actors: for example, if both players attempt to employ a Stackelberg strategy in a two-player game, inconsistency results. In all of the work by Brock, Young and me, the parties are Stackelberg leaders vis-à-vis their own lobby, while the lobbies are Stackelberg leaders relative to the voters and the economy. The logic behind this construction is that as an empirical matter, parties have more information and power than lobbies and lobbies have more power than individual economic actors and voters. Feenstra and Bhagwati (1982) have the government act as a Stackelberg leader to the protariff lobby, whereas Findlay and Wellisz (1982) have both lobbies Stackelberg lead vis-à-vis an unspecified political process.

Three other results were provided in Magee and Brock (1975). First, positive distortions will emerge in the political equilibrium only if the parties Stackelberg lead relative to the lobbies. If the parties are not Stackelberg leaders (if they act in Cournot–Nash fashion vis-à-vis the lobbies or the lobbies are Stackelberg leaders), free trade emerges. Second, with parties acting as Stackelberg leaders, the rational lobby will give only to its favored party in a two-party race: e.g., it is irrational for a free trade lobby to contribute to the protectionist party. Third, the Hotelling equilibrium (both parties quoting the same tariff) should not emerge in these models. Why? If both parties quoted the same tariff rate, neither lobby would contribute, and tariff rates cannot be positive without contributions.

FREE TRADE VERSUS PROTECTION

One desirable property of an endogenous tariff model is that it be capable of explaining both free trade and protection. In the Brock and Magee models in Table 3-1, zero levels of lobbying resources will produce free trade, and free trade quotations by both parties will produce no lobbying expenditures in equilibrium. Young and I (1982) find that a party favors distortionary policy when its probability of election is sensitive to resources but insensitive to policies, whereas it favors free trade when its probability of election is insensitive to resources and sensitive to policy. In Mayer (1983), free trade would emerge if the distribution of factor endowments was symmetric (the mean and the median endowments of capital per man were identical) in the Hecksher-Ohlin-Samuelson (HOS) model; in his factor-specific Jones-Neary model, free trade will be adopted if the distribution of factor ownership, voting costs and voting probabilities are all symmetric.

NOTES TO CHAPTER 3

1. For more recent work in this area, see for example Otani 1980.
2. Bhagwati (1982c) has also attempted to introduce a new nomenclature by renaming rent-seeking as *directly unproductive profit-seeking* (DUP) activities. This innovation is being welcomed with about the same enthusiasm as the American switch to the metric system. While it might have caught on a few years earlier when the field was younger, there are social costs to establishing a new nomenclature, quite apart from the arguments. Railroads, politicians, and even academics are reluctant to change gauges after the track has been laid. At the same time, the "pro-rent seekers" should heed Bhagwati's admonition that only the returns from exogenous policies are rents; those from endogenous policies are not. Bhagwati is correct that lobbying to obtain endogenous policies is incorrectly described by the term "rent-seeking."

CRITIQUES OF RENT-SEEKING AND DUP ACTIVITIES

4 A CRITIQUE OF RENT-SEEKING THEORY

Warren J. Samuels and Nicholas Mercuro

The thesis of this chapter is that the analysis of rent-seeking cannot properly and conclusively sustain many of the analytical or policy uses to which it has been put. Whatever prominence the recent literature on rent-seeking has attained, it has been done on the basis of selective, restrictive, and question-begging assumptions.

In the traditional Ricardian notion of economic rent, rent is a return to a factor of production in permanent inelastic supply, a return over and above the minimum necessary to induce its offering onto the market. Alfred Marshall expanded the concept of rent to include temporary inelasticities of supply, calling these *quasi-rents*.[1] Over time, the concept of rent has been broadened, so that *rent* is now generally defined as income received over and above the amount that would be received under a different institutional, or rights, arrangement.

In the relevant specialized literature, rent-seeking is variously defined. In the preface to an important book on rent-seeking we read that "it is meant to describe the resource-wasting activities of individuals in seeking transfers of wealth through the aegis of the state." (Buchanan, Tollison, and Tullock, 1980: ix). In the same book we read that the term "is designed to describe behavior in institutional settings where individual efforts to maximize value generate social waste rather than social surplus" (Buchanan, 1980a: 4) and that "an individual who invests in something that will not actually improve productivity or will actually lower it, but that does raise his income because it gives him some special position

We are indebted to James M. Buchanan, David Colander, Betsy Johnston, Lawrence Martin, Allan Schmid, James Shaffer, Gordon Tullock, and Stephen Woodbury for comments on an initial draft of this chapter.

55

or monopoly power, is 'rent-seeking,' and the 'rent' is the income derived" (Tullock 1980a: 17; see also McCormick and Tollison 1979). In another book, rent-seeking is designated as "activities of monopolization," or efforts "to procure the shelter of the state from competition and thereby to earn monopoly rents" (Ekelund and Tollison 1981: 6) and also "activities whereby individuals seek returns from state-sanctioned monopoly rights" (p. 13). A working paper identifies rent-seeking as "the activity of getting a monopoly or getting some other government favor" (Tullock 1978: 2) and as the use of resources in attempts "to achieve government granted monopoly, change regulations in your favor or protect yourself against these activities" (p. 5; see also pp. 9-11). This paper also speaks of such resource use as net social waste (p. 11). In a recent article surveying rent-seeking theory, rent-seeking is defined as the "activity of wasting resources in competing for artificially contrived transfers" (Tollison 1982: 577). Thus, rent-seeking theory, so-called, seems to center on the alleged unambiguous waste of resources spent in the pursuit of altering legal rights (or their equivalents) in competitive activities designed to influence the distribution of income and wealth through the state.[2]

A critique of the literature was begun in 1980, focusing on the purported unambiguous wastes associated with rent-seeking activities. The central point of these critics was that resource diversions into rent-seeking, in a second-best legal-economic setting, may not represent a social loss but, in fact, may well result in an increase in welfare (Bhagwati 1982c: 988-1002; Bhagwati and Srinivasan 1980: 1069-87; Bhagwati 1980: 355-63). Summing up their argument Bhagwati and Srinivasan wrote: "Conclusions based on first-best intuitions, that is, that resource diversion to 'unproductive' activities must be wasteful, will not carry over into the analysis of [rent-] seeking activities" (1980: 1086).

Our purpose here is to extend the critique of rent-seeking theory along different lines by indicating its flaws and severe limitations as well as to suggest the correct legal-economic context in which rent-seeking activity is to be understood. We fully recognize that our analysis is predicated upon an interpretation of welfare economics and of law and economics quite contrary to the conventional approach adopted by many of those who have written on rent-seeking. We believe our approach is more descriptively accurate, much less ideologically slanted, and open to fewer abuses.

RENT-SEEKING: THE CONVENTIONAL WISDOM

The intellectual construct employed by most contributors to the literature on rent-seeking is that of a competitive market economy; that is, firms are viewed as price takers and attempt to maximize profits accordingly. Given these "natural" prices, the net revenues or income that obtain are defined or at least perceived to be legitimate profits. When individuals attempt to expand their net revenues they have at least two options. First, they can work through the usual marketplace and make marginal adjustments, adopt new technologies, alter their scale of plant, exit or enter, and so on, in which case the profits they garner remain "legitimate" profits. However, it is also recognized that a firm might undertake to expand net revenues by lobbying. That is, given the opportunity cost of scarce resources, the firms may choose to work through the state in a variety of ways to obtain an increase in the price of commodities or a decrease in factor prices. Firms will pursue such activities as long as the marginal benefit of lobbying (the increase in prices of commodities or reduction in factor prices) exceeds the marginal cost of lobbying. As the conventional wisdom goes, if output is not altered, the increase in net revenues or profits is termed *rent*; and such lobbying activities are termed *rent-seeking* and characterized as "waste" since output remained constant. The normative thrust of the rent-seeking literature is to promote policies designed to avoid the wasteful rent-seeking activities. In all this, theorists of rent-seeking make implicit assumptions as to individual preferences, social preferences, and the structure of rights as well as the role of government. The result is that they trivialize the major issues by selectively treating what are in reality very complex, important, and subtle matters.

The basic idea of government as a source or means of largesse—rent, or transfers—is by no means new. For example, there is an 1872 Currier and Ives political cartoon in which a politician holding something labeled "Government Cake" and saying "Let us have peace" is being pulled at by figures (all well-dressed and male) crying "Let us have a piece." To the extent that theorists of rent-seeking can construct viable economic models to explain better the use of government as a source of rent they are doing something important. There *is* rent-seeking activity. There is rent achievable and achieved through control of market positions. There is cost to rent-seeking; that is, it uses resources that have an opportunity cost. In different legal-economic settings, the pursuit of rent can result in either an increase or decrease in society's welfare, but these settings must be carefully stipulated. Ours is a gain-seeking society and economic system. It comes as no surprise to anyone that such advantage-seeking activity takes place or that it affects society's welfare. If rent-seeking theory were held to express only these points, there would be little if anything over which to quibble. However, as will become evident, it attempts to do much more.

NO "CORRECT" RENTS

In order to understand the nature of our criticisms of rent-seeking theory, this section is intended to provide an outline of the essential interrelationships between law and economics as related to rent-seeking that can serve as a benchmark of our criticisms.

1. Physical goods and services have little present significance beyond the rights that attach to and sometimes (or in some respects) define them. An

"effective commodity" is defined as the specific physical commodity plus the associated property rights that govern the use and exchange of the commodity (Furubotn and Pejovich 1974: 4-5). Further, legal rights in part define the good (through various legal specifications). It is in this sense that one can alter a commodity by changing rights and that changing rights can alter the value of the good. This conception of commodities together with the understanding that alternative structures of rights affect the allocation of resources, composition of output, and distribution of income help unmask the real nature of commodities. In a parallel treatment, the factors of production can be termed *effective resources*.

2. The prevailing prices of commodities and resources are in part a function of the past use of the state and, among other things, past rent-seeking activities. In the context of the market economy, the state is (like it or not) a principal vehicle for achieving values and interests. The state is thus an object of control, an object of competition, and an arena in which conflicts of values and interests are worked out. The pertinent questions become: Who uses government to set the initial assignment of rights to commodities and resources? Who uses government to define effective commodities and resources? Who subsequently uses government to change rights through law? And, who uses government to alter commodity and resource prices to garner net revenues, i.e., income?

The state governs rights, which in turn govern resource allocation and income and wealth distributions, which influence the future composition of output. Efforts to change the values and interests given economic effect by law are inevitable. The minimalist or protective conception of the state (Buchanan 1980a: 8-9) is narrow and misleading, particularly but not solely with regard to (1) the profound consequences of state action and (2) the inevitability of legal change. So, too, is the conception that the economy is a system of noncoercive exchange relationships, whereas the polity is the system of coercive or potentially coercive relationships.[3] In this context, rent-seeking activity is related to the use of government, where the use of government is seen as inevitable. There is not, fundamentally, more government influence on the distribution of wealth than formerly, but more conspicuous activity oriented toward legal change and influence.

One point to be understood is that legal change is intimately connected with other facets and processes of socioeconomic change. Legal change, and efforts to bring it about, are seen negatively only through a particular ideology. The market economy itself developed and evolved in part through a process of legal change—that is, through efforts to remake the system of rights from the predominance of a system of landed (feudal) property to one of nonlanded (capitalist) property. The transformation of the economy from a postfeudal to a business system did not just happen. People were seeking rents. The law of England, for example, changed to accommodate industrial and mercantile interests, resulting in part in the absorption of the Law Merchant in the common law. There was not only the repeal of the Corn Laws but also the gradual evolution of the law of negotiable instruments, business corporations, and so on. This was a dynamic process interpretable in terms of rent-seeking by individual commercial interests attempting to reform the law in their favor. If mercantilism was a rent-seeking society, so too was capitalism. This is the very stuff of which political economy and public choice is made.

3. Models of the economy predicated on price-taking behavior are in reality models of rights-taking behavior. Since the market prices governing revenue and cost calculations are a partial function of rights, such a model has meaning only within the context of the specific structure of rights that is specified in the analysis of rent-seeking or the structure of rights being ignored if left unspecified in the analysis.

In this context the virtues of rent-seeking theory are many. It does focus on the allocation of resources resulting from the competition over the control or use of government for private advantage. It does reinforce the often neglected fact that prices in the market are a partial function of the operation of government, and are a part of a larger process wherein resource allocation and income distribution are determined by the self-interested behavior of individuals seeking favorable market results, including so-called rents. Rent-seeking theory does help clarify that legal rights help govern who can participate in the economy in efforts to secure positions in the market from which one is more capable to receive income.

4. Since the prevailing market prices that make up the firm's revenue-cost calculations are property-rights specific, so too is the net revenue calculation property-rights specific. That is, prices are not absolute, predetermined, and independent of law but are a product, in part, of the structure of rights. The genesis, structure, and distribution of economic rent is a function of power, rights, asymmetrical transaction cost systems, and other variables. There is no unique pattern of rent and no pattern of rent independent of law. Rights govern the realization and distribution of gains from trade, including rents.

5. Given the evolving nature of law (rights) and the past and present ubiquitous use of government to secure positions in the market, there simply is no way of unambiguously determining which activities make up profit seeking and which make up rent-seeking—that is, which portion of net revenues is rent and which is "legitimate" profits. Criticisms (as wasteful) of certain rent-creating opportunities engendered by government often, if not typically, take as given other existing rent-creating actions of government. Accordingly, rent-seeking theory criticism is selective. The reality is that rent is a function of many, if not all, government activities.[4]

6. A policy that purports to eliminate the "wastes" associated with rent-seeking activities is as artificial as the artificial distinctions drawn to delimit rents from profits and wastes from production. There are no *correct* rights, price, and rent structure and attendant distribution. There is, rather, a contest over rights,

prices, and, in the present context, especially over the creation and acquisition of economic rents.

THE PROBLEM OF "WASTE"

One of the principal assertions of rent-seeking theory is that the quest for rent inexorably involves waste. Although this seems to make sense on a superficial level, several problems with it severely restrict the analytical and policy significance of the theory.

The theorists of rent-seeking contemplate *waste* in reference to *productive* outputs, the criterion of which involves the creation of real assets, or social assets in the physical sense (Tullock 1980: 23). When the theorist says that rent-seeking produces nothing of net value, he means that resources are utilized in countervailing, or competitive, efforts to produce rental income (net revenues in one form or another) that do not involve the creation of real assets of use to the community.

One problem with this, of course, is the strictly physical conception of productiveness. This conception ignores the rights surrounding the commodity and the very rights that define the commodity, both of which impart value to the commodity.

A second, more important problem is that the market test of productiveness is rejected. The mainstream conception of economics is that the use of scarce resources is productive of value, and that value is determined in the market, as a matter of demand vis-à-vis supply. The rent-seeking theorists' conception of waste clearly rejects the preferences of individual economic actors as to how they will utilize their resources, which is a principal foundation of market-based productiveness. These preferences may well include the desire or opportunity to hire lawyers and lobbyists to bring about changes of legal rights in order to enhance revenues.

Third, one clear result—perhaps the objective—of rent-seeking theory is to rule out distributive results as an aim of individual economic actors (Buchanan 1980b: 359). Only production counts, not distribution. But this is every bit as presumptive of individual utility functions as is a physical conception of productiveness. Individual economic actors are entitled to think differently, no matter what some economists prefer to stipulate.

We are aware that the theorists of rent-seeking specify that there will be "social waste, even if the investments involved are fully rational for all participants" (Buchanan 1980a: 9). But the problem is whether economic well-being is to be defined in terms of the accumulation of real assets *or* personal utility functions. Quite aside from the very important question of whose capital accumulation or personal utility functions are to count, there is no reason why the former definition of well-being should be preferred to the latter. Further, as established earlier, critics of rent-seeking theory have shown that a decrease in output can be consistent with enhanced welfare. Nonetheless, to pursue rent-seeking analysis in physical terms by postulating a physical real-asset notion of productiveness and thereby of waste is to conduct analysis at a level independent of the human preferences and institutional organization of society.

Fourth, whenever rent-seeking theorists conclude that certain law-related (or legal-change related) activities are wasteful because they do not lead to the creation of real assets, they are placed in the position of assuming the propriety of all other laws governing the production of economic goods. The asserted welfare loss of which they speak is a function of altering the assignment or definition of a particular subset of rights, which assumes as given (and legitimate) all other rights and laws governing the production of economic goods.

Nowhere is this point more evident than in the rent-seeking theorists' use of the usual welfare-triangle calculation to define as rent the deadweight loss associated with the competitive use of resources over and above the traditional triangle.[5] The welfare-triangle diagram has on its respective axes only the price and quantity dimensions of a particular commodity. Conclusions of deadweight loss and, especially, resource-wasting rent-seeking activity, the latter so central to rent-seeking theory, presume the given physical commodity. However, as has been made clear, effective commodities are in part a function of law. What is called rent-seeking activity often comprises efforts to change the law to alter the commodity. There being no unique structure of rights surrounding a commodity nor a unique definition of a commodity, conclusions as to waste predicated upon solely physical definitions of commodities are neither proper nor conclusive guides to policy matters.

In addition, the triangle that has attracted so much of their attention is predicated upon a given demand (revenue) curve and a long-run marginal cost curve.[6] Both curves and thus the triangle are property-right specific being a partial function of past laws (rights) and changes in those laws as well as past rent-seeking activity. It is in this sense that the use of the diagram to delimit wastes can only be accomplished by lending propriety to all other laws governing the production of economic goods.

Viewed from another perspective, the "characteristics" approach to demand theory suggests that commodities may and perhaps must be defined not physically but by attributed characteristics, the attribution being made by economic actors and not intrinsic to the commodities themselves. "Safety" could be one characteristic by which a commodity is subjectively defined (arguably an important Austrian economics point). Thus, among the processes of the economy are those that establish the effective identity of commodities in terms of various characteristics. As Frank Knight wrote, "There are important values in production itself which tend to be overlooked in economic theory" (1952: 18). Commodities are, in the real world, defined in terms of certain values, and it remains an ongoing problem to (re)work their definitions.

The activities deemed rent-seeking may be understood to be directed, in part, to the solution of the fundamental problem of the structure of rights that define effective commodities and resources. Commodities and resources are not given by nature; they are defined by society (including actions by groups that establish material product and resource standards). That is a normative matter, and economic actors are understandably engaged in it given their preferences and observed activities. It is they who have to produce and consume commodities. Unless one is prepared to take some (for example, the status quo) definitions of commodities and resources as given, rent-seeking theory cannot condemn so-called rent-seeking activities as wasteful. Allocation *is* distribution-specific and society has the burden of working out the rights associated with commodities and resources and in doing so determines whose interests are to count. That ultimately *is* a distributional matter. Insofar as economic actors are motivated by a desire to maximize their respective incomes and wealth, distribution cannot be ruled out of analytical bounds, as rent-seeking theory so clearly would do.

It would appear that a complete analysis of rent-seeking activity would not interpose a selective notion of productiveness in place of the actual choices by economic actors of what they want. It would recognize that both the origin and distribution of rent are in part a product of all law, not just an instance of altered law singled out for condemnation as wasteful. Rent-seeking theory would recognize that one can achieve conclusions as to wastefulness only by the introduction of selective assumptions as to the antecedent structure of rights governing definitions of commodities, assumptions that substitute for the subjective preferences of economic actors as to commodity definitions and how they will use their effective resources.

THE ASSUMPTION OF (STATUS QUO) RIGHTS

Narrow conceptions of waste and productiveness are not the only severe limits to the theory of rent-seeking as it is conventionally understood. As indicated in the previous section, the theorists of rent-seeking also assume the existence of and lend propriety to, the already defined and assigned rights. Theirs is a model of rights-taking behavior that postulates some particular rights structure, typically one selectively deemed most consonant with a market system, *or* simply "some" rights structure—the status quo structure. Given the propriety of status quo rights, however defined, waste thus becomes the result of all, or substantially all, efforts to change and defend them.

Rent-seeking theorists grant that government is involved in the initial identification and assignment of rights. But the thrust of their efforts is guided by what has been called "Buchanan's ever-vigilant efforts to prevent conceptual over-extension of the economic rationale" (Burkhead and Miner 1971: 139) for further governmental activity. That is, the rights defining wealth are to be considered as essentially unalterable features of the world (Congleton 1980: 153). For all practical purposes Buchanan adopts a once-and-for-all-time position with regard to government action concerning rights. Once rights are set in place, the only permissible mode of change is through market exchange. Buchanan is quite candid about this:

> to the extent that property rights are specified in advance, genuine "trades" can emerge, with mutual gains to all parties. However, to the extent that existing rights are held to be subject to continuous redefinition by the State, no one has an incentive to organize and to initiate trades or agreements. This amounts to saying that once the body politic begins to get overly concerned about the distribution of the pie under existing property-rights assignments and legal rules, once we begin to think either about the personal gains from law-breaking, privately or publicly, or about the disparities between existing imputations and those estimated to be forthcoming under some idealized anarchy, we are necessarily precluding and forestalling the achievement of potential structural changes that might increase the size of the pie for *all*. Too much concern for "justice" acts to ensure that "growth" will not take place, and for reasons much more basic than the familiar economic incentives arguments. (Buchanan 1972: 36–37)

This is the mind-set underlying much of rent-seeking theory (see also Krueger 1980: 69–70). It deliberately or inadvertently postulates the preeminence of some given, status quo structure of rights—and the nature of the bundle of commodities that make up the pie together with the rights-specific market prices. By giving such preeminence to the status quo structure of rights it has the effect of ruling out of analytical bounds most if not all efforts to change rights. Indeed, such efforts are selectively denigrated as wasteful. The effect is to perpetuate status quo rights. If the only permissible change is through exchange, the price structure will reflect the high reservation demands of the already wealthy vis-à-vis all other persons. This would have rent-seeking theory adopt what has been called "the attitude of the established classes, the people who have arrived and secured their positions. They feel that the problems of life have been settled at last, and that what remains is merely to take this settlement as fixed for all time and make the most of it" (Small 1924: 263).

NO DISTINGUISHING PRINCIPLES: SELECTIVE LEGAL CHANGE

Whatever else one may find in the theory of rent-seeking, the theory makes it perfectly clear, by assertion, that if only there were no possibilities to influence the distributions of income and wealth through the state by jockeying for change of legal rights, there would be no waste of resources in the manner contemplated by the theory. Rent-seeking is described, it will be recalled, as "the resource-wasting activities of individuals in seeking transfers of wealth through the aegis of the state" (Buchanan, Tollison, and Tullock 1980: ix). The only way to avoid such activities is through the negation of such legal change. The fundamental problem is that the theorists of rent-seeking offer as a benchmark for their theories situations in which there would be selective legal changes, but with no principle by which conclusively to distinguish permissible from impermissible legal changes. In a fundamental sense they are more interested in limiting the right to try to change the law than looking openly at the society that could emerge under changing law.

Given that the prevailing market prices (necessary for rent calculations) are in part a function of status quo rights, there is simply no other benchmark structure of rights from which to identify rent-seeking behavior. Needless to say, this has created something of a tension and an ambiguity in the literature on rent-seeking. The choice seems to be either to assume and give effect to status quo rights or to ambiguously finesse government as a mode of change. Just as Buchanan, preferring exchange of legal rights to legal change of legal rights, nonetheless would permit some constitutional change, the rent-seeking literature recognizes that "the right to alter rights seems to be one of the most enduring, though the methods that must be used vary greatly from place to place and time to time" (Tullock 1980: 28) and that certain changes of rights and thus certain transfers "can be justified to rectify previously illegitimate holdings" (Anderson and Hill 1980: xiv—the example given is slavery).[7] But the theory of rent-seeking provides no unequivocal basis on which to distinguish between legitimate and illegitimate previous rights' definitions and assignments. The thrust of much of the literature on rent-seeking is to identify as wasteful all efforts both to change the law and defend against change of the law.

But, change there will be; the operative questions are what will change and who will determine the change. As Frank Knight expressed the matter, "the immediate practical problem confronting society at any time is that of progressively remaking its institutional system" (1947: 221–22). The legal system that identifies and assigns rights must have a process for reconstituting the structure and distribution of rights. Socioeconomic change, including technological change, brings about new subjects and new problems for reassessing and potentially changing the definitions of effective commodities and resources and assignments of rights to them. There must be the possibility for changing the interests given protection as rights as new conceptions of justification, entitlement, and consequence emerge as a result of the explorative and emergent processes of social living. The phrase "explorative and emergent" is Knight's, and it stands in marked contrast to the central thrust of the theory of rent-seeking. It simply will not do to offer a theory so lacking in realism and discrimination as to condemn as wasteful the utilization of resources involved in working out solutions to this necessary, progressive remaking of the institutional system.

The theory of rent-seeking offers a pretense of a state without a process of legal change. It does not deny the inevitability of law governing the allocation of resources and the distributions of income and wealth, but it seems systematically to denigrate the inevitably and *a priori* desirability of efforts to change the law. But no final assignments by law are possible in a democracy or, for that matter, in any other society. Knight wrote that immediate social problems arise in situations "where a complex set of rules of social living already exists and functions in some way" and "because the 'progress of civilization' makes men critical and constantly more critical of their inherited laws and institutions and makes them desirous of *changing* them" (1952: 21). He recognized that each citizen in his or her own way strives "to bring it about that the law itself shall conform to the highest attainable ideal of justice and the general good, and shall afford accurate guidance to the individual, as far as possible" (p. 14). Knight did recognize that this process may be offensive to freedom because of the coercion it involved, but he recognized that coercion resided in *any* system of law, even one unchanged, and argued for a system neither of violence nor of unilateral fiat but of discussion. But legal change had to come about. He recognized both that "new forms of moral responsibility and need for law and enforcement to maintain 'standards'" will emerge and that "since freedom allows organization for power ... organization for power creates a vital problem for social action and a type of political responsibility for the citizen" (p. 18).

Contrary to much of the current rent-seeking literature, it would appear more sensible to recognize that the process of determining the legal change of economic interests to be protected as legal rights is *the* critical legal-economic process and is one that people apparently value as indicated by their revealed preferences, rent-seeking theory notwithstanding. Legal change of interests to be protected as legal rights is a vehicle for economic gain and advantage as individuals and subgroups jockey for position to participate in the economy, engaging in a struggle over the distributions of income and wealth. We may or may not prefer it to be different, but certainly that is how matters are. To say that this type of competition, in contrast to that over the production and exchange of "real" goods and services, is wasteful, appears naïve and certainly is presumptive with regard to both wastefulness and the problem of legal change.

The policy prescriptions set forth by some of the contributors to rent-seeking rest on weak (perhaps unfounded) assertions. Consider the scope of participation in decisionmaking. The rent-seeking theorists aver that "rent-seeking has become more important because institutional changes have opened up opportunities that did not exist in the nineteenth and early twentieth centuries," that is, because governmental action has moved "significantly beyond the limits defined by the minimal or protective state" and has done so "on a sweeping scale" (Buchanan 1980a: 3, 9). One objection to such reasoning is that it neglects the opportunity for and reality of rent-seeking behavior in earlier periods in this country's history. Moreover, although there never has been a solely "minimal or protective" state, if one existed it would involve efforts to change the law. If rent-seeking theory understands past forbearance from action as something other than preserving the status quo, it is misguided: the power to prevent legal change is no less a power than that exercised to accomplish legal change.

But the present problem lies elsewhere. The reason for this *apparent* increase in governmental activism is the conspicuousness of legal change in a system in which the proportion of the population having nominal access to government has increased (especially via the franchise). It is this wider access to and participation in government that has increased the conspicuousness and absolute amount of resources entering the competition to control and use government law in efforts to bring about legal change of the interests to be protected as rights or otherwise.

In addition, consider the implication that the elimination of wasteful utilization of resources in rent-seeking efforts to change the law requires a serious modification of democratic access to and participation in government. That is, they argue that "If political allocation is to be undertaken without the emergence of wasteful rent-seeking, the differential advantages granted to some persons as a result of the allocation must be eliminated." On this basis it is suggested "that all persons in the community must be allowed equal access to the scarcity values created by governmental intervention in the market economy" (Buchanan 1980a: 11). We are not sure precisely what this means, but we note in passing that this potentially involves a radical redistribution of income and wealth, indeed, a massive effort at and through legal change—and certainly one in which great investments of resources of a rent-seeking kind might reasonably be expected. If the proffered solution to rent-seeking is held to involve greater access to and use of the law and if the level of rent-seeking resource use ("waste") is a function of greater access to and participation in government, we do not see how this solution would minimize wasteful rent-seeking.

Finally, by positing the possibility, if not the desirability, of a system in which resources are not wasted in rent-seeking, the theorists of rent-seeking appear to permit legal change selectively and to set up a presumably workable base in which "existing rights" are *not* "held to be subject to continuous redefinition by the State" (Buchanan 1972: 367).[8] Yet Buchanan acknowledges that it would be "absurd to think that a politically determined allocation of resources could be frozen once and for all and that resource owners and entrepreneurs would not continually seek more profitable opportunities in politics as in markets" (Buchanan 1980a: 11). We think that this last statement is eminently realistic, however displeasing to a certain state of mind. But Buchanan, as do most theorists of rent-seeking, goes on to condemn as wasteful virtually all use of resources in efforts to change the law.

CONCLUSION

In a review of a book whose authors represent the opposite end of the ideological spectrum from that of most or all of the writers on the theory of rent-seeking, Alfred Kahn described the volume as "an ideological tract masquerading as objective research." He noted that "a disinterested reader will feel compelled to quarrel every inch of the way. But the phenomenon the authors forcefully describe cries out for serious attention. Even though I found their analysis distorted, their explanations simplistic and their remedies of dubious efficacy, I commend their message to anyone interested in where America is and where it is going" (Kahn 1982: 11). Much the same can be said of the literature on rent-seeking. For issues as important as these one has to be concerned that the rough and tumble world of democracy not be sacrificed on the altar of narrow and myopic principles. If we grant what is important and viable about rent-seeking theory, we must also recognize its severe limits. As Knight argued, we must "emphasize the limitation of principles. I often say that all principles are false because all are true; that is, no one can be completely true, because opposed principles also contain partial truth (1952: 6). It is simply fatal to all sound political thinking to ascribe absolute validity to any simple principle" (p. 20). Knight laments the tendency to romanticize, "to go to any extreme, to over-simplify, and [to] attempt to solve any serious problem by a formula or especially by name-calling" (pp. 6-7).

The problem with the theory of rent-seeking is that it is credible only if one is willing to accept certain limiting assumptions and selective perceptions with regard to output, waste, legal change, and the state. These assumptions and perceptions mislead positive analysis and generate artificial distinctions and thereby provide no real basis for distinguishing between permissible and impermissible activities. It is an artificial, indiscriminate analytical tool that misguides normative analysis inasmuch as it cannot properly sustain the conclusions it reaches.

The theory of rent-seeking rejects the system of business- and nonbusiness-government interrelations in the total social decisionmaking process in the modern economic system. It does so in favor of a stylized conception of static efficiency in a closed economic system that necessarily and tautologically assures a negative view of rent-seeking activity.[9] In assuming the definitions of effective commodities and resources and the structure of legal rights, rent-seeking theory cannot address problems of their change without being presumptive about some structure of rights—a structure that must be worked out through the social decisionmaking process. The theory of rent-seeking, like so many other manifestations of the "public choice" approach, would effectively rule out continuing public choice. The irony, of course, is that advocates of the theories of rent-seeking and public choice, although they seemingly reject legal change motivated by ideology,[10] are themselves engaged in precisely such activity. Interestingly, the work of Douglass North and Richard Posner, both also on the conservative end of the political spectrum, suggests that statute and common law, respectively, reflect wealth-maximizing efforts by government in part in response to efforts by interested individuals, an argument that itself goes too far (Samuels 1981). One cannot properly argue that legal change is optimal, except presumptively *ex post* on the basis of the interests actually given legal support in the process of legal change. Similarly, one cannot conclude, except presumptively, that jockeying for position to redesign legal arrangements is suboptimal (wasteful).

What, then, is the theory of rent-seeking saying? Is it denying the realism of legal change in order to make a presumptive case against certain uses of resources? Is it condemning all such resource use as wasteful? Where is the principle by which we can distinguish between cases and situations in which rent-seeking legal change activity is permitted and those in which it is not permitted? Given all the occasional qualifications found in the literature, the theorists of rent-seeking operate in an arena of analytical ambiguity.

But one thing is clear. The theory of rent-seeking subtly, and with much irony, affirms the moral propriety of the competition for the control of the state. The state is a principal vehicle for achieving values and interests, no less through and within a market system than any other. There is, then, an inevitability to efforts to redesign and redirect state activity. And that is precisely what the theorists of rent-seeking are seeking to do while analytically castigating and normatively trying to eliminate rent-seeking. They are rent-seeking with regard to their ideological position, using the theory as a Schumpeterian handle, as it were, to change the structure of social power. They are participating in the processes through which are determined who will use government to change rights by law. It is but another chapter in a long—and honorable—quest for building blocks with which to erect a conservative intellectual fortress.

NOTES TO CHAPTER 4

1. Economic rent as a conceptual category is to be distinguished from the actual rent payments that distribute economic rent and that are derivative in part from varying land tenure and other rights structures (see Marshall 1920; book 6, chs. 9, 10).

2. It is recognized that rent-seeking need not entail the use of government but can be accomplished in the private sector. For instance, one author in commenting on the applicability of rent-seeking theory wrote that it "does not depend on a government-propped-up monopoly right" and "includes institutional processes in the private sector," that is, within nominally private firms and other institutions (Tollison 1982: 587). See also Bhagwati (1982c: 991).

3. Buchanan, "What Should Economists Do?," *Southern Economic Journal* 30 (January 1964), p. 220, quoted in Burkhead and Miner 1971: 165. Compare Hale 1923: 470–94.

4. For example, with regard to the increasingly scarce energy coal resources, the distribution of rent is a function of required state (or, in the case of Canada, province) royalty payments of minerals, severance taxes, property taxes, income tax deductibility of royalty payments, price controls, distinctions (if any) between "old" and "new" reserves, land restoration requirements, import quotas, prorationing, and depletion allowances, Connally Hot Oil Act provisions, provisions for deferral of taxes on unrealized appreciation of reserves, and, *inter alia*, a variety of conservation policies and techniques. See Gaffney and Samuels (1977: 252–58).

5. See Tullock, Krueger, and McCulloch, each quoted by Bhagwati (1980: 355–56).

6. For one such illustration, see Tollison (1982: 580).

7. One further problem involves the use by the theorists of rent-seeking of such terms as "natural" and "artificial." We read of "artificial interferences with markets by the state" (Buchanan, Tollison, and Tullock 1980: ix), "arbitrary and/or artificial scarcity created by government" (Buchanan 1980a: 9; see also Ekelund and Tollison 1981: 18, 20), rent "contrived *artificially* through, for example, government action" (Tollison 1982: 575), and "artificially created" transfers (ibid.: 578). The use of such terms is presumptive and question begging. The tendentious use of *natural* tends to involve, as Bentham put it, nonsense upon stilts, deliberately to obscure important questions. Surely theorists of rent-seeking would have identical objections to claims that "the modern industrial wage-earner [has become] a characteristic representative of that artificial race of men now growing up in cities" (Sombard 1904: 792) and that the institution of the corporation has led to special privileges, "artificial values," "inequitable contracts," and other means "by which some are enabled to thrive and prey upon the public" (Joshua K. Ingalls, *Social Wealth*, New York: The Truth Seeker Company, 1885, quoted in Hall 1980: 392, 294.) The use of such terms as *artificial* and *natural* provides the appearance of closure but actually is indefinite and selective. As Knight argued, the distinction between artificial and natural has no general validity and rests on "sentimental" grounds (see Knight's Introduction to Menger 1950: 27). Ultimately, the problem here is the same as with the attempt to distinguish, with regard to the market plus framework approach to the economic role of government, between framework filling activities and other, particularistic interventions of government (Samuels, 1966: ch. 1) — that is, to define the minimal or protective state. There is, however, no possibility of an unequivocal classification of government actions into one or the other of these categories, so the distinction breaks down. The same is true of "artificial" versus "natural" interferences with markets by the state in the theory of rent-seeking. The result is an empty rhetorical device that serves to abet analysts in introducing selective antecedent normative premises as to acceptable and unacceptable legal-change actions of government, at least when all government legal-change action is not summarily denigrated. The result, in other words, is an exercise in power-thought, not description; emotion, not science.

8. If it were not contemplated that there might be such a situation, then, one wonders, how it is possible and why it is deemed useful to say, "However, if the world is not clearly understood by all, or if one's opportunity set is not entirely determined externally by forces beyond the influence of an individual actor, situations are very likely to arise in which an economically rational individual will use the resources at his disposal to influence his range of options at the expense of others" (Congleton 1980: 154). Buchanan also has written, "In a positive, empirical sense, many of our social-legal institutions have 'grown' independently of design and intent. But man must look on *all* institutions as potentially improvable. Man must adopt the attitude that he can control his fate; he must accept the necessity of choosing. He must look on himself as man, not another animal, and upon 'civilization' as if it is of his own making" (1977: 136).

9. With regard to the condemnatory application of the theory of rent-seeking to foreign trade, see Bhagwati (1980, 1982c) and Bhagwati and Srinivasan (1980), as well as Samuels (1980).

10. Buchanan, "Foreword," in Anderson and Hill (1980: xi).

5 LIMITS ON SELF-SEEKING
The Role of Morality in Economic Life

Michael S. McPherson

Although economists have always recognized that some sort of moral (or "normative") thinking is required to evaluate the economy, they have generally brought in morality from *outside*, as a standard of external judgment. Recently, however, economists have recognized that morality plays a central role within the economy and that the moral ideas of the participants in the economy *themselves* — their willingness to restrain their pursuit of self-interest within morally prescribed limits — is essential to normal economic functioning. Thus morality is an important part of the reality economists try to understand. Even market economies (to reduce a central theme of this literature to a slogan) are built not only on mutual interest but also on mutual trust.

Importing moral notions into our understanding of the economy is in a way inverse to "economic imperialism" — of which rent-seeking theory is a prominent example. The goal of such imperialism is to employ the traditional economists' assumption of self-interest to explain noneconomic phenomena without relying on notions of "morality," "fairness," "public interest," and the like. Indeed, the rent-seeking literature derives valuable insight from probing the disturbing asymmetry of theoretical views that postulate rigorous self-interest in economic conduct and some vague notion of moral or public-spirited conduct elsewhere. It is illuminating to see what follows from assuming that people pursue the same self-interest in trying to influence the rules of the economic game that we usually assume they pursue in playing the economic game.

My thanks to Lee J. Alston, Albert O. Hirschman, Dennis F. Thompson, and Gordon C. Winston for encouragement and helpful comments. Eric Stein supplied valuable research assistance. This chapter was prepared with the help of a grant from the Ford Foundation.

The approach of this chapter is to attack the same asymmetry from the other side: If views about morality and fairness in fact affect a wide range of non-economic conduct—for example, in politics, religion, and the family—it might also be illuminating to see what implications moral conduct has for economic behavior and performance. The two approaches to the asymmetry are not mutually exclusive, unless one assumes (as some "imperialists" seem to) that self-interest is not just a helpful working assumption but, rather, a deep truth about human nature. Indeed, an approach that emphasizes morality may usefully remind us that the self-interest postulate is partial and that theories built upon it (like all theories), by shedding light on some features of reality, cast others into darkness.

I shall take up two major issues. First: What makes morality economically valuable? Second: Given that morality matters to the economy, what accounts for people's willingness to be moral? The second is a difficult question for economists, who are professionally predisposed to postulate a self-interested basis for action. But even attempting to be more neutral—assuming, let's say, that it is just as natural to help an old lady across the street as to shove her in an alley and take her purse—we are interested in how social arrangements may foster or undermine our willingness to be moral.

THE ECONOMIC VALUE OF MORALITY [1]

The most relevant dimension of morality from the standpoint of economic interaction is what might loosely be called "honest dealing": a general willingness to tell the truth, to keep promises and contracts, and more broadly, to refuse to "take advantage" of others—to live up to the spirit as well as the letter of our commitments and obligations.

Honest dealing would lose its point—indeed even its sense—in a world of complete certainty. (In fact, increasing attention by economists to the consequences of uncertainty is probably the major impetus behind this new economic focus on morality.) The possibility of deception or dishonesty depends on one party to an agreement exploiting the ignorance of the other. Even more than simple uncertainty, the need for morality arises because of an *asymmetry* of information between parties. It is because one actor knows something the other does not (what he knows may be simply his own intentions) that opportunities for exploitation arise.

Insurance markets provide a useful starting point to illustrate these ideas. The institution of insurance is based on the *fact* of uncertainty and on the notion that a large group of people can, by agreeing to share risks with one another, help cushion the impact of that uncertainty on any individual in the group. For example, we all, through the mediation of a fire insurance company, in effect agree to chip in to help buy a new house for someone whose house has burned down—trading the certainty of a small loss (the premium) for the small risk of a devastating one.

Insurance agreements are, however, notoriously prone to the problem of "moral hazard." The fact that one has been insured against a risk makes it less worthwhile to take precautions to avert it. I have less reason to avoid overloading the electrical system in my house if it is insured for fire than if it is not, and in the extreme I may deliberately burn down my house to collect the insurance. The problem of moral hazard thus arises because of an asymmetry of information between insurer and insured. The insured, presumably, knows he was negligent or an arsonist; the insurer knows less. If information were equal between the parties—if, say, the insurer could know effortlessly and immediately exactly how neglectful each homeowner was, and exactly how fires started, there would not be a problem of moral hazard. Instead, insurers would merely link premium payments to the degree of neglectfulness.

It is clear that the presence of moral hazard makes insurance markets work less well than they otherwise could. Insurance will be more expensive, partly because greater negligence will lead to more fires and other losses and partly because policyholders wind up paying the costs of policing the insurance agreements (investigating for arson, inspecting establishments, administering physicals). Some kinds of insurance simply will not be available because the incentives to cheat are too great: that is why you cannot in general insure your home for more than it is worth.

But moral hazard is in part a moral problem. It is alleviated to the degree that people are honest or keep their word. For example, if insurance companies could expect an honest answer to the question, "Did you burn your building down?," fire insurance would be both cheaper and easier to get in the South Bronx. More modestly, honest answers to medical questions, a willingness to continue to take reasonable precautions against hazards even when insured, a disposition to report claims truthfully—such moral qualities make insurance more economical and effective.

The same points apply to any economic relationship in which one actor has an informational advantage over another, and a private incentive to exploit it. An obvious example is the doctor–patient relationship (see Arrow 1963), where the doctor knows more about the need for and risks of a surgical procedure than the patient does but where the doctor may also have a private incentive to perform more operations than "good medicine" warrants. Medical codes of ethics, which require the doctor to put the patient's interest first, can be viewed as a kind of institutionalized morality that helps protect patients against this opportunity for exploitation.

A vivid illustration of the economic value of morality is the market in human blood for transfusion (see Titmuss 1971; Arrow 1972; Singer 1973; and Alchian and Allen 1973). Since there is no reliable way to detect serum hepatitis in human blood, blood donors are not allowed to give blood if they say they have had the disease. "Altruistic" blood donors, whose aim is simply to help others, have no reason to *lie* about their medical histories. But those who sell their blood have an incentive to lie, especially since it is almost impossible to trace contaminated blood back to the individual donor.

This difference in incentives among types of donors has dramatic consequences. In one controlled study of cardiac surgery patients, more than half the patients who received blood from commercial sources contracted hepatitis. Among those who received blood from unpaid donors, none did (Arrow 1972: 44).

The danger of hepatitis provides good reason to attempt to avoid the purchase of blood altogether, as Britain does. It is even possible, as Richard Titmuss (1971) argued in his study comparing British and American experience, that people would be more likely to give blood if they understood that there were no commercial alternative, so that the supply of blood might be higher if its sale were prohibited. For Titmuss, this practical advantage of a voluntary donation system was only a part of a larger view of the moral significance of "the gift relationship." I shall return to these larger questions below.

Remaining at the practical level, this case reveals a trade of one dimension of morality for another. To the degree that we cannot trust paid donors to tell the truth about their medical histories when they have an individual incentive to lie, we may instead be forced to rely on the willingness of voluntary donors to give freely when they have only a moral incentive to give. Either way, the market for blood will not work well unless people are moral.

These medical examples are particularly telling because the uncertainties are so great and the stakes are so high, but less spectacular examples of the need for morality are pervasive in economic life. In fact, as Thomas Hobbes recognized so clearly, any transaction in which the performance of the two parties is separated by time involves an element of trust. In such cases, morality acts not as a replacement for the market, but as an almost indispensable backdrop for it.

Obviously, we do not usually rely simply on blind trust; we take steps to protect ourselves against dishonesty. We investigate the background of people we deal with; we write elaborate contracts and enforce them in court; and we promise repeat business as an incentive for people to "deal straight" with us. But all these devices are costly of time and money. As in the insurance examples, the more we can trust people to be honest, the less we have to protect ourselves, and the more efficiently markets will work. Furthermore, try as we might, we are often enough *forced* to rely on people's honesty. The next time your car breaks down in a small town in Idaho, you have little recourse but to hope that the local mechanic lives by the maxim, "Virtue is its own reward."

Let me turn from relationships across markets to relationships within the firm or enterprise. The value of morality may be even greater in this latter case.

Economists have traditionally seen the firm as a black box with inputs of machinery, raw materials, and labor poured in at one end, and output flowing out the other. This rather mechanical picture is useful for some purposes, but in many ways it is more accurate to see the typical firm as a little society, marked by conflicts and commonalities of interest, and with a need for a measure of moral behavior by the participants to hold it together.

The fundamental role of morality within the firm is grounded in the presence of informational asymmetries and differential incentives among the members. In many kinds of work, the worker has significant control over the information the boss receives concerning his effort and contribution to production, and a substantial incentive to minimize the effort he expends.

Firms will try to discourage such "shirking."[2] They can increase the level of supervision, although that costs time and money and brings the problem, "Who will watch the watchers?" Firms can motivate individual workers through promotions or production bonuses, although this presupposes the ability to measure the workers' output accurately. They can even redesign the production process itself to make work effort easier to monitor and control, which in fact is a strong motive for the lock-step work patterns of assembly-line production (see Marglin 1974, 1975; Edwards 1979).

However, such monitoring devices are expensive to firms, and at best they cannot eliminate all possibilities for opportunistic behavior. Almost any organization can be brought to its knees if the employees simply work according to rule, doing only the parts of their jobs where performance can be explicitly enforced. As recent experience in Poland illustrates, even the threat of machine guns cannot effectively motivate performance in a complex organization. Without a tolerable level of willing cooperation from its workers, few firms could long exist (Sen 1976).

Workers must trust managers and employers in some measure. Just as workers have some leeway in their jobs, managers have discretion in the way rules are interpreted, rewards are handed out, and employees are evaluated. Such discretion is held in check by the accountability of managers to higher-ups in the organization and by grievance procedures and the like that protect workers. But, again, the supervision of managers is itself both costly and inevitably incomplete, so that there is no escaping some degree of reliance on the good will of management.

The inflation problem points to a role for morality at the macroeconomic level. As Olson and Colander argue in this book, the capacity of many groups of sellers to make their power felt, either politically or in the market place, causes a higher level of equilibrium unemployment when this combativeness or "bloody-mindedness" is fought with what Albert O. Hirschman (1981) has called "countervailing bloody-mindedness," a staunch refusal by the Federal Reserve Bank or the Central Bank to provide the monetary accommodation needed to sustain the inflationary spiral. If bloody-mindedness could be tempered with moral self-restraint—willing compliance, say, with voluntary wage-price guidelines—then the inflation problem could be contained with less unemployment and protracted struggle. That, of course, is a big "if."

These examples, which could easily be multiplied, suffice to demonstrate the moral underpinning of the normal functioning of our economy, both as a support for efficient exchange and in some spheres as a substitute for it. Moreover, at least within limits, an increase in people's voluntary inclination to behave morally would further improve the system's functioning—with benefits ranging from less spending on locks and lawyers to (perhaps) less painful solutions to our current inflation problems. To put it perhaps a bit crudely, the moral character of a society's population is a valuable economic resource.

Viewed in those terms, morality is a most peculiar resource. One cannot in any straightforward sense buy it. If, for example, I pay you $20 in exchange for a promise not to lie to me, how much will you charge me to keep your promise? Or again, one cannot, in any straightforward sense, *coerce* people into being moral either. It is precisely because morality enables one to avoid the expensive tools of coercion and policing that willing moral cooperation has economic value in the first place.

MORAL MOTIVATION

So we reach our second question, one that is—perhaps especially for economists—more puzzling than the first: Where does all this wonderful moral stuff come from? And how can we get some more?

Here economists, including those who have made the major contributions to the analysis of the economic *value* of morality, have done less well. Partly this is because they have not thought so much about this question as about the other, but also, I think, because the approaches they use have some important limitations. I will identify, and briefly criticize, three such approaches, which I shall call *reductionism, functionalism,* and *instrumentalism.*

Reductionism

Reductionism attempts to show that all apparently moral behavior is actually rooted in self-interest. This project reflects the strong inclination of many economists to explain *everything* in terms of self-interest. Two different versions of this reduction of morality to self-interest can be distinguished. One is the idea that because moral behavior is in the interests of *all*, it must, ipso facto, be in the interest of each. The logical confusion here, of which even David Hume may have been guilty, is the familiar "tragedy of the commons," the "free-rider problem," or "prisoner's dilemma." Each of us may benefit from cheating on an agreement whose observance would make us all better off.

Economists do not usually make the mistake of reducing morality to self-interest via any such confusion between the individual and the collective interest. In fact, the whole of the rent-seeking literature, dating back to Mancur Olson's influential *Logic of Collective Action* (1965), relies heavily on the proposition that self-interested persons will normally not lift a finger to achieve results that are collectively valuable, even when they benefit too, unless they are provided a "selective incentive," an individualized reward, to do so. Proponents of rent-seeking, then, if they want to maintain the self-interest hypothesis as basis for a general theory of social conduct, find themselves forced to search for the selective incentives, the subtle individual rewards that *really* account for seemingly moral behavior.[3]

When we ask, for example, why merchants and traders are often honest, not relentlessly seeking gain by trying to "sharp" their customers, the rent-seeking answer must be that, while it seems to be in the merchant's interest to cheat, really it is not. There is always the risk of being detected and hence either damaging one's reputation (losing future trade) or going to jail. Even on a strictly self-interested but long-run calculation, it is alleged, it pays to be honest. The obverse, of course, is that the politician or moralist mouthing pieties or citing high-minded reasons for his actions can always be found to have a personal interest, either overt or covert, in the way things come out.

But these arguments, like the related ones that seek to explain why it is in one's narrow self-interest to vote,[4] are balanced awkwardly between tautology and falsehood. If whatever moral concerns people have are simply redescribed as peculiar forms of self-interest—she tells the truth because she'll feel guilty if she lies; she voted against the farm bill because it made her feel good to defy the "interests"—then the self-interest hypothesis becomes empty. On the other hand, if acting for moral reasons does not *ex definitione* count as self-interest, then the self-interest hypothesis looks false as a general explanation of behavior. There are too many subtle opportunities to cheat, and too few police officers, to make it plausible that the *only* effective motives supporting moral behavior are the prospects of financial or criminal penalties for immorality.[5] After all, people do sometimes leave tips in restaurants they will never see again; they put litter in trash barrels when no cop is in sight; even judges and politicians sometimes take stands because they think those stands are right.

Self-interest, rewards, and sanctions do play a large and presumably indispensable role in stimulating honest behavior. As that great moralist Al Capone is reputed to have said, "You can get so much further with a kind word and a gun than you can with a kind word alone" (McKean 1975: 42). What is odd (and it can be seen in the work of some though not all proponents of rent-seeking) is the desire to derive *everything* from self-interest as if that were a natural or necessary starting point. It is a peculiar feature of the sociology of the present-day economics profession that this odd ambition should be so prevalent. (Economists who follow this line may think of themselves as following in Adam Smith's footsteps. But the project of reducing all human psychology to self-interest is really Hobbes's rather than Smith's, and Smith's work as a whole, like much of the Scottish enlightenment, can be viewed as an attempt to refute Hobbes by basing an account of society on a broader understanding of human motivation.)

Functionalism

The functional approach assumes that the fact that morality is economically beneficial, or "functional," for society is enough to explain its presence. Functional explanations in the social sciences form a tricky subject, to which I cannot here do full justice. Pointing to the benefits of morality does give people a moral, not a self-interested, reason for acting morally. But this mechanism only operates to the degree that people are aware of the benefits and act because of them. However, the functional explanations usually assume that the conduct is sustained despite the fact that people are *unaware* of its larger benefits. The social scientist then explains behavior by revealing its previously hidden benefits, as Kenneth Arrow does in his valuable book *The Limits of Organization* (1973) by accounting for moral codes and dispositions as "unconscious agreements." This phrase explains obedience to such codes through reference to their mutually beneficial, though "unconscious," consequences. But such an explanation begs the crucial question of *how* the agreements are sustained. "Unconscious agreement" is really a terribly opaque metaphor, which raises in sharper form familiar difficulties posed by the notion of "tacit consent."

In other writings, Arrow shows more awareness of the limits of functional explanation.[6] The great virtue of his subtle and insightful treatment of morality, in contrast to the reductionist view, is his clear recognition of the *fact* of and the *need* for moral bonds, and his explicit denial that morality can be derived from individual self-interest. Functionalism is a convenient bulwark against reductionism.

But the functionalist is blank about where these "agreements" come from, and what social mechanisms sustain them.[7] Functionalism may also encourage complacency by implying that society will get what it needs. There is perhaps some ground for saying that more efficient societies or institutions will out-compete others, so that society will evolve toward well-adapted institutions. But these evolutionary forces are much less binding on social institutions than on natural selection in animals, the theory that presumably inspires the argument.

Arrow (1963: 947) at one point remarks that "when the market fails to achieve an optimal state, . . . non-market social institutions [including morality] will arise attempting to bridge [the gap]." Though it makes sense to look around for such institutions, to be accurate one must add that they will arise except when they don't. The interesting questions concern when and why they do and do not arise and for this, functionalism is not much help.[8]

Instrumentalism

This approach is similar to functionalism in assuming that moral conduct exists because of the social benefits it produces, but it differs in assuming that the "rulers" of society consciously aim to produce those benefits.[9] Institutions like the family, the church, and the school deliberately *indoctrinate* children into acting "morally," it assumes.

Obviously, instrumentalism has some validity. It is indeed helpful to call attention to the enormous social energies that *do* go into inculcating moral attitudes, energies that would appear wasted to reductionists, who see all action as self-interested.

However, as a general view of moral development, this approach seems implausibly deliberate and calculated. Surely a great deal of a child's moral development is an unintended by-product of the way her parents treat her, of the kinds of relationships she develops with friends, and so on. The actual role of conscious indoctrination—the effectiveness of preaching—may be relatively small.

Writers in the instrumentalist vein also tend to view moral education as conditioning and the moral conduct it produces as a conditioned response—a nonrational or even irrational constraint on individual free choice. Implicitly for such writers, an internalized fear of authority or a fear of God motivates morality. Such aspects exist in moral motivation, especially as a stage in the moral development of children, but exclusive stress on them produces an excessively negative and antirationalist picture of the motives for moral conduct.[10]

The stress on childhood development and on extraeconomic institutions like church and school has the further problem of diverting attention from the role that *economic* institutions may have in shaping and reinforcing the moral attitudes and conduct of *adults*. It is possible to grant the great importance of childhood influences and of noneconomic institutions and still make the point that, to the degree that *economists* are interested in moral development, the moralizing effects of *economic* interaction may be a more useful focus than is child psychology.

There is an important difference between followers of the reductionist approach and of the other two. The first group wants to *explain away* moral conduct by showing that it is simply a subtle form of self-interest, while the others recognize that economically relevant moral attitudes are real and must be *explained.* So writers who have tentatively adopted functionalist or instrumentalist approaches are much more open to recognizing that these particular approaches may be inadequate or incomplete. Indeed (as I have tried to show in the notes) even authors drawn to these latter approaches show in some of their writings an awareness of their limitations. But among those who work at the project of reducing morality to self-interest, at least some seem to feel sure on a priori grounds that a real explanation of these phenomena *must* take that reductive form. If their particular attempts at reduction are faulty, they do not question their underlying approach, but simply produce subtler versions of it.[11]

Having criticized these approaches to explaining moral motivation in economic life not so much for being wrong as for being importantly incomplete, let me now consider some interesting directions that might further our understanding. Probably the most surprising aspect of the recent literature is the lack of connection between writing on the economic functions of morality and the question of the influence of *economic* institutions on moral development, a point noted previously in regard to the instrumental approach. One reason for such neglect may be that raising such a question reverses the usual way economists approach the problem of economic organization. That usual view is to see economic institutions and outcomes as the products of individuals' choices, taking preferences as pregiven, rather than seeing the individuals themselves, their desires in general, and their moral attitudes in particular, importantly as products of the economic institutions that surround them.

This neglect of the socializing role of economic institutions (a neglect that is much more evident in contemporary economics than in classic writers like Marx and Veblen, or even Mill and Marshall) is reinforced by the tendency for economists to focus on formal models of anonymous buying and selling among strangers. Such impersonal arrangements (the hallmark of perfect competition) do not leave room for moral (or for that matter immoral) conduct, and do not seem promising as a seedbed for developing moral views.

But the very uncertainty that makes morality valuable (and that is generally abstracted from in these formal models) also makes it worthwhile to develop personal relations between buyers and sellers, or employers and employees, or among workers. These relationships may be based in part on an instrumental desire to protect oneself from deception by getting to know one's counterpart, but once in place they may also provide the foundation for developing more genuine moral cooperation.[12]

Noting these economic relationships that are not solely mediated by prices is only a starting point for analyzing their social effects. Prisoners and their guards, after all, have long-term relationships rooted in uncertainty, but those relations rarely blossom into feelings of trust and mutual respect. The *character* of the relationships matters greatly. Moreover, a mutually trusting group may not always serve the larger social interest, as in the old saying about honor among thieves or the more recent work by Olson and Colander on the negative effects of "coalition equilibrium."

An implication is that whether an institution will generate moral cooperation among its members depends in part on the members' view of how that institution functions. Are other participants in the institution doing their part? Is the institution genuinely cooperative and worthwhile? Does it treat its members fairly? It seems reasonable to believe that willingness to "pull one's oar"[13] — to forgo opportunities to free ride — depends on the belief that others will do the same and that the institution will treat its members with fairness and respect.

It follows that moral motivation can readily be undermined by lack of information about whether one's fellow participants are doing their part in a cooperative venture. In many social settings it is hard to allay suspicions that others are not taking their responsibilities seriously. The need for assurance about the motives and performance of others can be met by enforcement, some suggest, but that is an incomplete solution,[14] for it does not resolve the question of how easily people can get around the enforceable rules. Ironically, the very need for enforcement may be itself a mark of *distrust* rather than a ground for assurance.

The dilemma results from the fact that in most situations good behavior is elicited *partly* by sanctions and incentives, so that the moral component is difficult to identify. This difficulty helps clarify Titmuss's claim that the voluntary donation of blood was not only an efficient way to get healthy blood, but also made people more altruistic in general. The claim seems plausible, but in his book Titmuss never gives a real argument for it.

A possible explanation is this: if you really can manage to supply an urgently needed social good through genuinely—and visibly—uncoerced and unrewarded cooperation, you demonstrate a very important fact about people in your society. If they (or enough of them) are so clearly and undeniably trustworthy in this situation, it is more reasonable to believe that they are trustworthy in other situations, and so we will have the assurance we need to do our part in these other situations. By keeping certain important goods out of the market, we create an opportunity for citizens to confirm an optimistic theory of human nature in practice.[15]

Moral allegiance depends not only on a perception that other people are doing their part, but also on a belief that one is part of a genuinely cooperative venture, from which all participants benefit on fair terms. This suggests that the performance of an economic enterprise—whether a firm or a whole economy— depends on its capacity to make people *believe* it is fair. The firm in this perspective is not merely a technical device for organizing production, but a socializing and moralizing agent in society.

John Rawls, in the latter part of *A Theory of Justice* (1971), examines what might be called "the political economy of moral development," the way in which one's "sense of justice" builds upon experience participating in genuinely cooperative institutions. In one passage, Rawls pictures a just society as a "social union of social unions," with the institutions of which one is part building upon linkages of community and self respect among citizens. It is clear in Rawls's account that productive institutions, firms and factories, are important elements in this matrix. A difficulty, though, in mapping this picture onto our society is that it would be easier to view the corporation as a social union or a cooperative venture if it were a *cooperative* venture.

This, of course, is a common theme in radical analysis. Hierarchy and ownership relations are held to be exploitative, concerned with protecting profits rather than promoting efficiency. On this view, corporate claims that under capitalism the organization is cooperative and management demands for moral cooperation from workers therefore justifiable are deceptive.[16] This radical critique focuses attention on the question of how and why one would expect the moral and motivational structure of a worker-controlled or socialist firm to differ from that of a capitalist firm. The easy answer is that socialism will transform the motivational structure by replacing individualist with collective consciousness because with worker control all will participate and share in rewards, all will have a common goal and will work harmoniously together.[17]

Neoclassical writers are quick to note here a confusion between collective and individual interests (see Alchian and Demsetz 1972; Williamson 1980). If I add $10 to the revenue of a 500-member revenue-sharing firm, I receive 2¢ for my efforts. Rather than common interest in hard work, there is a powerful incentive in a cooperative firm to free ride. To overcome this, continues the neoclassical critique, would require the same hierarchy, supervision, and wage differentials as in a capitalist firm. So what's the difference?

The difference, I think, is subtler than either the radical or the neoclassical analysis conveys. A better treatment can be derived from some of John Stuart Mill's remarks on the cooperative movement in nineteenth-century England. Mill suggested that the organization of the capitalist firm in his day divided "the producers into two parties with hostile interests and feelings, the many who do the work being mere servants under the command of the one who supplies the funds, and having no interest of their own in the enterprise except to earn their wages with as little labor as possible" (Mill 1965: 769). The efficiency problem is that to the degree that workers *do* cooperate, they are liable to do so in *minimizing* effort, resisting capitalist demands.

In a worker-controlled enterprise, however, the incentives would be subtly different. Mill does not assume that all forms of hierarchy, supervision, and wage payment could be dispensed with. But the arrangement is now cooperative. The worker has become not a "mere servant" but a democratic *partner* in making the rules. There is more ground for "oar-pulling": "The rules of discipline [of a worker-controlled firm]," Mill argued,

> instead of being more lax, are stricter than those of ordinary workshops; but being rules self-imposed, for the manifest good of the community, and not for the convenience of an employer regarded as having an opposing interest,

they are far more scrupulously obeyed, and the *voluntary* obedience carries with it a sense of personal worth and dignity. (1965: 792)

The cooperative enterprise is able to capture this Rousseauan element of "giving the law to oneself" in a way that a capitalist firm has difficulty in doing. Mill also argued that the moralizing effects of such arrangements would tend to spread beyond the workplace, which would become, in his phrase, "a school for the social sympathies and practical intelligence." This, of course, is precisely what Rawls's picture of society as a social union of social unions requires the firm to be.[18]

Issues of worker loyalty and commitment are relevant not only to the Great Debate between capitalism and socialism, but also to the everyday workings of capitalist firms. And indeed, managers of contemporary firms, unlike the nineteenth-century firms Mill described, go to considerable lengths to lend legitimacy to their authority. Substantive measures, like grievance procedures and various organs for participation and voice, and propaganda efforts, like the old IBM practice of assembling the workers every morning to sing the company song, exist. Currently attention is paid to possible trade-offs between rigid autocratic hierarchy and the cultivation of a sense of community and trust among workers. There is an edge of hypocrisy to such talk of community within a capitalist enterprise, for corporations are certainly more inclined to stress the essentially cooperative nature of the enterprise when there are losses instead of gains to be shared. And there is a quality of "blaming the victim" in suggesting that our productivity problems can be laid to a sudden decline in the moral commitment of American workers. Nonetheless, the relation between the form of corporate organization and the level of commitment of workers deserves more attention from economists than it has received, both within capitalism and in comparing alternative systems.

THE STATUS OF EFFICIENCY AS A NORM

An important way in which this analysis of morality is incomplete is in its nearly exclusive focus on moral conduct as contributing to the efficient performance of the economy. Other values, such as distributive justice or community, have entered the story principally through their role in promoting moral commitments that are economically valuable. This is inadequate. Although more equality or a healthier sense of community may sometimes promote economic well-being, rather than always being traded-off against it, justice and community are not just instruments of prosperity; they are values in their own right. Indeed, there is something to be said for turning the relationship around. In a fuller view, the real importance of economic efficiency as a social goal may lie in its capacity to provide the basis for relations of justice and community among a society's members. In any case, a fuller treatment of the economic significance of morality would require an analysis of the proper relation between economic efficiency and other valued social ends.[19]

That cannot be attempted here. Nonetheless, the exaggerated emphasis in this chapter on the efficiency-enhancing aspects of morality may serve a useful purpose. For although it can be argued that an economist who neglects morality fails to be a good *person*, this chapter argues that an economist who neglects morality fails to be a good *economist*. Recognizing limits on self-seeking is not only morally but analytically necessary.

NOTES TO CHAPTER 5

1. The following account was helped especially by the treatments of similar issues by Hirschman (1981), Reder (1979), McKean (1975), and Arrow (1972, 1974).
2. On the general problems of monitoring and rewarding effort, see Alchian and Demsetz 1972, Barzel 1980, and Williamson, Wachter, and Harris 1975.
3. Besides being advocated by Olson himself (and his book is concerned more with political action than with moral conduct as such), such an approach is adopted explicitly by Stigler (1980) and by Schotter (1981). The frequent attempts by economists to explain the behavior of organizations, either public or private, without reference to moral motives, reflect a similar presupposition, although without the conscious intent to explain moral behavior as such. (See the discussion of this literature in Sen 1976.)
4. These articles often appear in the journal *Public Choice.*
5. For an effective statement of this point, see North 1981: ch. 5.
6. See especially Arrow 1973. On p. 315 of this essay, Arrow observes that "I've said that ethical codes are desirable. It doesn't follow from this that they will come about." This is really the point I want to make here, and the point that it seems to me Arrow neglects in some of his other work on this subject.
7. Richard Posner (1981) relies on functional explanations for morality in primitive societies and presumably elsewhere. See my review (McPherson 1982b).
8. For recent contributions to the perennial discussion of functionalism in social science, see Elster 1979 and Hardin 1980.
9. This approach is quite explicit in Reder (1979), although his treatment is quite brief and may not reflect a considered view. Douglass North (1981) shows an ambiguous attachment to the instrumental view. Although stressing at times that "ideologies" are (presumably unintended) consequences of people's economic and social situations, he elsewhere in the same volume lays great stress on the instrumental view that the "rulers" of society dictate outcomes: "Institutions are a set of rules, compliance procedures, and moral and ethical behavioral norms designed to constrain the behavior of individuals in the interests of maximizing the wealth

or utility of principals" (pp. 201–202). The instrumental approach in general is of course akin to that of so-called instrumental Marxists.

10. I am indebted to Lee Alston for emphasizing this point.

11. I find it helpful to draw an analogy between those social scientists who think explaining morality requires reducing it to self-interest and those philosophers who think that justifying morality requires justifying it to a rational egoist. A more neutral starting point for the philosophical argument is to imagine justifying morality to one who is not committed either way on whether to be an egoist. Analogously, we need not start the explanatory argument by *assuming* a prior commitment to self-interest. (On the philosophical side, see Rawls 1971: 86; on the explanatory side, see Parfit 1979: 544; Carens 1981: ch. 2.)

12. These paragraphs rely heavily on insights gleaned from Albert O. Hirschman.

13. I owe to Albert O. Hirschman the suggestion to use this term as a way of evoking a helpful counterimage to free riding. The term "reciprocity" is used in Rawls (1971) for what I here call "oar-pulling." McKean (1975) distinguishes similarly between "altruism" and "trust." Parfit (1980) has an extremely useful taxonomy of attitudes and mechanisms, including "reciprocity," that may help overcome the prisoner's dilemma.

14. The assurance problem was first identified and named by Sen (1967). The notion of enforcement as a source of assurance plays an important role in Rawls 1971.

15. I would not claim that this beneficial result explains *why* blood in England is supplied outside the market; presumably the effect I am describing is an unintended by-product. In fact, I suspect that if one actually tried to rig up such an arrangement for the purpose of demonstrating the effect, it would take on a manipulative cast that might cause the demonstration to backfire. But even if nonmarket institutions do not arise in the first place to produce such demonstration effects, those effects may provide a reason for not doing away with such institutions where they do exist.

16. Examples are Gintis 1977, Bowles and Gintis 1976: ch. 3, and references therein.

17. Vanek (1970: ch. 12), though not radical, is similarly starry eyed. A somewhat more cautious view is held by Reich and Devine (1981).

18. These paragraphs are not intended as a decisive argument for worker control of socialism, the feasibility and desirability of which raise a variety of difficult issues. But my remarks do call attention to an aspect of the issue that is often handled badly by both conventional and radical economists.

19. Richard Posner (1981), a proponent of the "economic analysis of law," recently argued that the ultimate goal of morality (and law) is economic efficiency (or, as he terms it, "wealth maximization"). The main effects of advancing this argument seem to have been (1) to provide Ronald Dworkin (1980) with a particularly choice target for his formidable dialectical skills and (2) to make life a little awkward for other free market economists who may actually *believe* efficiency is the only thing worth paying attention to but who have not been so reckless as to defend that implausible proposition in writing.

THEORETICAL MODELS

6 TOWARD A MODEL OF ENDOGENOUS RENT-SEEKING

Ronald Findlay and Stanislaw Wellisz

The political economy of rent-seeking is a subject that has grown rapidly in interest and significance without there being any well-defined theoretical core that commands the assent of the majority of contributors to the field. While the insights of a number of pioneers such as Anthony Downs, Mancur Olson, James Buchanan, Gordon Tullock, and others are appreciated and acknowledged by all, there is as yet no consensus at all on the appropriate ways in which to model the intersection of the economy and the polity in positive terms and to evaluate the normative implications of the consequences. This lack of methodological self-consciousness and unity is perhaps inevitable and healthy in any growing and exciting new area of research.

One of the most important unanswered questions is the role of the hypotheses about the nature of the political regime that conditions the operation of the economic model of rent-seeking behavior and the implications of these for the cost-benefit evaluation of the alleged waste of resources expended in the process. We shall see that the assumed nature of the political system has an important bearing on the relevance and applicability of the results, especially in the case of endogenous rent-seeking.

In considering this question, a fundamental consideration is the appropriate equilibrium concept. In economic theory, particularly in its general equilibrium manifestations, the assumption of perfectly competitive markets has been the dominant one. Although it could be argued that the associated political "markets" or regimes should also be taken as competitive, alternatively it could be

The second part of this chapter is a summary of an earlier article that appeared in *Kyklos* 36 (1983): 469–81. It is reprinted with permission.

argued that there is an asymmetry between the political and economic spheres, with monopoly or oligopolistic Nash equilibria in the political system and Walrasian competitive equilibrium in the economic system. We argue that the latter alternative is preferable.

THE KRUEGER MODEL

To develop our points, we begin with an examination of Anne Krueger's seminal model, which introduced the vocabulary of "rent-seeking" into our discipline (see Krueger 1974). Krueger's paper is the ideal starting point for our discussion because it is not only familiar but it advances the claims of a new approach in a clear and forceful way on the basis of a simple, yet appealing, model. The original presentation, however, was obscured, in our opinion, by some unnecessary complications related to a "distribution sector." What follows therefore is a streamlined version of the original that preserves all essential results and enables clear perception of the crucial assumptions underlying the analysis.

In our streamlined version, labor is the only scarce factor of production and the total available is fixed at $\bar{L}$. Only one good, Y, is produced according to a production function $Y = \alpha Ly$ where Ly is labor engaged in production and α is the marginal and average productivity of labor. Another good M is consumed, in addition to Y, and it can be imported from the rest of the world at a fixed price $\bar{p}$ in terms of Y. Individual consumers have identical and homothetic tastes represented by a set of indifference curves that reflect "social" as well as individual demand. Given these assumptions the free trade equilibrium will be as shown in Figure 6-1. Output of Y is equal to F', the relative price is $\bar{p}$, the slope of the M line, imports are M^* and exports are equal to $\bar{p}M^*$. Consumption is at point a^* and utility is at U_1.

Suppose now that a quota of $\bar{M} < M^*$ is imposed. The new equilibrium price will be p^*, the slope of the $M'' F''$ line, which is equal to the slope of U_2 at b^*. The premium on imports is therefore $(p^* - \bar{p})$ and the "rent" for the right to import will be equal to $(P^* - \bar{p})\bar{M}$. Traditionally this rent was regarded as a redistribution from consumers to whomever is fortunate enough to receive the rent. It was not therefore regarded in any sense as a *cost*. The sole cost in the conventional analysis is the reduction of consumer welfare from U_1 to U_2 due to the reduction of the "gains from trade" induced by the imposition of the quota.

Krueger's innovation is to propose that the rent $(p^* - \bar{p})\bar{M}$ be considered as up for grabs and to assume that it is allocated in some fair way on the basis of free entry and open access. Thus, one may simply assume that the import quotas are distributed proportionately to the number of applicants. The activity of applying for the licenses and complying with the rules, however, takes time, the opportunity cost of which is the real wage in production (measured in terms of

Figure 6-1. Social Cost of Rent-Seeking.

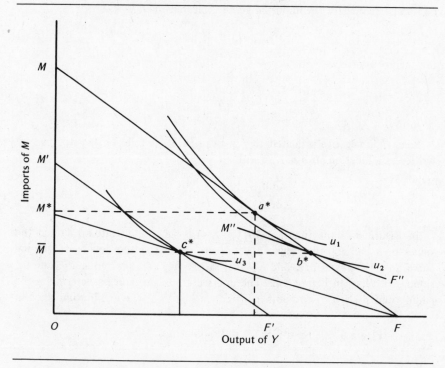

good Y the *numéraire*). If entry is free, the equilibrium income received by the holder of an import license would be equal to α, the marginal product of labor.

The number of these applicants, or "rent-seekers," can be determined from the equation

$$\frac{(p - \bar{p})\overline{M}}{L_R} = \alpha , \qquad (6.1)$$

where $L_R + Ly = \overline{L}$, L_R being the number of rent-seekers. In this equation $\bar{p}, \overline{M}$ and α are constant, but p is a variable that depends upon L_R itself because the diversion of labor into rent-seeking would reduce real income, demand for imports, and hence price.

The demand function for imports can be written as

$$M_D = M_D (p,I) , \qquad (6.2)$$

where p is the price and

$$I \equiv \alpha Ly + (p - \bar{p})\overline{M} = \alpha(\overline{L} - L_R) + (p - \bar{p})\overline{M} \qquad (6.3)$$

is equal to income from production αLy, *plus* the implicit quota revenue $(p - \bar{p})\bar{M}$. The market for the imported goods is cleared when

$$M_D(p, I) = \bar{M} , \tag{6.4}$$

in which of course we assume

$$\frac{\partial M_D}{\partial p} < 0, \quad \frac{\partial M_D}{\partial I} > 0 . \tag{6.5}$$

Since I is negatively related to L_R from (6.3), it follows that M_D can be written as a function $M_D(p, L_R)$ with

$$\frac{\partial M_D}{\partial L_R} < 0 . \tag{6.6}$$

In Figure 6-2 the function $M_D(p, L_R)$ is substituted into (6.4) and the values of p and L_R that make $M_D = \bar{M}$ are plotted as the downward sloping curve dd'. The values of p and L_R that satisfy (6.1) are plotted as the upward sloping curve ss' in Figure 6-2. The intersection of dd' and ss' determines the equilibrium price p^* and number of rent-seekers L_R^*. The equilibrium price in

Figure 6-2.   Rent-Seeking of Equilibrium.

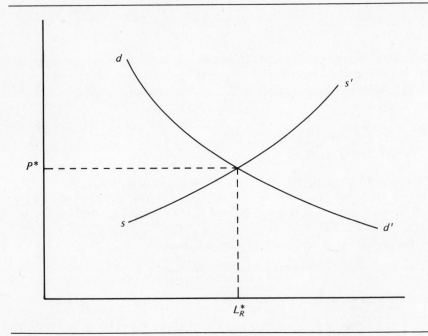

the Krueger case will differ from that in the conventional case since the value of $\bar{L}$ corresponds to $\alpha\bar{L}$ in the latter case and $\alpha(\bar{L} - L_R^*)$ in the former.

Going back to Figure 6-1, the Krueger equilibrium will be at point c^* and utility at U_3. The rent-seeking behavior thus results in a further loss over and above the conventional cost. This additional cost is due to the decline in real income from production to $\alpha(\bar{L} - L_R^*)$ from αL, leading to the decline in utility from U_2 to U_3. The rent-seeking process that uses up L_R^* workers leads to an outcome that is equivalent to the conventional situation with a loss of L_R^* workers, as can be seen by comparing point c^* with point a^*. Alternatively it is as if we had the conventional situation with $\bar{L}$ workers and a decline of $(\bar{L} - L_R^*)/\bar{L}$ in productivity. In Figure 6-1 the original output of Y was equal to OF. This falls to OF' in the Krueger case with FF' equal to $(p^* - \bar{p})\bar{M}$ being the income of the rent-seekers.

There are a variety of possible criticisms of Krueger's basic analysis. Its very special and simple production structure is *not* a legitimate criticism at all since the essential results can be shown to be quite robust in more general models, though the extent of the welfare loss may be less.[1] To us, the main criticism of Krueger's ingenious and stimulating paper is the naïveté of the *political* assumption of "free entry" into rent-seeking for the quota premiums. In most less developed countries, to which the analysis applies, the rents from import licenses are a jealously preserved privilege of political or bureaucratic cliques. The rents thus attach to persons or groups by virtue of their special position in an independently determined hierarchy. It is true that these privileges make such positions attractive for others to secure and hence can lead to expenditure of real resources to secure them. This points toward a spoils theory of government and political competition, into which the analysis would have to be embedded. We are a long way from having any serious attempt at such a theory as yet, though there are some scattered insights. In what follows we outline two alternative models that provide direction in developing a more comprehensive theory and insight into the question of how rent-seeking activity varies under alternative political regimes.

FACTIONAL EQUILIBRIUM UNDER DEMOCRATIC PLURALISM[2]

A typical political science approach to the analysis of the political process is one in which outcomes are determined by the interplay of competing interest groups in the manner described by writers such as Arthur Bentley, David Truman, and Robert Dahl, among others. It is anticipated and inspired by the tenth *Federalist* paper of James Madison, with its celebrated analysis of "faction" in a democratic republic. We can integrate this with the rent-seeking approach by linking the broad Madisonian "landed" and "manufacturing" interests with the specific inputs "land" and "capital" in the familiar Ricardo-Viner model of international trade. In this model we assume two goods are produced, with relative world prices exogenously given. Agricultural goods are produced with "land" and labor and manufacturers with "capital" and labor. Land and capital are specific to their sectors but there is a common pool of homogeneous labor that both sectors draw on. Perfectly competitive pricing and resource allocation are assumed.

Take at the start the free trade situation, with no real resources diverted to political activity. Given the endowments of all three factors, the production functions for the two goods and their relative price on world markets, the real wage and allocation of labor between the two sectors, hence also the rentals of the specific inputs, are all determined. We suppose that the production levels thus determined together with the demand functions for the two goods result in the manufactured good being imported and the agricultural good being exported.

We now introduce an endogenous political process into the model by way of a "tariff formation function."

$$t = F(L_K, L_T) \tag{6.7}$$

with

$$\frac{\partial F}{\partial L_K} > 0, \quad \frac{\partial F}{\partial L_T} < 0, \tag{6.8}$$

where t is the level of the tariff and L_K and L_T are the real resources (assumed for the sake of simplicity to be labor only) allocated to influencing the outcome of the political process by each of the Madisonian interests. Taking the political constitution, the structure of parties and so on as given, the tariff is an increasing function of the input by the protariff manufacturing interest and a decreasing function of the input by the countervailing free trade landed interest group. Politics, ideology, and international obligations are thus taken as exogenous influences through the form and level of the function F, which relates the inputs by the two pressure groups to the tariff. The analogy with technology and the familiar concept of a production function is a direct one. The economists' focus is on how the relevant inputs are connected with the ultimate outputs, the details of the process of conversion in each case being inside a black box.

This method of introducing the political element into the model, though purely formal, has the advantage of showing that there is no necessary conflict between a pressure group approach to tariff determination and recognition of the importance of ideology and the "autonomy of the state," as some political scientists seem to think. A strong free trade bias in public opinion and in the executive branch of the government, based either on purely intellectual grounds or foreign policy considerations, for example, simply makes the task of the protariff pressure group harder. The greater the strength of the free trade proclivity in the society, for any input by the countervailing interest group, the larger the input by the protectionist group is necessary to achieve a given tariff level.

Owners of the specific inputs are competitive price-takers in the "economic" sphere but act collectively in the "political" sphere to promote their group interests. The internal organization of each group, such as the mechanism for levying contributions in the face of the well-known free rider problem, is a subject of obvious interest that is not pursued here. It is assumed that a collective organization exists for each of the factions and that it acts rationally to promote the aims of the group as a whole with regard to the level of the tariff in the light of what it perceives the actions of the countervailing group to be.

The political struggle to determine the tariff level can be conceptualized as a Cournot-Nash process in which each faction, taking the input by the other side as given, calculates its own optimal input in the light of the tariff formation function and the structure of the economy. Thus, given L_T the manufacturing group will increase L_K until at the margin the increase in the total real income of the capitalist class resulting from the effect of the higher tariff in raising the internal relative price of manufactures and hence the rental of capital is equal to the cost of increasing their political effort. We imagine stationary conditions and a repetition of the struggle over a tariff bill enacted each time for a fixed period so that eventually each side can be assumed to calculate correctly what its optimal behavior should be.

A possible outcome of this Cournot-Nash process is depicted in Figure 6-3. The dashed line t^*t^* shows combinations of L_K and L_T that result in a tariff level of t^*, the positive slope given by the properties of the tariff formation function, an increase in L_T reducing the tariff and so requiring an increase in L_K for t^* to be restored. The curves KK' and TT' are possible reaction functions for the capitalist and landed interests, respectively. Given L_K an increase in L_R will reduce the tariff and so make the capitalists worse off. It is assumed that the optimal reaction for them would be to increase L_K in response to the increase in L_R, raising the tariff level by comparison with the lack of any response but not sufficiently to restore the former level. The tariff level thus *falls* from left to right along KK'. Symmetrical reasoning implies that the tariff *rises* from left to right along TT', with intersection of KK' and TT' at the endogenous equilibrium tariff level t^*. Multiple equilibria are, of course, possible but, for simplicity, we assume that the equilibrium is unique. A sufficient condition for this equilibrium to be stable is that KK' be steeper than TT'.

The intersection of KK' and TT' in Figure 6-3 determines the equilibrium levels of the "political" inputs L_K^* and L_T^* and hence the labor force employed in production as

$$L^* = \bar{L} - (L_K^* + L_T^*) . \tag{6.9}$$

The "political" activity thus deprives the society of $(L_K^* + L_T^*)$ amount of labor that could have been productively employed. It imposes a welfare loss on

Figure 6–3. A Cournot-Nash Lobbying-Tariff Equilibrium.

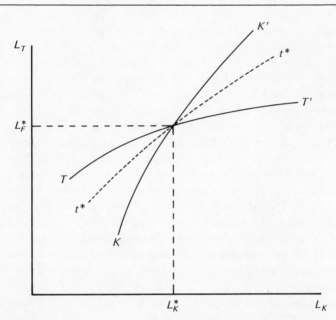

society of $\hat{w}(L_K^* + L_T^*)$ where $\hat{w}$ is the "shadow wage" of labor, equal in this case to the reduction in the value of total output at world prices resulting from one less unit of labor. This welfare cost of protection is over and above the conventional welfare cost arising from the misallocation of productively employed resources caused by the distortionary effects on production and consumption of the tariff.

The lobbying activities of the capitalist class increase its real incomes and reduce the real incomes of the landowning class. The real wage of labor falls in terms of manufactures (since the return on capital is increased) and rises in terms of agricultural goods (since the rental of land is reduced). Thus the effect on labor of the tariff depends upon the relative weight of the two goods in workers' consumption. In relatively low-wage countries labor might be in favor of the tariff on manufactures since it raises their purchasing power in terms of food, while in high-wage countries it would be opposed. A more elaborate investigation of the political economy of trade restrictions, taking account of coalitions among different interest groups, could develop these implications further.

THE "BUREAUCRATIC AUTHORITARIAN" CASE[3]

The pressure group approach is applicable only to democratic societies. A familiar alternative economic structure is the closed authoritarian system. We continue to use a simple two-sector, small, open economy general equilibrium model to analyze the effect of this political structure, though it will now be more convenient to adopt the Heckscher-Ohlin-Samuelson (HOS) version of this model rather than the Viner-Ricardo one. However, on the "political" side, we replace the pluralistic system with a closed authoritarian system, dominated by a bureaucratic central administration. A state of this kind could have been established by a revolutionary political party or a military coup d'état. Contemporary examples from the Third World are plentiful and the absolutist states of early modern Europe also fit the pattern.

We postulate that "the prince," be he hereditary monarch, revolutionary leader, or ambitious general, is driven to justify his rule by maximizing the output of his regime, considered as a composite public good that requires real resources for its production that have to be acquired from the private sector by means of taxation. In the present context a natural simplifying assumption is that the sole source of revenue is a tariff. (Most less developed countries do in fact rely on foreign trade levies for the bulk of their revenue since the machinery for direct income taxes is not available.) The tariff rate will thus be determined at the level that enables the governmental authority to maximize the provision of the public good.

The traditional approach to the provision of public goods is, of course, in terms of the Wicksell-Lindahl process, which determines the optimal level of public goods with reference to the preferences of the individual citizens. Much of the modern literature has been concerned with the problem of "incentive compatibility" in this context, of how to induce people honestly to reveal their true preferences. Here instead of the welfare-oriented demand approach, we postulate that the level of public goods in an authoritarian state is determined on the supply side by a bureaucratic regime intent on providing a functional justification for its existence. This view is in conformity with the seminal work on the economics of bureaucracy by William Niskanen (1971), with two important differences. Niskanen was considering a single "bureau" within a pluralist democratic framework, whereas in our case the entire government is a single bureau writ large. Consequently, Niskanen's model is a partial equilibrium one, while ours is one in which the allocation of resources between the private and public sectors has to be determined in a general equilibrium fashion.[4]

The economy is endowed with fixed quantities of capital $\bar{K}$ and labor $\bar{L}$ and produces two private goods, a capital-intensive exportable X and a labor-intensive importable M. The relative price on the world market of the two goods is given. Both private goods have constant returns to scale neoclassical production functions. The public good G is produced with labor Lg applied to a fixed quantity of specific capital. The government and the private sector hire labor competitively from a common pool $\bar{L}$. The wage-bill in the government sector is paid by the revenue arising from the proceeds of a tariff t, the level of which has to be endogenously determined, along with Lg, by the solution to the following maximization problem:

$$\text{Max } G(Lg) \quad \text{subject to} \quad w(t)Lg = R(Lg, t) \quad , \tag{6.10}$$

where R denotes the revenue obtained by the government from the tariff in which

$$\frac{\partial G}{\partial Lg} > 0 \; ; \quad \frac{\partial w}{\partial t} < 0 \; ; \quad \frac{\partial R}{\partial Lg} < 0 \; , \quad \frac{\partial R}{\partial t} \gtreqless 0 \tag{6.11}$$

and R and w are measured in units of the exportable good that serves as *numéraire*.

The first of these partial derivatives is positive for the obvious reason that government output is an increasing function of employment in the public sector. The negative dependence of the real wage w on the tariff rate t follows from the Stolper–Samuelson theorem since the importable is capital-intensive and the tariff raises the internal relative price of this good. Given the tariff, the revenue R is a decreasing function of Lg since employment in the private sector falls when Lg increases, thus leading to a contraction in the output of the labor-intensive exportable X and an increase in the domestic output of the importable M by the Rybczynski theorem. As a consequence, demand for imports is reduced and so is the revenue from the tariff. Given Lg, and hence employment in the private sector, the revenue from the tariff first increases as the tariff rate increases and then declines when the rate exceeds the level that maximizes revenues. The partial derivative of revenue with respect to the tariff rate is thus positive or negative depending upon whether the rate is below or above the maximum revenue level.

The necessary conditions for solving the maximization problem are obtained by setting up the Lagrangean expression

$$G(Lg) - \lambda [w(t)Lg - R(Lg, t)] \tag{6.12}$$

and putting the partial derivatives with respect to Lg and t equal to zero, so that we have

$$\frac{\partial G}{\partial Lg} = \lambda [w(t) - \frac{\partial R}{\partial Lg}] \quad ; \tag{6.13}$$

$$Lg \frac{\partial w}{\partial t} = \frac{\partial R}{\partial t} \quad . \tag{6.14}$$

Figure 6-4. General Equilibrium in the "Bureaucratic-Authoritarian" State.

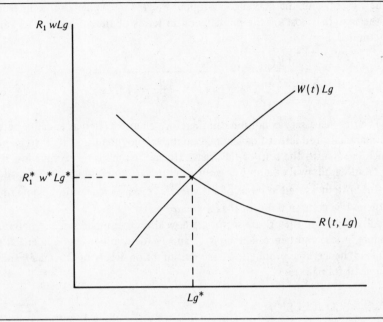

The second of these two conditions states that the marginal reduction in the wage-bill brought about by increasing the tariff for a given Lg (resulting from the Stolper-Samuelson effect of the tariff on the wage rate) should be equal to the marginal reduction in revenue resulting from the increase in the tariff. The tariff yields revenue that the government uses to hire labor and also lowers the real wage in the economy, which means that with a given revenue the government can hire more employees. It follows that a public sector employment maximizing tariff is higher than the maximum revenue tariff. Another way of looking at this relation is that for given Lg the tariff should be set so as to minimize the deficit $[w(t)Lg - R(t, Lg)]$ or maximize the surplus.

In Figure 6-4 we plot revenue R and expenditure wLg as functions of Lg, with t being set at the optimal level as indicated above for each value of Lg. At each value of Lg the tariff level t is set in such a way as to maximize the vertical distance between $R(t, \bar{Lg})$ and $w(t)\bar{Lg}$ where $\bar{Lg}$ is the given value of Lg. The revenue function slopes downward since even though the tariff is being adjusted optimally at each point of the curve the greater is Lg the less is the revenue that can be obtained from the reduced volume of trade. The expenditure function slopes upward since the higher Lg is likely to dominate any possible reduction in the real wage that may result from the tariff levels being lower at higher levels of Lg. The optimal level of public employment is where these two curves intersect at L_g^* and t^* is the associated optimal endogenous tariff level. The two first-order conditions and the government budget constraint are sufficient to determine L_g^*, t^*, and the Lagrange multiplier λ. This multiplier can be interpreted as the marginal cost of the public good in terms of the *numéraire*. Its value is determined as

$$\lambda = \frac{\partial G(L_g^*)}{\partial Lg} \cdot \frac{1}{w(t^*) - \dfrac{\partial R}{\partial Lg}(t^*, L_g^*)} \tag{6.15}$$

The first necessary condition can therefore be interpreted as equality between the marginal productivity of labor in public employment and its marginal cost, which is equal to the sum of the wage-rate and the marginal revenue loss resulting from withdrawal of a unit of labor from private employment in the tradeable sector, both measured in terms of the *numéraire*, times the "price" equal to $\frac{1}{\lambda}$ of the public good in terms of the *numéraire*.

All variables in the private sector are now also determined since t^* determines product prices and hence factor prices and L_g^* determines employment at $(\bar{L} - L_g^*)$ and hence the production and consumption levels of X and M and the volume of foreign trade.

CONCLUSION

The foregoing two models come to different conclusions as to relative price and as to the amount of rent-seeking behavior. This is not surprising. Depending on their political structure, societies are likely to experience quite different amounts of rent-seeking behavior. Although these models have only scratched the surface, in both cases they have arrived at determinant results and, we believe, provide a useful guide to further research.

NOTES TO CHAPTER 6

1. Bhagwati and Srinivasan (1980) showed that lobbying may under certain conditions paradoxically *increase* welfare when it is directed at attempting to secure the proceeds of tariff revenue. Anam (1982) showed that rent-seeking for quota premiums cannot lead to such paradoxical outcomes in the two-sector Heckscher–Ohlin–Samuelson type of model used by Bhagwati and Srinivasan.
2. This section is essentially a summary of Findlay and Wellisz (1982).
3. See also the important study of the fiscal "Leviathan" in Brennan and Buchanan (1980) for a closely related approach.
4. The common sources of inspiration for both our approaches is Parkinson's law. There is also of course an obvious affinity with the "sales maximization" hypothesis of William Baumol and others regarding corporate managers in the private sector.

7 PURCHASING MONOPOLY

Harold Demsetz

The theory of monopoly presumes the condition of monopoly, much as the theory of competition presumes the condition of competition. Both proceed to deduce profit maximizing output policies for firms operating within the constraints appropriate to the assumed conditions of the market. Neither theory seriously attempts to explain how these conditions arise, and so they are more aptly named the *theory of pricing under monopoly* and the *theory of pricing under competitive conditions.*[1]

These theories lead to conclusions about the level of price, its relationship to marginal cost, and normative matters. The normative propositions are associated with theoretical measurements of the deadweight loss associated with monopoly (and, in rent-seeking theory, with resources used to secure monopoly). This chapter examines the case where monopoly is simply purchased, how the price paid to acquire monopoly affects the usual positive and normative conclusions derived from the monopoly model, and how the standard calculation of the deadweight loss underestimates the impact of monopoly. Before turning to these issues, it is useful to remind ourselves of the dangers in drawing any normative conclusions from a comparison of pure monopoly and perfect competition.

THE NORMATIVE INCOMMENSURABILITY OF MONOPOLY AND COMPETITION

The equilibrium of perfect competition is deduced by invoking a short list of important assumptions. These impose on the analysis full information about prices and technology and costless transactions. They are useful for the purpose of exploring coordination achieved by the price system when decisions are decentralized. The analysis of the basic role of prices in coordinating resource decisions is more direct and simpler with these assumptions than without them. If these same assumptions are applied to monopoly pricing (given the monopoly), the consequences of monopoly would be purely distributional. There would be nothing to prevent a monopolist from finely discriminating in the prices he charges for each unit, or from exacting "all or nothing" payments from buyers. Such fine discrimination creates little or no deadweight loss if this loss is measured in the standard manner by the deadweight loss triangle. This attempt to make the welfare analysis of pricing in monopoly and competition commensurate by applying the perfect competition assumptions to the monopoly pricing model undermines the standard inefficiency deductions from monopoly pricing. Positive information and transaction costs are required to generate a monopoly caused deadweight loss, but this destroys commensurability with the competitive model's assumptions.

If we attempt to achieve commensurability by importing nonzero information and transaction costs into the analysis of competitive equilibrium, thus preserving the inefficiency of monopoly, we can no longer use the perfectly competitive equilibrium as the standard of efficiency. Instead, we are left with a yet to be derived pseudo competitive equilibrium exhibiting characteristics similar to "workable" or monopolistic competition. We are not quite sure about the equilibrium properties of such "contaminated" competitive situations, and it is doubtful that it can be argued convincingly on the basis of what we now know that monopoly is necessarily less desirable. Indeed, the real question becomes how much monopoly (or contaminated competition) is desirable. The present state of economic theory does not allow us to answer this important question, so I set it aside and return to a reexamination of conventional aspects of the monopoly problem.

SOURCES OF MONOPOLY

Once we move outside the narrow framework of the monopoly pricing model, which begins by assuming monopoly, we encounter a variety of statements about sources of monopoly. The most analytical of these is economies of scale. If scale economies are significant over the range of output required to satisfy demand when demand equals marginal cost, then unfettered rivalry can be expected to yield a one-firm industry. The impact of the competition to be that one firm is important to a determination of the price that results, and if this competition "for the field" is intense, it is clear that price will not reach the level deduced in the monopoly pricing model.[2] In any case, the assumption of scale economies sizable enough to yield one firm is such a special case, with so little apparent empirical relevance, that it hardly can explain much monopoly pricing even if there were no competition to be the single seller.

In a world of positive information cost, monopoly (short-run) could be achieved by superior performance. It is doubtful that this Schumpeterian case implies any welfare loss, and it is not even clear that dominance achieved by a firm in this way is best described as noncompetitive.

Government protection of markets constitutes another source of monopoly pricing, but one that cannot be maintained in the absence of the higher level of coercive force excercisable by political institutions. It is difficult to evaluate the impact of this source of monopoly on either the positive or normative consequences of monopoly pricing until a more fully developed and widely accepted theory of government behavior is available. In particular, it would be useful to be able to understand the methods used to acquire protection and the nature of the controls imposed by government on the recipients of such protection.

A fourth source of monopoly pricing is found in collusion. Much has been written about collusion, but virtually all non-game-theoretic models of collusive pricing, from Cournot to Stigler, implicitly assume no entry. Like the theories of monopoly and competition, models of collusion are models of pricing that begin with a given set of firms or industry structure. How the colluded price is maintained in the face of entry is unanswered.

There is a fifth source of monopoly pricing power, but it plays no prominent role in economic literature. This is monopoly acquired by pure luck, for example, by purchasing or, better yet, by inheriting land containing the only supply of uranium just *before* the energy potential of uranium becomes known. This unusual source of monopoly, because no expenditures are made to secure the monopoly and no entry threats are possible, seems to be a source of monopoly that is best fitted by the standard theory of monopoly pricing.

The sixth source of monopoly does answer the question about entry, and it does it in a purely private way. The source is described in the folklore of the "robber barons," who are alleged simply to have established and maintained a monopoly by buying out rivals. The ratio of evidence to "his story" in this literature is pitifully low, but this purely private resolution of the problem of entry, with its apparent deadweight loss, makes this case worthy of further theoretical analysis. Most of the remainder of this chapter carries forth one such analysis.

THE PROFIT OF MONOPOLIZATION

It is important to distinguish the logic that yields the profit maximizing output rate, and the resulting profit, for a given monopoly, from that which yields the profit from *monopolizing* a market. This distinction lies at the heart of the analysis to follow. Consider two alternative scenarios for settling farmland and marketing farm products. In scenario 1 the government auctions land to the highest bidders under the condition that farm products are to be sold in competitive markets. In scenario 2, the government promises to set product prices at monopoly levels (at taxpayer expense). The profit to monopolization is measured by the excess of the sum of bids in scenario 2 over those of scenario 1. This difference is not equivalent to the profit calculated from the standard monopoly model, which pays no heed to the value of forgone competitive rent. The maximization of monopoly rents, in the context of the standard monopoly, yields a correct answer to the question "What is the profit maximizing output rate?" but *not* to the question "How much is the monopoly worth?" The answer to the second question leads to a correct calculation of the maximum profit attributable to monopolization, and this answer sets the limit to which the cost of monopolization is to be compared when judging the profitability of creating a monopoly where none now exists. What one is willing to pay to monopolize the sale of a product depends on the magnitude of the competitive rent that can be secured in the absence of the power to set price.

Variations on this theme occupy much of the remainder of this chapter, but before turning to these it is useful to repeat its basic logic from a different perspective. How much would sellers in a price-taker market pay an agent for the service of making it possible for them to set price collusively? The maximum amount they would pay is not the standard monopoly profit, but this profit minus the competitive rent they can obtain without the services of the agent. The "agent" in what follows is the robber baron who monopolizes the industry for himself, but he could just as well be the paid agent of sellers in a price-taker market. The maximum profit (payment) to the robber baron (agent) is the difference between the rents to monopoly and the rents to competition. Whether he receives this maximum depends on how competitive is the activity of monopolization. Intense rivalry between robber barons (agents) may yield only a normal rate of return to the activity of monopolization.

I begin my analysis of this process by adopting initially the standard monopoly model's implicit assumption that monopoly already exists. However, the monopoly that I assume to exist is not in the industry that is the target of the monopolizer but in the activity of monopolizing. Assume that only one entrepreneur seeks to profit from the conversion of a competitive industry to a monopoly.

Barriers to entry play no important role in this chapter, so the task faced by this one monopolizer is not one of purchasing a legal barrier to competition but of purchasing the power to set price in the face of unblockaded entry. Open entry makes it unprofitable to monopolize an industry if there are constant returns to scale. A price that yields supracompetitive returns cannot be maintained under conditions of infinite supply elasticity. Moreover, if we are to begin with a "normally" competitive target industry, we also rule out "natural" monopoly. (A more elaborate treatment of the problem could include scale economies, once the possibility of competing to be the single producer is recognized.) Hence, the prospect for *profitable* conversion of a competitive industry to a monopoly is restricted to rising supply conditions, precisely the situations in which competitive rents are real alternatives to monopoly rents.

To simplify the discussion, I define a firm as a unit of capacity sufficient to produce one unit of output. By implication, the marginal cost to each firm of producing more than one unit of output is infinite. The rising supply curve thus reflects the greater opportunity cost borne by successively entering firms. I also consider only the long run, in which we may assume that all costs are variable, and, to simplify still more, that all costs are "capacity" costs. The simplifications achieved by these assumptions are that we need not be concerned with how to interpret the degree to which a firm "remains in the industry," as we would if its output could vary over alternative positive amounts, or with how to treat separate types of cost. The logic of the discussion can be revealed fully by using linear demand and supply functions.

The cost of purchasing a monopoly depends on the process that determines the price to be paid per unit of capacity acquired by the monopolizer. One process must be rejected at the outset if monopolization is to offer the prospect of profit. The owners of existing capacity cannot know for certain that the industry is to be monopolized, for they would not then sell their specialized resources for less than what they could earn by continuing to operate with price raised to a monopoly level. Profitable monopolization (if possible) requires that the monopolizer be able to acquire at least some capacity at lower prices.

The standard monopoly model assumes that the monopolist's marginal cost schedule is the supply schedule that would face the industry were it to operate competitively (and if there were no cost advantages or disadvantages associated with either of these forms of market organization). I wish to examine the profit to monopoly in this case for the purpose of portraying graphically the standard monopoly model's overestimate of this profit.

In Figure 7-1, the standard monopoly profit is given as area $\overline{P_M CAO} = P_M \cdot Q_M - OAQ_M$. This suggests that if Q_C were produced competitively, the owners of firms would be willing to pay $\overline{P_M CAO}$ to an agent who secures for the industry the power to set price at P_M. Clearly this is incorrect even if existing competitors fully cooperate to secure the monopoly, for these owners can secure competitive rent $\overline{OP_C E}$ in the absence of monopoly pricing power. The profit to monopolizing the industry is $\overline{P_M CAO} - \overline{OP_C E}$. Thus, under the conditions implicit in the present context, the profit to monopolization, shown in Figure 7-1, is the difference between the vertically shaded rectangle and horizontally shaded triangle.

This measurement of the profit of monopolizing the industry assumes that resources are securable at their supply prices to the industry when functioning

Figure 7-1. The Profit of Monopolizing.

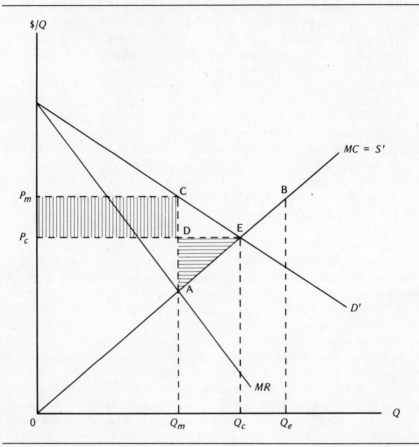

competitively, for this underlies the calculation of competitive rent, and that those resources that would be attracted into the industry by price P_M can be put, or kept, in alternative uses at no special cost to the monopolizers. $Q_E - Q_M$ resources would be attracted into production at price P_M; if these resources could be kept in alternative uses by paying their owners an infinitesimally small increment of funds above the value of these resources in these alternative uses, then area $\overline{DEA}$ measures that part of competitive rent forgone by resorting to monopoly organization. Even in this case, the profit to monopolizing the industry is considerably less than is portrayed by the standard monopoly model.

If $Q_E - Q_M$ can be kept out only by paying owners a significant fraction of the monopoly rent they forgo by refraining from entering the monopolized industry, then the amount that must be subtracted from standard monopoly profit to calculate the profit to monopolization is larger. If potential entrants receive the total of the monopoly rent they forgo by keeping their resources outside the monopolized industry, $\overline{ACB}$ must be subtracted from $\overline{P_M CDP_C}$ to calculate correctly the (per period) profit of monopolization. The elasticity of supply beyond A need not be infinite to make monopolization unprofitable. In the limit, where resources already in the industry also must be purchased to make the monopolization effective, the payment to monopolize the industry could rise to $\overline{P_M BO}$, but this has been ruled out by assuming the monopolizer can acquire the resources he uses to produce Q_M at their competitive supply prices.

The profit to monopolization (per period), then, can be thought to vary between $\overline{P_M CDP_C} - \overline{ADE}$ and $\overline{P_M CDP_C} - \overline{ACB}$ depending on the payment required to keep "price-reducing" capacity in other industries. The minimum subtraction from standard monopoly profit $\overline{P_M CAO}$ is the forgone competitive rent $\overline{P_C EO}$. The maximum subtraction adds the forgone monopoly rent of potential entrants, $\overline{CBED}$, to the amount that must be subtracted. These limits, of course, also determine the limits that would be paid in aggregate by rival monopolizers of a competitive industry under conditions of open entry into the business of monopolizing.

Even the case of a free monopoly, one achieved through pure luck, is misrepresented by the standard monopoly model. Maximizing the difference between revenue and cost of production does inform the monopolizer about the output rate that yields maximum profit when exercising his power to set price, but the profit so calculated is not a measure of how much it is worth to him to maintain his monopoly price. If price is set at its competitive level, he would still receive competitive rent, so the maximum amount he would pay to prevent the "confiscation" of his right to set price above its competitive level is the difference between monopolistic and competitive rents.

THE PROPENSITY TO MONOPOLY

The tendency to monopoly is thus a function of the difference between the rents to monopoly and to competition. *Ceteris paribus*, the more inelastic the market demand, the greater is the monopoly rent, and the more elastic is the supply, the smaller is the competitive rent. It would seem that perfectly elastic supply, given the market demand, would be conducive to monopoly were it not for the problem created by open entry.

There are two ways in which elastic supply can be promotive of entry. Figure 7-2 shows how elastic supply can combine with the positioning of demand to create a large propensity to monopoly. The intersection of D' at the right angled kink of $\overline{SS'}$ yields a positive monopoly rent in combination with a zero competitive rent. Should D' be moved higher into the region of the vertical branch of supply, competitive rent would increase relative to monopoly rent,

Figure 7-2. Propensity to Monopolize.

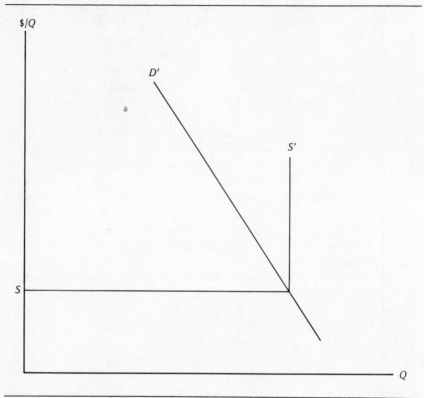

thus diminishing the propensity to monopoly. Should D' be moved leftward into the region of horizontal supply, monopoly rent falls relative to the (zero) competitive rent. The closer supply conditions are approximated by SS'; and the closer competitive price is to a zero rent price, the greater the incentive to monopolize. The cornering of a given periodically supplied agricultural commodity seems a case in point, and the history of the organized commodity exchanges is replete with attempts to achieve such corners.

The other way in which elastic supply can become attractive to a monopolizer is, of course, to obtain a regulated barrier to entry after a position of dominance has been achieved. The purchase of that position becomes trivially cheap under the assumed conditions if economic rent is zero.

A reasonable pattern of acquisition prices requires the monopolizer to pay more to acquire competitive assets the closer he is to completing the monopolization of the industry. This implicitly ties the price of the specialized assets being purchased to the expected price of the good to be produced by the industry, an increase in the probability of monopoly implying an increase in the

Figure 7-3. The Problem of Entry.

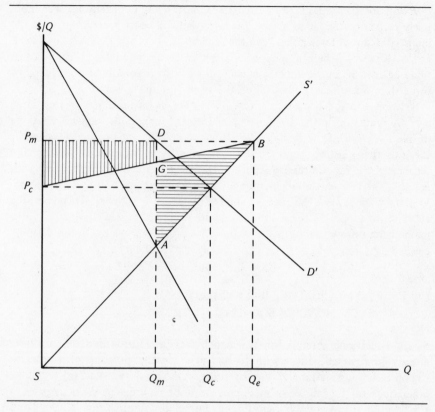

expected price of the good. The question then arises as to how to specify the
buy-out price as a function of the fraction of the industry's capacity acquired by
the monopolizer. The absence of theoretical groundwork tolerates a wide variety
of specifications. At the very beginning of the acquisition process, the probability of successful monopolization is close enough to zero that the price paid for
specialized assets should be no greater than their value under competitive conditions. At the end of the monopolization process the price paid should be very
close to the monopoly rent.[3]

If the probability of monopoly pricing is strictly proportional to the quantity
of assets acquired by the monopolizer, the path of capacity acquisition prices
might approximate line $P_C B$ in Figure 7-3. The return to monopolization, if by
this we mean the maintenance of price P_M, is then area $P_C P_M DG$ minus area
AGB. This difference easily can be negative, so that even a relatively inelastic
competitive supply can wring the profit out of monopolization in the absence of
barriers to entry.

To the extent that there is rivalry to monopolize the target industry, the line $P_C B$ will approach line $P_M B$, so that the return to monopolization is even more likely to be negative. In aggregate, the most that will be spent to monopolize the industry is the difference between the vertically shaded and horizontally shaded areas. Moreover, where monopoly is acquired through purchase, the only real resource cost of rent-seeking behavior is the cost of negotiating the exchange of ownership. The sum actually paid for the assets is simply a transfer.

Price P_M no longer can be thought of as the profit-maximizing price, however. A reduction in the price maintained by the monopolist reduces the slope of line $P_C B$ by shifting B toward the origin along SS', thus reducing somewhat the total that must be spent to acquire the capacity necessary to allow the maintenance of the now lower monopoly price. If P_M is the profit-maximizing price ignoring entry, then the open-entry profit maximizing price set by the monopolizer must be lower. The precise amount by which it is lower depends on the elasticity of supply. In the limiting case, with supply infinitely elastic, the profit-maximizing price certainly is the competitive price. But even with finite supply elasticities it may not pay to monopolize the market when entry is open.

ESTIMATING THE WELFARE LOSS
FROM MONOPOLIZATION

Serious questions about normative conclusions in regard to monopoly have already been asked, but I wish to set such considerations aside in order to examine the implications of the foregoing analysis for the standard economic evaluations of the impact of monopoly on resource use. The older measure of the "waste" of monopoly—the value of output lost through restriction of output—has been supplemented in recent years by adding to this the value of the resources used to compete for monopoly. In the purely private purchase of competitive capacity, this added value will be mostly a simple transfer, so the appropriate measure becomes again the familiar deadweight loss triangle. In a world free of antimerger laws and other impediments to the straightforward purchase of rival assets, there would be little or no drain on real resources because of the competition to secure monopoly (even if monopolization were a profitable activity).

Most empirical estimates of the welfare loss are based on the estimation of the value of the deadweight loss triangle, and the calculated estimates are generally quite low. A variety of assumptions are utilized to ease the estimating procedure. Harberger (1954), for example, assumes horizontal cost curves and unitary elastic demands, and these assumptions, as other have noted, lead to errors in the estimates. The present analysis suggests another source of error.

In Harberger-type estimates, the deviation in an industry's profit rate from the average of manufacturing profit rates, or some such measure, is used as an

Figure 7-4. The Bias in Dead-Weight Loss Estimates.

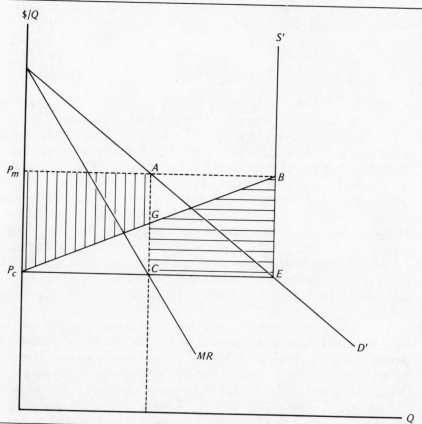

index of the deviation of monopoly price from competitive price. But monopolization via purely private purchase of assets should yield to the winner a smaller recorded profit for successful monopolization, and this reduction in profit is more significant the greater is the rivalry between would-be monopolizers. Even in the case of the lone monopolizer, the profit that will obtain under correct accounting procedures is the difference between the vertically and horizontally shaded areas with which we have been working (if we ignore the downward pressure on price exerted by the cost of acquisitions).

In Figure 7-4, we use D' and P_CES' to represent demand and supply for a Harberger study of the deadweight loss of monopoly. The deadweight loss triangle is $\overline{AEC}$. Harberger theoretically indexes the size of this triangle by vertical line AC, with AC empirically estimated from recorded profit rates. However, in the present analysis, recorded profit rates reflect the difference between the vertically and horizontally shaded areas $\overline{P_M A G P_C}$ and $\overline{GBEC}$. If monopoly is the source of higher recorded profit rates, the empirical estimate of AC must understate the real magnitude of AC and, therefore, of the deadweight loss triangle.

THE RISKS OF MONOPOLIZATION

A departure from the "easy monopolization" assumptions with which we started makes it clear that attempts to monopolize are fraught with risks of various kinds. (1) The monopoly may turn out to be a more costly producer than is the competitive industry being monopolized. (2) The monopolist may find it costly to enforce contracts meant to bar the return from other industries of capacity that the monopolist sought to retire; either this capacity will need to be retained in idle condition by the monopolizer or he must deploy this capacity himself in diversified employments outside the monopolized industry; both alternatives reduce profit relative to the profit projected by the "easy monopolization" assumptions. (3) The supply of output may be more elastic beyond competitive output than is supposed, in which case the cost of excluding new capacity may more than dissipate the profit from monopolization. (4) Rival monopolizers (or holdouts) may raise the price for purchasing competitive capacity.

All these possibilities increase the risks that accompany an attempt to monopolize an industry, and several present a would-be monopolizer with asymmetrically poor risks. Possibilities (1) and (3) might pose symmetric risks; the monopoly firm may be less costly to operate and supply may turn out to be less elastic than anticipated. But (2) and (4) present downside risks for which there seems no upside counterweight. Relative to the profit prospect deduced from the assumptions with which we began, themselves yielding a lower profit than is suggested by the standard monopoly model, the profit prospects of any real attempt to privately monopolize an industry must be gauged as dimmer still.

Purely private monopolization is surely less promising of profit than the folklore of populism suggests, at least for cost conditions that do not offer economies of scale to the monopolizer. Some of the risks of monopolization, and some of the costs of deterring entry, can be offset by abandoning the purely private approach in favor of securing government aid. Entry barriers imposed and policed by the government present a formidable hurdle to the reentry or new entry of capacity. Abandonment of monopolization in favor of cartelization of an industry also reduces the financial stake required of any one firm in retiring unwanted capacity from the industry; where monopolization requires one firm to bear the entire cost of purchasing and retiring such capacity, cartelization permits a sharing of cost. The disadvantage of cartelization is the risk that one or more firms will cease cooperating, but this risk may be worth bearing to reduce the financial commitment required of a monopolizer who seeks to raise price on his own. Regulation or collusion could easily dominate purely private monopolization as the preferred route to profit. A combination of discovering and prosecuting collusion and of rejecting legal bars to competition represents a more potent and less risky antimonopoly policy than the prevention of mergers and various pricing practices thought to signify a campaign to privately monopolize industry.

NOTES TO CHAPTER 7

1. The assumed relationship between the number of firms in the industry and the constraints guiding a firm to its output decision does not bear close scrutiny because it ignores the problem of entry. Because of this ommision, we are left without explanation of the market structure other than one based on economies of scale.
2. See my discussion of this in "Why Regulate Utilities?" 11 *Journal of Law and Economics* 55 (October 1968).
3. If predation is meaningless, as it would be with efficient capital markets, a "holdout" price might emerge, in which case the seller asks for more than simply the monopoly rent that will accrue to his assets when price is set at monopoly levels. If predation is not meaningless, the price he can ask, in the limit may be pushed to the opportunity cost of his assets. I assume that neither extreme holds.

8 COALITIONS AND MACROECONOMICS

David C. Colander and Mancur Olson

In the sixteenth century the French political philosopher Jean Bodin (1530–1596) pointed out that an increase in the quantity of money raised prices and led to increased consumption and production, whereas monopolies — which were in his day mainly guilds — tended to restrict total output. Since that time, much work in macroeconomics has been devoted to the first two issues mentioned by Bodin but little to none has been done on the third. That is, there has been little concern in macroeconomics about the contemporary counterparts of the guilds of his day, the modern-day distributional coalitions that seek monopoly power or governmental favors. Even when research turned to the microfoundations of macroeconomics, the focus was usually on essentially competitive markets; the effects of trade restrictions imposed by collective action to lobby or to cartelize were not usually considered.

In part this focus resulted from Keynes's attempt to develop a novel theory of unemployment that did not appear to rely on the supracompetitive wages that had previously been invoked to explain unemployment. In recent times, Keynes's theory has been attacked by rational-expectations or "equilibrium" macroeconomists. In their sophisticated reconstruction of classical theory they usually assume perfect competition, or at least a coalition-free environment, and with this and other assumptions demonstrate that traditional macroeconomic policies can play no useful role. This chapter does not address the specific issues raised by the debate between Keynesian and equilibrium macroeconomists. Rather it argues that, to the degree that this debate assumes a perfectly competitive or even a coalition-free environment, it misses the main point. In the United States, and in most other countries today, distributional or rent-seeking

115

coalitions not only exist but are widespread, and their existence can be predicted on purely economic grounds in any long-stable society. For macroeconomics to abstract from this phenomenon is to overlook a type of rational, self-interested behavior that any theory that is properly grounded in microeconomics must include. The explicit introduction of the logic of distributional coalitions into macroeconomics also makes it possible to incorporate valuable insights from both Keynesian and equilibrium macroeconomics into one integrated framework.

Incorporating an analysis of the collective action of coalitions into macroeconomics is helpful for at least four additional reasons. First, it explains the incentive that gives rise to involuntary unemployment of labor and other resources, and in doing this provides the explanation of why the equilibrium or the non-accelerating inflation rate of unemployment (NAIRU) is above what macroeconomists have considered full employment. Second, it provides the needed explanation of sticky wages and prices and thereby provides an explanation of why monetary shocks can have real effects. Third, by showing that the incentive that gives rise to involuntary unemployment and underutilized capacity is not eliminated or even weakened by inflation, even though unexpected increases in the money supply or nominal spending temporarily increase employment and real output, it explains the political pressures for expansionary policies and the inflationary bias in the highly organized modern economy. Finally, an analysis of collective action and rent-seeking can help explain what types of public policies will be able to solve macroeconomic problems.

WHY IS THERE INVOLUNTARY UNEMPLOYMENT?

Equilibrium macroeconomists attack the Keynesian and disequilibrium macroeconomists for making the ad hoc assumption of sticky prices or wages. They correctly argue that this assumption has been given no microeconomic justification. In a coalition-free environment, it is in fact inconsistent with rational behavior: Individuals will trade with one another until they have obtained all the gains that are available from such trades, and thus must end up explicitly or implicitly with the only prices at which joint gains and output levels are maximized—competitive prices.

It follows that whenever there is "involuntary unemployment," there are potential gains from trade and it is advantageous for both employees and employers to get together and to make employment contracts that eliminate that unemployment. Thus the natural place to begin any theory of unemployment is with the question, "Who might have an interest in blocking the mutually advantageous transactions between employers and the involuntarily unemployed?"

The answer is straightforward: any coalition of workers of the same or a similar skill, or any coalition of employers that has brought about a less-than-competitive wage for such workers. Any such monopolistic or monopsonistic coalitions must block mutually advantageous transactions in order to maintain a noncompetitive wage level. As Olson (1965, 1982) has shown, rational actors can organize or collude to block the mutually advantageous transactions between involuntarily unemployed workers and individual employers if (and only if) they are few in number or have access to "selective incentives." Similarly, coalitions in the markets for factors of production other than labor, and in product markets, must also block mutually advantageous transactions to maintain noncompetitive prices. These noncompetitive prices can generate unemployment of capital and reduce social income. This will depress real income and the demand for output, thereby also exacerbating the problem of unemployment of labor.

Macroeconomists have not incorporated this manifestation of rational behavior into their theories because their analyses have usually assumed an institutional framework within which all individuals are price takers, passively accepting whatever price the market determines, or at the least act in isolation rather than in coalition. Such an institutional structure is, however, unstable. The issue can be shown very simply in Figure 8-1.

If those who supply the product or labor at issue have the necessary small numbers or selective incentives, they can obtain an increase in rents of the kind depicted in rectangle A. As a consequence, other suppliers lose an amount at least equal to triangle B (and more than this if they are among the inframarginal suppliers with the lower costs depicted to the left of Q_0). Demanders lose area A and triangle C. The increase in rents in rectangle A can, of course, be obtained *only* if the mutually advantageous transactions that would realize the

Figure 8-1. The Incentive for Rent-Seeking.

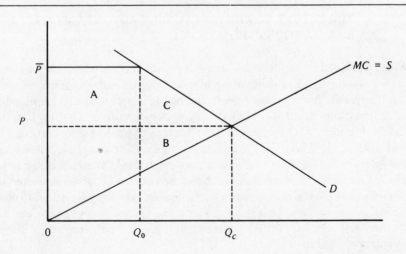

gains in areas B and C are blocked. The social loss is accordingly not only areas B and C, but also the costs of maintaining the coalition and blocking the mutually beneficial transactions that would otherwise occur.

A game theorist might initially object that those who are excluded will form coalitions of their own and that with everyone able to form coalitions there may be a tendency toward a "core" allocation of resources with Pareto efficiency and full employment. But this argument is erroneous because it neglects the fact that only those groups that have access to selective incentives or are small in number can organize to further their common interests. Some groups, such as consumers and the unemployed, are so numerous and so spread out over so many locations that picket lines and other selective incentives are not available, and they are not organized in any society. There are small groups of *buyers* in some industries that have organized to obtain monopsonistic or political power, and they block mutually advantageous transactions of others just as monopolistic cartels of sellers do. But most coalitions represent particular groups of producers, so that most noncompetitive prices are at higher-than-competitive levels and markets with excess supplies are more common than those with excess demand. Empirical support for this prediction has recently been supplied by Katherine Abraham (1983). Looking at excess supply (vacancies) and excess demand (unemployment) in postwar United States, she found that unemployment has exceeded vacancies by an average of about four times, and that, as the theory here also predicts, this ratio has probably increased over the postwar period. We conclude that a purely competitive economy is accordingly institutionally unstable in any long-stable society with rational self-interested behavior; many markets eventually come to have disequilibrium prices, mainly at supracompetitive prices that generate excess supply and unemployed resources.

THE EXTENT TO WHICH MUTUALLY ADVANTAGEOUS TRANSACTIONS ARE BLOCKED

When, as here, the focus is on coalitions that block mutually advantageous transactions of others, the extent of the blockage and the unemployment or social loss that results from it cannot be determined so simply as in the case of monolithic firms with monopoly or monopsony power. A profit-maximizing firm that faces a downward sloping demand curve because of product differentiation, for example, will, as is well known, equate marginal cost and marginal revenue, and the extent of the social loss is then uniquely determined. When a coalition rather than a monolithic firm exercises monopoly or monopsony power, however, the determination of the extent of the excess burden can depend on a great many factors. If the coalition consists of workers who cannot "merge" or "own" one another, and who have differing reservation prices for their time, the matter is even more complicated.

This can readily be illustrated by supposing that the coalition that blocks the mutually advantageous trades shown in Figure 8-1 is a workers' cartel and that its members are not in every case those workers whose reservation wages are the lowest (i.e., those to the left of Q_0). If somehow the members of the workers' cartel had happened to be those with the lowest reservation wages, and we could assume the number of workers in the coalition was given, and the unity and strength of the cartel were beyond question, we could readily calculate the extent of the blocked transactions by equating the marginal cost of the time of the workers, which under these assumptions can be read from the supply curve, with the marginal revenue received from selling this type of labor. If, more plausibly, the workers who are initially in the cartel are not always those with the lowest reservation wages, and devices such as seniority systems, or the political hazards of conducting a public auction to sell places in the cartel, prevent trades that would staff the cartel with just these people, then the marginal cost of labor will be greater than otherwise and the monopoly wage correspondingly higher.[1]

There is a similar ambiguity in the extent to which a coalition of firms will raise prices. Whereas a monolithic monopolist will strive to produce the whole of its chosen level of output at the lowest possible cost, this often will not happen in a coalition of firms. If there is an antitrust law, or even a fear of governmental regulation if the monopoly becomes conspicuous, a coalition of firms is likely to be hesitant to bribe high-cost producers to close down and switch production to more efficient firms; this may make the existence of the coalition and the monopoly gains it is reaping at the expense of the rest of the society more conspicuous. In such a circumstance the firms may, for example, elect to divide whatever industry output they decide to supply among the existing firms in proportion to precartel levels of production. In such a situation of "qualified joint maximization" the industry marginal cost curve will in general be higher than it would have been had there been complete joint maximization and the profit-maximizing level of output would also be different. There would also generally be disagreement among the members of the cartel about what price should be chosen, with the low-cost members wanting a larger output than the others. The continued production by member firms whose output could be provided more cheaply by other firms is analogous to the presence of marginal workers of the kind described (in the previous paragraph) in a workers' cartel.[2]

Another determinant of the extent to which mutually advantageous transactions are blocked is the number of members in the cartel. The number of members is influenced, among other things, by two conflicting forces. One is the desire of each member of the cartel to share the opportunity to sell at the supracompetitive price with as few others as possible: each participant seeks to be a member of a minimum winning coalition. But more-than-normal returns can be earned by selling at the supracompetitive price, and so the other force is the desire of incumbents to remain in the favored group. The relative political strength of different members of the coalition will therefore be important in determining who is allowed to remain in the cartel and who is forced to leave the industry. In general, a long-established position in the industry and in the cartel implies greater power, and this is one of the reasons why the seniority, or last-hired are first-fired, system is so commonplace in labor unions. (Another reason is that this simple system spares the cartel continued divisive decisionmaking about who will get the benefits.)

Despite these complications, in the *very* long run an otherwise unchanging economy would reach a condition in which every group with the access to selective incentives or the concentrated, small-number clientele needed for organization would have overcome the difficult task of organizing for collective action. In fullness of time each organized group would also have fully exploited its political or market power. As Gary Becker and John Flemming have previously argued in criticizing or extending Olson's argument,[3] the gains to both political and market entrepreneurs from resisting or undercutting a distributional coalition would rise with the extent of the excess burden it generated, so some of these coalitions would have to settle for lower prices and wages than they would have chosen in the absence of opposition.

When all this is sorted out in the historical long run there is, then, a coalitional or institutional equilibrium. *It is this equilibrium*, not the perfectly competitive equilibrium assumed by many macroeconomic theorists, toward which the economy tends in the really long run. The implications of this simple point for the modeling of the macroeconomy are enormous. The truly long run macroeconomic equilibrium is accordingly one in which there is continuing disequilibrium, and most often disequilibrium with excess supply, in many of an economy's markets. In the long run we are not only all dead, but we have in addition bequeathed a coalitional equilibrium to our descendants that makes the new classical or equilibrium macroeconomics inapplicable.

GENERAL EQUILIBRIUM:
WHERE DO THE UNEMPLOYED GO?

Our assertion that markets in excess-supply disequilibrium imply unemployment of resources requires elaboration. In general equilibrium analysis, the normal assumption is that the excluded group will leave the activity and undertake other activities; barriers to entry misallocate resources, but they do not create unemployment. In our coalitional equilibrium, individuals remain involuntarily unemployed, in that they would be willing to accept a job at the same wage that some others with the same endowment of human capital as they have are currently receiving, and even at the marginal revenue product they would have in a coalition-free economy, but sometimes cannot obtain such a job however much they may search. As Olson (1982) explains, countries in which only a small segment of the economy has fallen under the thrall of special-interest groups will normally not have any significant unemployment, because the much larger flex-price sector will absorb the unemployed with no great reduction in the wages and prices in that sector. If large parts of a country's economy are, by contrast, under the control of distributional coalitions, the exclusion in the controlled sectors will have kept an important part of the factor supply in the whole economy from being employed in the sectors in which they would otherwise have been employed. The shift of resources to the flexprice sector will then be so great that *large variations in the returns to homogeneous factors will emerge.* So many people will be crowded into the "selling apples on the street corners" sector that employment in this sector can in depressions come to be regarded as synonymous with involuntary unemployment. At an extreme, the flexprice wage can be driven below the reservation wages of even the relatively industrious or even to zero.

The more extensive the special-interest groups and the non-market-clearing prices that lobbying and cartelization bring about, the more extensive are the disparities in the rates of return for homogeneous resources. The greater these disparities, the more it pays to invest in searching and queuing for positions in the distributional coalitions. The extra search in such a case is not, like the search in a purely competitive economy, a socially efficient investment in information; it is a search for rents that would otherwise accrue to others. The extra time spent searching and queuing is a type of social waste or involuntary unemployment arising from the distributional coalitions that created the disparities in rates of return.[4]

We can summarize our first proposition as follows:

1. Distributional coalitions, if sufficiently numerous, will raise the "equilibrium level of unemployment" by increasing the level of search unemployment above the socially optimal amount, and by creating a degree of underemployment so serious that it is often not distinguished from unemployment.

CYCLICAL UNEMPLOYMENT AND DISTRIBUTIONAL COALITIONS

A second effect of the existence of special-interest organizations is that they take longer to make decisions than do private individuals and are less likely to come to rational (group-optimal) decisions. One need only compare the decision process in a group to an individual decision process to recognize how important this effect is. Because all important decisions of a collusive organization must be made collectively, it will normally have a crowded agenda and bargaining tables will also be cluttered. This slow decisionmaking means that wages and prices are unlikely to change quickly, even if conditions change in such a way that a different wage or price would be optimal for the special-interest group under the new conditions. Additionally, each member of the special-interest coalition does not have an incentive to become fully informed, because information about collective goods is also a collective good. In such cases prejudice and general feelings are more likely to control the decisionmaking process where collective decisions are concerned than they are when individuals make decisions about private goods. Others, such as Arthur Okun (1981), have offered other explanations of price and wage rigidities, and we do not deny that other factors could also help to generate price or wage stickiness. The present explanation, however, appears to be consistent with the *variations* in such stickiness across societies and historical periods (Olson 1982). We can summarize our second conclusion as follows:

> 2. Many prices and wages in long-stable societies will be slowly adjusting and will not reflect the best trades open to the society. Thus shocks to an economy will likely have significant repercussions, and Keynesian type feedback effects (as described by Clower) will occur. Such societies will therefore experience cyclical variations in unemployment levels.

THE INTERACTION OF PROPOSITIONS 1 AND 2 AND THE UNIT OF ACCOUNT

Proposition 1 was that eventually distributional coalitions, mostly on the supply side, push prices in many markets above the supply/demand equilibrium price, and proposition 2 that prices determined or influenced by coalitions adjust slowly. What is bad for the coalition need not be bad for the economy as a whole. Members of coalitions do not have the incentive to be fully informed. For this as well as other reasons, at low rates of inflation most distributional coalitions lobby or bargain for prices and wages expressed in terms of the unit of account, not in indexed or real terms. Thus inflation, or a rise in the unit of account, can temporarily improve the efficiency of the economy by reducing the degree of monopoly and the height of non-market-clearing prices and wages. Since the typical cartel or lobby would have gained from setting a supracompetitive or monopoly price, unexpected inflation will make the relative price it receives less monopolistic than intended. The interaction of propositions 1 and 2 may also give the society an inflationary bias. Unorganized consumers and suppliers excluded by the distributional coalitions do not have the selective incentives or small numbers needed to form countervailing coalitions. But presidents and political parties interested in votes and in a booming economy have an incentive to use demand-management policies that are unexpectedly expansive to reduce, if only temporarily, the extent to which prices exceed market-clearing levels in the organized sectors. This leads to proposition 3.

> 3. An "unexpected" inflation will reduce the losses from monopoly due to cartelization and lobbying and will therefore reduce the amount of involun-

tary unemployment. Thus in a period of unexpected inflation, an economy with a high level of special-interest organizations and collusion will be more productive than it normally is.

If the inflation continues and becomes fully expected, the gains will be lost since special-interest groups will index their bargains. Since all methods of indexation are quite imperfect, the imperfections in the indexes and the time it takes to prepare and publish them will in such circumstances be important. These imperfections keep proposition 2 relevant, and will sometimes induce political leaders concerned about consumers, excluded suppliers, and the general level of output to expand demand even in already inflationary environments.

EMPIRICAL EVIDENCE

The foregoing three propositions account for aspects of the postwar economic experience in the United States that other macroeconomic theories do not: the initial low levels of unemployment as unexpected inflation reduced the real prices charged by suppliers' coalitions; the large increases in unemployment due to the oil price shocks; the procyclical movement in productivity, and the progressively worsening inflation/unemployment trade-off. The framework offered here also explains why contractionary monetary policies designed to end inflation, even when credibly announced in advance, have brought substantial recessions in countries with a dense coalitional structure. Given the theory's emphasis on the duration of a stable political system, the most relevant periods for international cross-sectional comparisons are in the first few decades after World War II. Olson (1982) and Choi (1983) have considered that international data and have concluded the theory is generally consistent with the data, as are the broad outlines of historical change in the West and Japan since medieval times.

We consider a second test of the theory below. If the theory is correct, then jurisdictions with more distributional coalitions will have higher rates of unemployment. It has been shown elsewhere (Olson 1983) that *within countries* labor unions are the main coalitions that influence modern state and local economic life, especially where the unemployment of labor is concerned, even though things are very different when separate national economies or other historical epochs are at issue. We therefore consider the percentage of the labor force unionized by state for the 48 contiguous U.S. states in 1976, UNON76, and regress unemployment rates by states, UN7681, against this variable. The results (with the absolute values of T statistics given in parentheses) are

$$UN7681 = 4.54 + .887UNON76 \quad R^2 = .32 ; \qquad (8.1)$$
$$(4.68)$$

$$UN7681 = 4.60 + .765UNON70 \quad R^2 = .27 . \qquad (8.2)$$
$$(4.10)$$

It is possible that the percentage of the labor force that is unionized is correlated with other variables that cause unemployment, and that this explains the foregoing results. To test for this possibility, the percentage of a state's labor force that was employed in manufacturing industries (which are relatively sensitive to the business cycle) in 1976, PCMF76, was included in the regression equation:

$$\text{UN 7681} = 3.68 + .730 \text{ UNON76} + .601 \text{ PCMF76} \qquad R^2 = .43 \ . \quad (8.3)$$
$$\qquad\qquad\quad (4.00) \qquad\qquad (2.99)$$

As a further precaution, the percentage of the population that was in urban areas in 1970, RB1970, was also added as an independent variable:

$$\text{UN7681} = 3.21 + .668 \text{ UNON76} + .618 \text{ PCMF76}$$
$$\qquad\qquad\quad (3.33) \qquad\qquad (3.05)$$
$$\qquad\qquad + .857 \text{ RM1970} \qquad R^2 = .44 \ . \qquad\qquad (8.4)$$
$$\qquad\qquad\quad (.757)$$

Though the preceding results are only preliminary, it does appear that there is a highly significant positive relationship between unionization and unemployment. The lower significance levels of the percentage of manufacturing employment and urbanization levels, and the modest increase in explanatory power that results from adding these independent variables, also suggests that the relationship between unionization and unemployment is probably not due to a correlation of unionization with some third variable, although a good deal of further research is required before this can be attested with certainty.

There is the possibility that the foregoing results are an artifact of the stagflation that the U.S. economy has suffered in recent years, and that results would have been different in the relatively prosperous years of the 1950s and 1960s. Unfortunately, the unemployment statistics before 1976 were collected on a different basis and are open to question. Regressions on the data of the fifties and sixties do nonetheless reveal exactly the same strong positive association between unionization and unemployment rates, even after taking account of the relationship between the percentage of employment in manufacturing and unemployment rates.[5]

Regardless of what evidence we present, a monetarist is likely to look at our structural analysis and argue that it merely obscures the fundamental relationship between money and prices. That may be, but it should be also clear that the propositions advanced above *do not* imply that the long-run relationship between money and prices does not hold. They merely imply that this relationship is not sufficient to understand macroeconomics, since it does not provide any explanation for fluctuations in real output or for involuntary unemployment. Monetarists who believe that macroeconomics should be grounded in microeconomic theory should have no objection to the argument here.

The coalition theory upon which this chapter draws also is supported by the progressive structural change that has occurred in the real/nominal split. Milton Friedman and Anna Schwartz (1963) argue that the closest comparison to the 1930s depression is the 1839-1843 contraction. A close comparison of these, as has been done by the economic historian Peter Temin (1969), shows that, although the contraction in the money supply was greater in the 1839-1843 period (-42 percent in 1839-1843 versus -31 percent in 1929-1931), real gross national product moved the opposite direction; it *increased* 16 percent from 1839-1843, whereas it had *decreased* 30 percent in the 1929-1933 period.

This suggests that something changed in the interim and we believe that something is the change in economic institutions. Philip Cagan (1979) has found similar tendency for the period from 1890 to 1979. He states:

> The distinctive feature of the post-war inflations has not been that prices rose faster in periods of cyclical expansion—many previous expansions had much higher rates—but that they declined hardly at all, or even rose, in recessions. The startling failure of the 1970 recession to curb the inflation was not a new phenomenon . . . but simply a further step in a progressive post-war development.

COALITIONS AND MACROECONOMIC POLICY

We would not claim that the present argument offers a totally different way of analyzing macroeconomics. The argument here borrows from both Keynesian and equilibrium approaches, embedding what is borrowed in the framework of a theory of political economy. Thus, without the existing macroeconomic theories, the theory of political economy that inspires this chapter would be quite incomplete. At the same time, we believe the existing theories are quite incomplete without the theory of political economy upon which we have drawn.

What is strange is not the predictions of the theory we offer; it is that the theory has not been used earlier. As we stated previously, Keynes went to great lengths to avoid any explicit appeal to coalitions or monopoly in his theory. He did so because classical economists were quite willing to accept the proposition that monopolies caused unemployment. In explaining why the 1930s depression was different from earlier fluctuations, classical economists referred to cartelistic restrictions and institutional rigidities in their discussion of both unemployment and policy. To differentiate his product, Keynes strongly avoided any reliance on monopolies or coalitions in his theory. Monetarists and the new classicals, in an attempt to meet Keynes on that same perfectly competitive level, likewise downplay institutional realities, leaving both sides debating about a world that almost all agree does not exist. The foregoing is not to argue that the Keynesian and classical theories were not colossal intellectual achievements.

For the 1930s Keynes was largely correct in his policy prescriptions; for the "new unemployment" of the 1970s and 1980s, which is at much too high a level even when there has been no unexpected deflation or disinflation, the old-fashioned Keynesian analyses and prescriptions are less useful. Given the institutional structure, we have pushed aggregate demand policy by itself about as far as we can. Without coming to grips with institutional realities, we are unlikely to significantly decrease the average rate of unemployment over the cycle (the NAIRU) or to increase the rate of growth. But neither the Keynesian nor the classical theory provides any insight into the type of institutional change needed. That is why the new theory is necessary. The theory outlined here explains that progressive development and suggests some policies to help to deal with it.

POLICY IMPLICATIONS

The most important macroeconomic policy implication following from the coalition analysis is that *the best macroeconomic policy is a good microeconomic policy.* To continue to discuss macroeconomic policy in reference to unfettered perfectly competitive markets when the heart of the problem is in coalitions generating monopoly or public favors makes policy recommendations following from traditional analysis suspect. Thus the new classical macroeconomics' policy prescriptions have only a limited relevance to a society like the United States today.

Within a microeconomic context, any theoretical case for policy must be based on "private" market failure or externalities.[6] Past macroeconomic theories and policy recommendations have not been grounded in an analysis of market failure and thus have lacked a microeconomic base. The coalitional theory we have presented provides a firm microeconomic explanation for involuntary unemployment and slowly adjusting prices. It accordingly can also provide a foundation in certain circumstances for an anticyclical stabilization policy. When many prices do not adjust quickly, total spending can for a time be too high or too low; government is merely offsetting the spending "externality."[7] Thus, with traditional theory, Barro (1979: 55) can find no micro foundation for "the frequently suggested macro-policy response to the oil crisis" (an expansion of the money stock or government deficit). But within the coalitional framework there is a theoretical basis for considering such a policy as long as it is temporary, and a political analysis indicating that such a program could be politically feasible.

The expansionary policy cannot continue forever, however. The coalitions of suppliers will eventually adjust, thereby keeping the expansionary policy from lowering unemployment. If it is to lower the average level of unemployment, expansionary policy must be coupled with institutional change that reduces the impact of distributional coalitions or the way they interact.

Here again, by providing a different conception of the nature of macro equilibrium, the coalition theory focuses on how alternatives can work. For example, in his discussion of tax-based incomes policies (TIP), Robert Barro stated, "I honestly have no idea what sort of private market failure or externality is supposed to rationalize this sort of government interference with the price setting process" (Barro 1979: 53). The coalition theory provides a justification. The long-run equilibrium the economy arrives at is one in which there are barriers to entry and unemployed factor supplies. This equilibrium is in no way optimal and includes involuntary unemployment. As James Meade (1982) nicely put it: "The natural rate of unemployment is unnaturally high."

If one thinks of the TIP proposals as devices to offset the effect of cartelistic or lobby-inspired prices and wages, one can understand how they can reduce the natural or equilibrium level of unemployment.[8] We do not claim here to have dealt adequately with all of the advantages and disadvantages of TIPs. We do, however, claim that the framework presented here is far more useful in considering these plans than are the competing "perfectly competitive" or coalition-free frameworks.

CONCLUSION

The theory presented here is complementary to, not competitive with, existing theories; it provides a different and, we believe, useful perspective on the macroeconomic problems facing the economy in the 1980s. A likely reaction is that by introducing coalitions into macroeconomic analysis, we have opened up a Pandora's box of theoretical problems. Our answer to that is sometimes, when a monster exists, it is best to admit its existence and deal with it.

NOTES TO CHAPTER 8

1. Note also that even when there is a socially inefficient allocation of persons to the cartel there is, however, still an incentive to form a cartel.
2. Because less efficient firms can be purchased or merged with more efficient firms, and no corresponding transactions are possible among workers in a society without slavery or indentured servitude, there is probably somewhat less efficiency in the allocation of places in cartels of workers than in those of firms.
3. John Flemming made this argument when criticizing Olson's theory in 1978; Gary Becker offered it in a different context at the W.I. Thomas and Florian Znaniecki Conference on Contemporary Social Theory in 1983.
4. Unemployment is, of course, not only a problem in the labor market. The same argument applies to the market for other factors of production and to product markets. Each of these can contribute directly or indirectly to un-

employment since, as Robert Clower (1965) and Edmond Malinvaud (1977) have shown, a non-market-clearing price in one market can contribute to unemployment in other markets.

5. We are thankful to Murray Ross and Fran Sussman for useful help with this statistical work, and to Charles C. Brown for providing both good counsel and helpful data. Natalie McPherson deserves exceptional thanks for contributing a large amount of most useful effort to the statistical study that has been briefly referred to here.

6. Robert Barro argues this in Barro (1979).

7. Abba Lerner (1960) suggested this as an appropriate micro foundation to macro much earlier. Also, Lerner's interpretation of Keynes focused on institutional rigidities.

8. For a more complete discussion of this point, see Colander 1982.

9 THE OPTIMAL TARIFF WITH REVENUE-SEEKING
A Contribution to the Theory of DUP Activities

Elias Dinopoulos

Recent developments in the theory of international trade have stressed the importance of relaxing the traditional assumption of Meade (1952) and others that the revenue generated by a tariff is redistributed to consumers in a lump-sum fashion. Thus, Bhagwati and Srinivasan (1980) introduced the concept of "revenue seeking" as an important example of what Bhagwati (1982c) has christened as *directly unproductive profit-seeking* (DUP) activities, and analyzed the welfare consequences of a tariff when the associated revenues are competed for by lobbies.

An interesting question that arises then is: How would the optimal tariff be modified for a large country (i.e., one with monopoly power in trade), if revenue seeking were present? Since the optimal-tariff argument is the oldest reputable exception to the case for free trade, this is undoubtedly a question of importance, for the real world must be considered to lie somewhere between the case where all revenues are redistributed as lump-sum transfers and the case where they are all competed for by revenue-seeking lobbies.[1]

The plan of the chapter is as follows. For a large Ricardian economy with revenue seeking allowed for, the following questions are answered: (1) What is the optimal tariff in the presence of revenue seeking? (2) Is the optimal tariff with revenue seeking smaller or greater than the optimal tariff without revenue

The author would like to thank Jagdish Bhagwati, Heraklis Polemarchakis, Richard Brecher, Robert Feenstra, and Ronald Findlay for valuable comments and suggestions. In addition, this chapter has benefited from the comments of I. Borsook, A. Hughey, M. Kercheval, and A. Venetoulias. Any errors are the sole responsibility of the author.

seeking? And (3), is the optimal-tariff-associated welfare higher or lower with and without revenue seeking?

Both full and partial revenue seeking are considered, utilizing further the model of a large Ricardian economy. Because the Ricardian economy can be forced to complete specialization, consider first the case where it is not, and then the case where it is (under trade). Those results are drawn together and contrasted with the results for the case of full revenue seeking in the conventional increasing-cost, not strictly convex Production Possibility Curve (PPC) model as analyzed partially in a pioneering paper by Anam (1982). Further concluding observations are offered as well.

NONSPECIALIZATION AFTER TRADE

Assume that the home country is a large Ricardian economy and produces both goods before and after trade. The implication of these assumptions is that consumer and producer prices are equal and fixed by technology.[2] The home country then chooses the level of net exports that maximizes national welfare, and the optimal tariff is determined by the associated difference between domestic and international terms of trade.

There are two countries and two traded goods x and y. The supply sector of the home country is characterized by

$$X = a_x L_x \quad , \tag{9.1a}$$

$$Y = a_y L_y \quad , \tag{9.1b}$$

$$\bar{L} = L_x + L_y + L^* \quad a_x, a_y > 0 \quad , \tag{9.1c}$$

where X, Y represent the output of x and y, respectively; $\bar{L}$ is the fixed labor endowment of the home country; L^* is the amount of labor going into the DUP revenue-seeking sector, which lobbies for some fraction of the tariff revenue and is assumed to be a nondecreasing function of tariff revenue R.

The social utility function of the home country is given by

$$U = U(C_x, C_y) \quad C_x, C_y > 0 \quad , \tag{9.2}$$

where U is a well-behaved function giving rise to convex social indifference curves and C_x, C_y are the quantities of x and y consumed domestically.

Without loss of generality, assume that the home country exports x and imports y. The foreign country is represented by a well-behaved foreign offer curve:

$$M = F(E) \quad F'(E) > 0 , \quad F''(E) < 0 \quad , \tag{9.3}$$

where M, E are net imports and exports of the home country, respectively, and the concavity of F reflects the monopoly power in trade of the home country. Assuming balanced trade, the terms of trade in international prices p_x^*, p_y^* are

$$\frac{p_x^*}{p_y^*} = \frac{M}{E} = \frac{F(E)}{E} . \tag{9.4}$$

Moreover, if p_x, p_y are domestic prices and t is the tariff imposed on home imports M, we have

$$\frac{p_x}{p_y} = \frac{p_x^*}{p_y^*(1+t)} = \frac{F(E)}{E(1+t)} . \tag{9.5}$$

If both goods are produced after trade, the wage in both sectors in our Ricardian economy should be the same, so $p_x/p_y = a_y/a_x$. Substituting in (9.5) and solving for the tariff, we have

$$t = \frac{a_x}{a_y} \frac{F(E)}{E} - 1 . \tag{9.6}$$

The tariff revenue R expressed in units of y is

$$R = t F(E) = \left(\frac{a_x}{a_y} \frac{F(E)}{E} - 1 \right) F(E) . \tag{9.7}$$

Thus, the tariff revenue is a function of net exports E. This simple model captures the basic characteristics of revenue-seeking lobbying. The government wants to maximize the social utility function $U(C_x, C_y)$ subject to the constraints (9.1), (9.3), and (9.7). Any tariff revenue increases L^*, the amount of labor going into the DUP sector, and decreases the output of x and y through the full-employment condition.

After the appropriate substitutions, the policy problem of the government is

$$\underset{L_y, E}{\text{Max}} \quad U(C_x, C_y) ; \tag{9.8}$$

$$\text{s.t. } C_x = a_x (\bar{L} - L_y - L^*) - E$$

$$C_y = a_y L_y + F(E) .$$

From the first-order conditions of (9.8) we can express the optimal tariff in the presence of revenue-seeking DUP activities as

$$t^* = e(1 + a_x \frac{\partial L^*}{\partial R} \frac{\partial R}{\partial E}) - 1 , \tag{9.9}$$

where

$$e = \frac{F(E)}{E} \frac{1}{F'(E)}$$

is the elasticity of foreign reciprocal demand and all expressions are evaluated at the optimal level of net exports E^*. We can then see that the optimal tariff t^* depends on the properties of the foreign offer curve and the intensity of revenue seeking. Expanding the expression $\partial R / \partial E$, we have

$$\frac{\partial R}{\partial E} = \frac{F(E)}{E} \left(2 \frac{a_x}{a_y} \frac{F(E)}{E} \frac{1}{e} - \frac{a_x}{a_y} \frac{F(E)}{E} - \frac{1}{e} \right) , \qquad (9.10)$$

where e is the elasticity of foreign reciprocal demand. Substituting (9.10) into (9.9), utilizing (9.6) and denoting by B the fraction of tariff revenue sought, we get a quadratic equation in t^*:

$$B(2 - e)t^{*2} + (B(3 - 2e) - 1)t^* + (1 - B)(e - 1) = 0 . \qquad (9.11)$$

It can be easily shown that, as long as $e > 0$ and $0 \leqslant B \leqslant 1$, Eq. (6.11) has at least one positive root. Although we can obtain the solutions of (6.11) algebraically, we cannot gain further economic insight because of the complexity of the solution formula.

Figure 9-1 presents the graph of the optimal tariff t^* for $e \geqslant 1, 0 < B < 1$ and $t^* \leqslant (1 - B)/B$.[3] There is a horizontal asymptote at $t^* = B^{-\frac{1}{2}} - 1$, which is the upper bound of t^*. Moreover, Figure 9-1 shows the graph of the no-revenue-seeking tariff $t_{NRS} = e - 1$, which is a 45° line intersecting the horizontal axis at $e = 1$. From Figure 9-1, as long as both equilibria with and without revenue seeking are characterized by the same e we can conclude that $t^* < t_{NRS}$. Moreover, it is obvious that as B, the fraction of tariff revenue sought, increases, the horizontal asymptote at $t^* = B^{-\frac{1}{2}} - 1$ moves downward, reducing t^* monotonically. Thus, as B increases, the optimum t^* decreases monotonically. $t^* < t_{NRS}$ would be true for instance if the foreign offer curve has constant elasticity e. However, in general, the two equilibria will be characterized by different values of e.

We can provide a local proof that in the presence of partial revenue seeking, the optimal tariff is less than the no-revenue-seeking tariff. Following Johnson (1951), we can express the maximum welfare attainable by the home country when partial revenue seeking is present as a function of the tariff imposed. For illustration, see Figure 9-2. We can then show that the slope of the welfare function with respect to the tariff evaluated at the no-revenue-seeking tariff is negative.

$$\left. \frac{\partial U}{\partial t} \right|_{t_{NRS}} < 0 .$$

Figure 9-1. Non-specialization after Trade: Ranking of Optimal with and without Revenue-Seeking Tariffs.

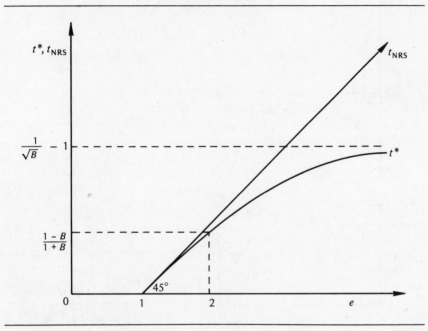

Thus, starting at the no-revenue-seeking equilibrium tariff a reduction in tariff increases national welfare, when partial revenue seeking is present. The first-order conditions of (9.8) imply that $C_x/C_y = k$, where k is a constant. Utilizing this result and (9.8), we can express the consumption levels C_x, C_y as functions of net exports E, and thus the tariff t:

$$C_x = kA \left(\bar{L} - L^* - \frac{E}{a_x} + \frac{F(E)}{a_y} \right) \quad , \tag{9.12}$$

$$C_y = A \left(\bar{L} - L^* - \frac{E}{a_x} + \frac{F(E)}{a_y} \right) \quad , \tag{9.13}$$

where $A = ((k/a_x) + (1/a_y))^{-1}$, which is a constant. We can substitute (9.12) and (9.13) in the welfare function $U(C_x, C_y)$ and evaluate its derivative with respect to t at the no-revenue-seeking tariff t_{NRS}, where $F'(E) = a_y/a_x$. From (9.10), (9.12), and (9.13) we get

$$\left. \frac{\partial R}{\partial E} \right|_{t_{NRS}} = - \frac{F(E)}{E} \ (e^{\frac{1}{2}} - e^{-\frac{1}{2}})^2 < 0 \quad , \tag{9.14}$$

Figure 9-2. Tariff Ranking and National Welfare in the Presence of Partial Revenue Seeking.

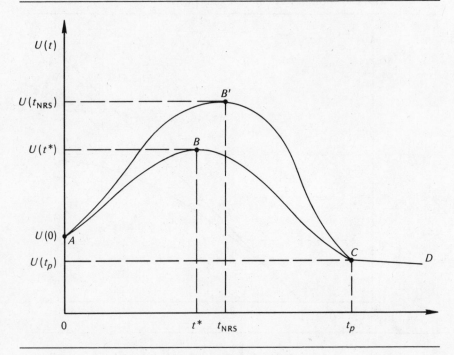

*In the case of nonspecialization after trade, we have $u(0) = u(t_p)$.

$$\frac{\partial C_x}{\partial t}\bigg|_{t_{NRS}} = -kAa_y \frac{\partial L^*}{\partial R} \frac{\partial R}{\partial E} \frac{\partial E}{\partial t} < 0 , \qquad (9.15)$$

$$\frac{\partial C_y}{\partial t}\bigg|_{t_{NRS}} = -AA_y \frac{\partial L^*}{\partial R} \frac{\partial R}{\partial E} \frac{\partial E}{\partial t} < 0 , \qquad (9.16)$$

where $\partial L^*/\partial R > 0$ and $\partial E/\partial t < 0$. Thus, the welfare change around t_{NRS} due to a small change in tariff is

$$\frac{\partial U}{\partial t}\bigg|_{t_{NRS}} = U_1 \frac{\partial C_x}{\partial t}\bigg|_{t_{NRS}} + U_2 \frac{\partial C_y}{\partial t}\bigg|_{t_{NRS}} < 0 , \qquad (9.17)$$

which implies that welfare increases if there is a slight tariff reduction around the no-revenue-seeking equilibrium point.

To complete the analysis in the nonspecialization case we examine the ranking of the two tariffs and national welfare in three special, but important cases.

Case 1. When $e = 1$, we are evidently in the small-country case. Equation (9.11) then gives us two possible solutions: $t_1^* = 0$ and $t_2^* = (1 - B)/B$. The first solution, $t_1^* = t_{NRS} = 0$, is the free trade solution and is consistent with the result that, in a small country for a given intensity of revenue-seeking DUP activities, welfare increases monotonically with the reduction of a tariff. Thus, the maximum welfare is reached when the tariff is zero. The other solution is related to the nonspecialization assumption, which will fail in general with $e = 1$. With full revenue seeking, $t_2^* = 0$; and, with no revenue seeking, t_2^* goes to plus infinity, suggesting the prohibitive tariff.

Case 2. Another special case is when we have a large Ricardian economy without any revenue-seeking DUP activities—that is, when $B = 0$. In this case from Eq. (9.11) we get $t_{NRS} = t^* = e - 1$; that is, in the absence of DUP activities the large Ricardian economy imposes the traditional optimum tariff. In terms of Figure 9-1, when $B = 0$, the horizontal asymptote goes to plus infinity and the t^* graph becomes the 45° line.

Case 3. Finally, in the case of full revenue seeking, $B = 1$ and the optimal tariff is zero. In Figure 9-1 both the horizontal asymptote and the expression $(1 - B)/B$ go to zero. This is the familiar result of Bhagwati and Srinivasan (1980) extended to the case of a large Ricardian economy.

A NOVEL ARGUMENT FOR FREE TRADE

The optimal tariff argument is based on three important assumptions. The elasticity of foreign offer curve has to be greater than unity, absence of retaliation, and lump-sum redistribution of tariff revenue.

Johnson (1953-54) showed that the case for the imposition of an optimal tariff, when there is monopoly power in trade, does not necessarily disappear if retaliation is incorporated into the analysis. However, if the assumption of lump-sum redistribution of tariff revenue is replaced by full revenue seeking, it is easy to show that free trade is the optimum policy for a large country when there is no retaliation.

Anam (1982) using the Heckscher-Ohlin-Samuelson (HOS) model and the full revenue seeking assumption, has shown that in the absence of Metzler effects free trade is the optimal policy for a large country.[4] The economic intuition for the preceding results is straightforward once we view the optimal tariff problem of a large country in terms of welfare costs and benefits. The monopoly power in trade allows a country to change the terms of trade in its favor and increase its welfare by imposing the appropriate tariff. However, the imposition of a tariff is associated to welfare losses once revenue seeking is present. Full revenue seeking by maximizing the welfare loss of the tariff forces the home country to the free-trade welfare level, unless the home country has excessive monopoly power in trade (Metzler effects).

Thus, in the absence of Metzler effects the policy implications of full revenue seeking are very important. Free trade becomes the optimal policy for a country independently of its size. The traditional divergence between national and world welfare disappears for a large country. Notice that in this case the welfare of the world is maximized in the first-best Pareto optimal sense, because under free trade there is no revenue to be sought and no resources are diverted into DUP activities.

HOME COUNTRY SPECIALIZES AFTER TRADE

Assume that producer and consumer prices are equal but not fixed. Without loss of generality, assume that the country after trade specializes in the production of commodity x.

Define the domestic price ratio as

$$q = q(C_x, C_y) = \frac{p_y}{p_x}, \quad \frac{\partial q}{\partial C_x} > 0, \quad \frac{\partial q}{\partial C_y} < 0 ; \qquad (9.18)$$

that is, q is a function of consumption levels of both commodities where we have assumed that both goods are normal.

With these qualifications, the government's problem is to maximize the social welfare function $U(C_x, C_y)$ by choosing the optimal level of net exports E, where

$$C_x = a_x(\bar{L} - L^*) - E \qquad (9.19)$$

$$C_y = F(E) .$$

Equation (9.19) gives C_x as an implicit function of E because L^* depends on tariff revenue, which in turn is a function of E, q, and C_x. From the foregoing maximization problem we can calculate the optimal E^* and thus, the optimal tariff. An equivalent formula for t_s^* is given by

$$(9.20)$$

$$t_s^* = e \left\{ \frac{1 + a_x \dfrac{\partial L^*}{\partial R} \dfrac{\partial R}{\partial E} + a_x \dfrac{\partial L^*}{\partial R} \dfrac{\partial R}{\partial q} \dfrac{\partial q}{\partial C_y} F'(E)}{1 + a_x \dfrac{\partial L^*}{\partial R} \dfrac{\partial R}{\partial q} \dfrac{\partial q}{\partial C_x}} \right\} - 1 .$$

If we compare Eq. (9.20) to Eq. (9.9), we can see that $t_s^* \leqslant t^*$ since $\partial L^*/\partial R > 0$ and normality of consumption implies that $a_x (\partial L^*/\partial R) (\partial R/\partial q) (\partial q/\partial C_y) F'(E) \leqslant 0$ and that $a_y (\partial L^*/\partial R) (\partial R/\partial q) (\partial q/\partial C_x) \geqslant 0$.

Following Johnson (1951) once again, we can evaluate the slope of the welfare function with respect to a tariff at t_{NRS}. Noting that

$$\left. \frac{\partial R}{\partial t} \right|_{t_{NRS}} > 0 \; ,$$

the tariff revenue around t_{NRS} increases with a small increase in the tariff, and utilizing Eq. (9.19), we have

$$\left. \frac{\partial U}{\partial t} \right|_{t_{NRS}} = - a_x \, U_1 \, \frac{\partial L^*}{\partial R} \, \frac{\partial R}{\partial t} < 0 \; , \qquad (9.21)$$

where all derivatives are evaluated at t_{NRS}. Equation (9.21) implies that welfare increases if there is a slight tariff reduction around the no-revenue-seeking equilibrium point.

Thus, in the presence of DUP activities, when the home country specializes after trade, the optimal tariff t_s^* is less than or equal to t^*, the tariff imposed in the nonspecialization case. Consequently, in the case of partial tariff-revenue seeking as long as $e > 1$ then $t_s^* \leqslant t^* \leqslant t_{NRS}$. When the domestic price ratio is constant, Eq. (9.20) implies that $t_s^* = t^*$.

SUMMARY AND CONCLUSIONS

This chapter analyzed the problem of optimum tariff in the presence of partial revenue-seeking lobbying in a large Ricardian economy. We saw that in general the optimum tariff depended on the fraction of tariff revenue lobbied for and the elasticity of foreign reciprocal demand.

Figure 9-2 summarizes the basic results by plotting the welfare level of the home country as a function of the tariff imposed with and without revenue-seeking lobbying, when the elasticity of the foreign offer curve is greater than 1. The line AB'CD represents the welfare level of the country for different tariffs without revenue seeking. The line ABCD represents the maximum welfare level for the home country when a fraction of the tariff revenue is sought effectively. As before, t^* is the optimal tariff with revenue seeking. t_p is the prohibitive tariff and t_{NRS} the optimal tariff without revenue seeking. At $t = 0$, and $t \geqslant t_p$, lobbying evidently does not have any effect on national welfare. The same is true for every tariff that is greater than t_p. However, for any tariff $0 < t < t_p$, there is a welfare loss due to revenue seeking, measured by the vertical distance between the AB'CD and ABCD lines. Moreover, the optimal tariff with revenue seeking t^* is always less than the optimal tariff without revenue seeking t_{NRS}.

The present model can be extended in a Heckscher–Ohlin–Samuelson framework, relaxing the assumption of a Ricardian production possibility curve. In this case though, the level of the optimal tariff would depend on the capital/labor ratio of the revenue-seeking DUP sector vis-à-vis the other two sectors, as well as the fraction of tariff revenue sought and the elasticity of the foreign offer curve.

NOTES TO CHAPTER 9

1. It might also be noted that Bhagwati and Srinivasan (1973) analyzed the consequences for optimal and maximum revenue tariffs of relaxing a yet different assumption of traditional trade-cum-public finance theory: namely, allowing for illegal trade or smuggling induced by the tariff. That analysis, of course, continued to assume that tariff revenues would be redistributed to consumers in a lump-sum fashion.

2. Nonspecialization after trade is possible in the context of a large Ricardian economy. The domestic terms of trade are fixed but the country can change the international terms of trade in its favor by imposing the appropriate tariff.

3. The elasticity of the foreign offer curve is usually greater than unity, except in the case of a Giffen home exportable good, some peculiar cases of increasing returns and perfect substitutability of exports for imports. The analysis in this part follows Johnson (1951). Moreover, when $t^* \leqslant (1 - B)/B$ the country can guarantee the autarkic welfare level. Since no-trade is always an option, we shall assume that this inequality always holds for the rest of the analysis.

4. Notice that in the case of a large Ricardian economy remaining unspecialized after trade, the possibility of Metzler effects is ruled out. Although Anam states this result, he does not discuss its implications. Finally, it should be stressed that the difference between the rest of the results in the present chapter and those of Anam is independent of the trade model used but depends on the assumption of partial (rather than full) revenue seeking.

IV APPLICATIONS AND EMPIRICAL TESTS

10 PROTECTION AND RENT-SEEKING IN DEVELOPING COUNTRIES

Stanislaw Wellisz and Ronald Findlay

The level of protection for manufacturing industries in most less developed countries (LDCs) is extraordinarily high, both by historical standards and in comparison with contemporary advanced economies. The empirical evidence to support this statement is unambiguous and overwhelming. It is documented and summarized in several authoritative recent works such as Bella Balassa (1971), I.M.D. Little, Tibor Scitovsky, and M.F.G. Scott (1970), Bhagwati (1978), and Krueger (1974). How is this fact to be explained?

One possibility is in terms of the economic mind-set or *Weltanschauung* of the politicians, planners, and bureaucrats in control of economic policy in these countries. Marxism and the influence of the Soviet model of planned industrialization, nationalist doctrines that associate free trade and comparative advantage with patterns of colonial domination, more narrowly technical arguments such as the Prebisch–Singer thesis and the "two-gap" theory can all be held to have contributed to such an attitude (see Bauer 1976; Johnson 1965; and Breton 1964). On this hypothesis protectionism in LDCs can be combated by an intellectual conversion of the key decisionmakers, showing them the irrationality of their views in terms of the neoclassical paradigm and by the evidence of the success of those few economies that have followed outward-looking, export-oriented development strategies.

We believe, however, that the stubborn persistence of rampant protectionism in the Third World is inconsistent with an explanation in terms of the hold of false doctrines alone. The ideas to which we have referred may simply be playing the role of an ideology, concealing the more deep-seated forces associated with

We would like to thank Jagdish Bhagwati for helpful comments.

the passions and the interests of the relevant parties. This approach to the explanation of protection in terms of the political economy of interest groups has recently been formalized by Brock and Magee (1978), Findlay and Wellisz 1982), Mayer (1983), and others.

The main purpose of the present chapter is to attempt to apply this framework to the problem of why protection is so high in most LDCs. The analysis is in the same spirit, though somewhat more formal, as the stimulating paper by Albert Hirschman (1968) and the interesting study by the political scientist Robert Bates (1981) on state intervention in some African economies. We also consider an important associated question, which is the cost to the economy as a whole of the resources used in attempts to obtain protection, or the revenue arising therefrom as in Krueger (1974) and Bhagwati and Srinivasan (1980), and the effect of government regulations or controls on such lobbying activities.

THE LOBBYING EQUILIBRIUM

Our discussion will be based on the familiar Ricardo-Viner small open economy. The two tradable products, manufactures and food, are competitively produced under the usual neoclassical assumptions, by applying labor to capital and to commercial land, respectively. In some cases we shall also take into account subsistence farming in which labor is applied to freely available land unsuitable for commercial purposes. The productive factors may also be used for various nontradable activities, such as lobbying. We shall assume that the commercially produced food is either consumed at home or exported, that food produced in subsistence farming is consumed on the farms, while manufactured goods are sold at home in competition with imports. It follows that capitalists benefit from protection whereas landowners favor free trade.

The trade regime is determined by the government, which has a "restriction-formation function" reflecting its own "preferences"—that is, its ideology, the self-interests of the governing group, public support considerations, international obligations, and so on (see Frey and Lau 1968). Lobbying expenditures by pro- and antirestriction factions enter the restriction-formation function as arguments and link the political with the economic system.[1] Governmental activities other than those dealing with the passing and the enforcement of trade regulations as well as the resources needed to carry out such non-trade-related functions are considered to lie outside the system.

The costs and benefits of lobbying to affect the trade regime may be shown in terms of Figure 10-1, in which, for the sake of simplicity, it is assumed that in the absence of group pressures free trade would prevail. The capitalists, who favor protection, consider whether to form a lobby, and what resources to devote to lobbying. The cost of lobbying $C(q)$ is shown in the third quadrant as a function of q, the sum to be raised. Because of organization (and policing)

Figure 10-1. Costs and Benefits of Lobbying.

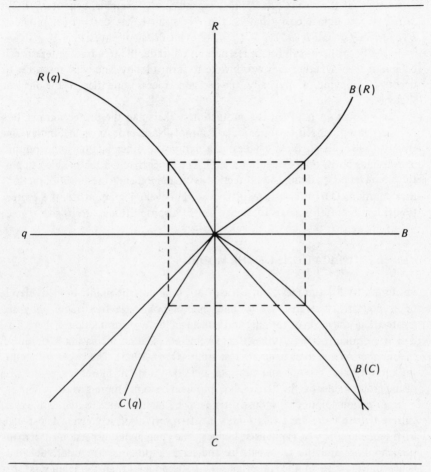

costs $C(q) > q$. Obviously, $C_q > 0$. It is also highly plausible the $C_{qq} > 0$—that is, that costs of raising money increase as the sum to be raised rises, putting a natural brake on the amount of lobbying expenditures. The severity of restriction R is shown in the fourth quadrant as an increasing function of q, the sum spent by lobbiests for purposes of influencing the government. Lobbying is worth while only if $R_q > 0$—that is, if the government responds positively to pressure It is plausible, however, to assume, that as the government is pushed further away from its preferred position, its resistance stiffens; so that $R_{qq} < 0$. This increasing resistance means that there are diminishing returns to lobbying. Finally, there are also diminishing benefits B to restriction; barring direct subsidies, absolute import prohibition sets the limit to possible benefits. Thus

$B_R > 0$ while $B_{RR} < 0$ (quadrant I). In quadrant II the benefits B are plotted as function of the costs C. At optimal expenditure q^* marginal benefit $dB/dQ = dC/dq$ the marginal cost—that is, the $B(C)$ curve has unit slope, provided $B(q^*) > C(q^*)$. If $B(q^*) \leq C(q^*)$, lobbying does not pay; hence $q^* = 0$.

Faced with the possibility of restrictions on trade, the free trade interests calculate, in turn, whether it is worthwhile to form a lobby, and what resources to devote to lobbying. Analytically, the decision process is identical to the one just sketched.

The interaction between the protection seekers and the protection resisters can be conceptualized in terms of a Cournot-Nash process as in Findlay and Wellisz (1982). Each faction takes as a datum the other faction's expenditure and decides on its own expenditure level. The process, under reasonable assumptions, converges, yielding the protection level and expenditures of both factions as a solution. Our task is to explain why, in developing countries, the protectionist faction often appears to carry a weight disproportionate to its size.

IMPLICATIONS OF THE MODEL

Let us start with a modest, but perhaps not unimportant point: In many developing countries the costs of forming and of policing a free trade lobby are greater than the costs of forming and policing a lobby of protection seekers. The cost of forming a lobby, other things being equal, is an increasing function of the number of members in an interest group (Olson 1965). The larger the group, the more costly it is to communicate and coordinate it; moreover, as the size of the group increases, the "free rider" problem becomes more severe.

In developing countries industry tends to be highly concentrated, while agriculture, where there are no latifundia, is often very dispersed, giving a cost edge to the organization of capitalists' lobbies. The geographic dispersion of agricultural holdings and the fact that, by and large, capitalists are better educated, hence more aware of the importance of trade policies than the landlords, also contribute to the higher cost of organizing the latter compared with the former.[2]

Given the marginal benefit of lobbying schedule, the higher the marginal cost, the lower the optimal lobbying expenditure. If organizational costs are sufficiently high, it will not be worthwhile to organize a lobby. In terms of Figure 10-1, as the marginal costs of lobbying rise, the $C(q)$ and $B(C)$ curves rotate clockwise, reducing q^*. Lobbying is uneconomical if the costs are so high that the $B(C)$ curve lies everywhere below the $45°$ line. Thus, if antiprotectionists are costly to organize, the protection seekers might find little or no opposition.

It is perhaps less obvious that, at early stages of development, capitalists are likely to benefit more and landowners to suffer less from a given protection level than in more developed economies.

In developing as well as in developed economies, protection of industry hurts landowners by turning the terms of trade against agriculture. In developed countries protection also raises wages reckoned in terms of the export good (food). As a consequence, the capitalists' as well as the landlords' rents are reduced. But in the presence of a subsistence sector in which farmers cultivate freely available land that is unsuitable for commercial cultivation, the wage is determined by the average product of subsistence workers. As a consequence, protection of industry does not lead to a wage increase, and redistribution from capitalists and landlords to workers does not occur.

Let OO' in Figure 10-2 represent the total labor force in the economy. Employment in the agricultural sector is measured to the right of O, while employment in industry is measured to the left of O'. The respective marginal product of labor curves in the two sectors, aa' and mm', are drawn for given land, capital stock, and product price ratio. In the developed economy the intersection of the two (free trade) marginal product of labor curves $a_0 a_0'$ and $m_0 m_0'$ determine the free trade wage Ow_0, as well as the allocation of labor, with OA workers in agriculture and $O'A$ workers in industry (Figure 10-2a). In the economy with a subsistence sector, the wage $O\overline{w}$ is determined by the subsistence workers' average product (Figure 10-2b). That wage, and the marginal product of labor schedules in the two organized sectors, jointly determine labor allocation: in Figure 10-2b, OA workers are in commercial agriculture, $O'B$ are in industry, and AB are in subsistence farming. The landlords' and the capitalists' rents are represented, in both figures, by the triangles lying below the respective marginal product of labor curves and above the wage line.

The restriction of manufacturing imports raises the marginal product of labor in manufacturing from $m_0 m_0'$ to $m_1 m_1'$, leading to an increase in the rent on capital. In the developed economy the wage rises from Ow_0 to Ow_1, reducing the benefits to capitalists, and imposing extra costs on landlords. Where there is a subsistence sector the wage remains invariant at $O\overline{w}$; hence the capitalists benefit more, while the landlords' surplus (in agriculture output terms) does not change. In both cases employment in the manufacturing sector expands (from $O'A$ to $O'A'$ and from $O'B$ to $O'B'$, respectively) expansion being greater in the latter than in the former case. In case 2a commercial farm employment shrinks, whereas in 2b the size of the subsistence sector is reduced, while employment in commercial farming remains invariant.

These conclusions hold, with only slight modifications, in developing countries in which there is no significant subsistence sector. As the imposition of a tariff of a given height, or of an equivalent quota, raises the wage, the more elastic the demand of labor in the protected sector, and the less elastic the demand for labor in the export sector. Where the industrial sector is small relative to the agricultural sector, demand for labor elasticity will, *ceteris paribus*, be low in the former and high in the latter, meaning that the impact of protection on wages will be smaller in such countries than in heavily industrialized ones.

The discussion assumes that the tariff-protected manufactures are not an input into agriculture. This assumption is realistic in that, in early stages of import-substituting industrialization, capital goods are generally tariff exempt.

Figure 10-2. Effect of Lobbying on the Wage Level.

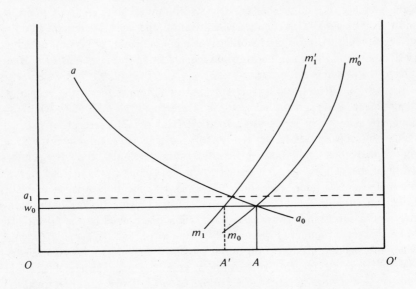

a

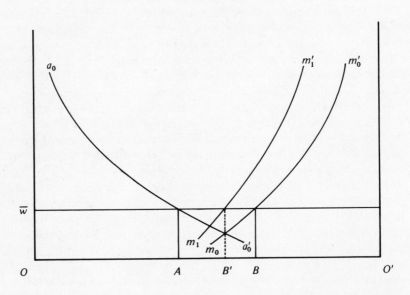

b

In some countries, indeed, the landlords are bought off by preferential treatment of imported farm inputs shifting the tariff burden to the sector least likely to form an organized lobby: the wage workers and subsistence farmers.

In developing countries the protection-seeking manufacturers can often count on the support of importers. Indeed, the two groups largely overlap. As Hirschman noted, "as industry is started primarily to substitute imports, those engaged in the foreign trade sector are likely to play a substantial role in the process" (Hirschman 1968: 96). For instance, importers or representatives of foreign automobile firms are likely to engage in assembly operations and in the fabrication of automobile parts.

It might seem at first blush that the importers' and the manufacturers' interests are diametrically opposed. Yet, if importers are able to capture the restriction-created rents, their interests, up to a point, coincide with the manufacturers'. If entry into the import business is itself controlled, importers maximize profits when the quota is set at a level of the maximum revenue tariff. Manufacturers maximize profits if imports are prohibited. A lobby that includes importers as well as manufacturers will seek a quote that is smaller than one that maximizes rents, but that does permit some imports.[3] The severity of the restriction sought by the protectionist lobby depends on the balance of forces. Here, perhaps, we have a clue why restrictions often tend to mount: as industrialization proceeds, manufacturers gain strength at the expense of the importers.

The government is another potential ally of the protection-seeking manufacturers. In most developing countries a large, and sometimes even the major, part of government revenues is derived from tariffs. An alliance between a revenue-maximizing or surplus-maximizing Leviathan and protection-seeking manufacturers would lead, as we have shown elsewhere (Findlay and Wellisz 1983), to a tariff that is higher than one maximizing revenue but that falls short of outright prohibition.

Manufacturers, other things being equal, are likely to prefer quotas to tariff protection. From their point of view the two are equivalent if there is certainty concerning the future relation between domestic manufacturing costs and foreign prices. In the presence of uncertainty risk-avoiding manufacturers would prefer a quota to a tariff. The imposition of a quota does not mean, however, that the government must forgo revenue: Import license sale is a device that is a distinct possibility and that does occur in practice.[4]

To sum up: In developing countries protection-seeking manufacturers are apt to find allies in rent-seeking importers and in revenue-seeking governments. Where the protected sector is relatively small, and a fortiori, where there is a subsistence sector, imposition of a trade restraint is likely to have little or no impact on wages, reckoned in terms of the export good (food). As a consequence, the adverse effect of protection on landlords' rents is lower than in more industrialized countries; hence landlords have less incentive to lobby for free trade.

THE COSTS OF LOBBYING

Let us now consider the economic cost of lobbying for protection or for rent- and revenue-seeking in developing countries. The LDC governments tend to be "soft," that is, vulnerable to group pressures,[5] and the trade systems to be highly distorted. Under these circumstances "favor seeking," to use a general term, flourishes. Paradoxically, however, the resource cost to the economy is likely to be relatively low.

To see this, consider a government that wants to stiffen its backbone by placing contracts on permissible lobbying activities. We shall quantify the severity of the control c in the following fashion. Let q be a lobby's expenditure on permitted activities, and let z be the recipient's valuation of the resulting "gift."[6] Write $z = (1 - c)q$, where $0 \leq c \leq 1$. From this definition it follows that the higher the c, the greater the gap between q and z. We can therefore utilize the relation between q and c to quantify z. Thus if $c = 0$, the recipient is indifferent between a gift in kind and one in cash. If $c = 1/2$, the recipient values the gift at half its cost to the lobby. If $c = 1$, then $z = 0$ for all q; in this case permitted gifts are valueless to the recipient regardless of their cost.

The stiffening of controls reduces the cost-effectiveness of lobbying; hence the more severe the controls, the less, other things being equal, the total lobbying expenditure.[7] The imposition of controls may be favored by all interest groups, provided it does not affect the relative balance of forces, much as mutual disarmament may be favored by militarily opposed countries. In both cases, there is the question of "balanced" reduction, and the question of enforcement; in countries with "soft" governments enforcement tends to be lax and controls nonbinding.

From an economywide point of view the laxity of lobbying rules is not necessarily a bad thing. The real resource cost of lobbying may be measured in terms of qr, the gap between the donor's cost and the recipient's valuation of the gift. If $c = 0$ the recipient values the gift at cost; hence the expenditure by the lobby is tantamount to a pure income transfer. For a positive c and a positive q there is resource cost qc. Since the optimal lobbying expenditure q^* declines as c increases, reaching 0 for a sufficient high c, economic loss increases, reaches a maximum, and then decreases as lobbying rules harden. It is therefore economically advantageous if the rules are either very hard or very soft, while intermediate levels may be advantageous to the opposing factions, but not to the economy as a whole.[8]

Can the economic cost of lobbying be equal to the lobbyists' expenditure? Clearly not, for in this case $qr = q$, hence $z = 0$; that is, the recipients derive no benefit regardless of the expenditure level. Under such circumstances lobbying, in the sense of economic inducements to the government, would cease. This does not necessarily spell the end of all lobbying activities, because there are other possibilities of affecting political outcomes, for instance by spreading information, or misinformation, among the voters.[9]

The extent of revenue or rent-seeking and the associated resource cost depends on institutional arrangements. If, as discussed earlier, the trade restriction is imposed through the efforts of an alliance of manufacturers and importers, the latter are bound to make sure that they reap the reward for lobbying by being granted exclusive import licenses. If licenses are transferable, their value is capitalized, and their transfer becomes simply a market transaction. No *additional* resource cost is involved in this case.

Rent or revenue-seeking is more likely to take place if the creation of rents or revenues is in the nature of a by-product, which was not sought by the protection-seeking groups. Under such circumstances a struggle might occur between groups or individuals to capture the rents (revenues), and this struggle might impose further real costs on the economy. Paradoxically, maximum waste is likely to occur if the licensing system is absolutely "fair" and if it brings no benefits to the licensor.[10] Graft and corruption reduce economic cost. Economic resource waste is entirely eliminated if the licenses are sold by the government on the competitive market. Here again we have the phenomenon of minimum waste if the government is either very soft, or if it is very hard and adheres to competitive rules.

To the extent that real resources are used in lobbying for trade restrictions or in revenue or rent-seeking, such activities may redistribute income within the economy, imposing costs on some sectors and bringing benefits to others.

Imagine first that lobbying entails the use of capital and labor in the proportion in which those factors are employed in manufacturing. In Figure 10-3a, which replicates Figure 10-2a, labor devoted to lobbying is shown by $O'O''$, with OO'' labor remaining in production. The marginal product of labor in manufacturing curve has to be redrawn with O'' as origin, but it also has to reflect the withdrawal of capital. As factor proportions in manufacturing remain the same as those prevailing prior to lobbying, the new curve $m_2 m_2'$ must intersect the original marginal product of labor in manufacturing curve at Q_0, the initial equilibrium point. Thus neither the equilibrium wage, nor the landlords' rent changes; that is, the manufacturers bear the entire cost of resources used in lobbying.

It is intuitively more plausible that lobbying may be more labor-intensive than manufacturing. To simplify the discussion, assume that labor is the only factor used in the former activity. In terms of Figure 10-3a, this means that the marginal productivity of labor in manufacturing curve has to be shifted to the left, and redrawn with O'' as origin, as shown by $m_3 m_3'$. The new equilibrium wage Ow_3 is higher than the prelobbying wage Ow_0: an extra cost is imposed on the manufacturers and landlords' rents are reduced, while labor benefits. Intensive use of the common resource (labor) is thus disadvantageous to both major interest groups. By the same token, lobbying that is intensive in the use of

Figure 10-3. Incidence of Lobbying Costs.

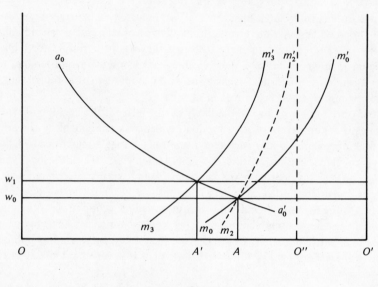

a

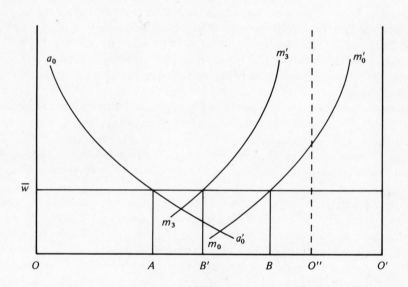

b

the specific resource reduces the equilibrium wage and favors both proprietory groups.

In the presence of a subsistence sector, which determines the wage (Figure 10-3b), the lobbying resource cost is borne entirely by the sector engaged in the activity. In this case, we may surmise, lobbying might be socially more acceptable than in economies where the burden is shared. Much the same arguments apply to rent-seeking; in the presence of a subsistence sector, people who queue for licenses do not impose costs on anybody except those who hired them.

We conclude by summarizing the main results of the chapter.

1. The high level of protection for manufacturing in LDCs is attributed to

   a. A bias in the cost of lobbying in favor of protectionist as opposed to free trade interests due to the greater geographical and sectoral concentration of the former and the smaller number of individuals involved.

   b. The prevalence of "surplus labor" conditions due to the existence of a subsistence sector which means that industrial protection does not harm agricultural interests by raising the real wage of labor employed in commercial agriculture and hence there is less countervailing pressure exercised by this sector.

   c. An alliance between importers of manufactures, who have an interest in imposing quotas if they can collect the resulting rents, and manufacturers who benefit from the protective effect of the quotas.

   d. An implicit alliance of manufacturing interests with the political elite in charge of the state, which has an incentive to maximize revenue from taxes on foreign trade, which tends to be the most lucrative source in LDCs.

2. The costs of lobbying activities to the economy as a whole are highest when regulations against lobbying are neither very hard, so as to make lobbying unprofitable, or very soft, so as to make all lobbying expenditure purely redistributive in nature, but at an intermediate level.

3. The economic cost of rent-seeking is not likely to be additive to the cost of protection seeking when protection is obtained by an alliance between importers and manufacturers because the securing of the rents is a condition for the support of the former group. Similarly there is no additional cost of revenue seeking when the protection is generated by a revenue-maximizing government. It is only when the rent or revenue is generated as a by-product of the activities of protection-seeking groups that there may be a further resource cost.

The general conclusion is that high levels of protection in LDCs, which are totally "irrational" in terms of the conventional theory of trade and welfare, are perfectly explicable in terms of the "rational" self-interest of the relevant pressure groups in the economy.

APPENDIX 10A

The purpose of this appendix is to present, in a somewhat more formal fashion, the relation between the severity of controls imposed on lobbying, total lobbying expenditure, and real resources used up in lobbying.

Let q be the sum that a pressure group devotes to lobbying, and let c be the control level. Thus, if a lobby spends q, the government officials benefit to the extent of $q(1-c)$ in money terms. Let us write $z = q(1-c)$.

Ignoring the cost of raising money, which is not essential to our story, let us set $C(q) = q$ as the cost of raising q dollars. The benefit function of the pressure group can be written as $B(z)$. The lobby thus faces the problem of maximizing.

$$p = B[z(a)] - q \quad , \tag{10A.1}$$

where c is exogenously given.

Let us now assume that the benefit function is of the form

$$B = A z^\epsilon \tag{10A.2}$$

where $A = 1/\epsilon$.

This assumption will permit us to investigate, in terms of easily understandable parameters, the effect of changes of c on the optimal q and also on real resources use. Substituting Eq. (10A.2) into (10A.1), and letting the derivative of (10A.1) in respect to q equal 0 we obtain the following first-order condition:

$$q^* = (1-c)^{\frac{\epsilon}{1-\epsilon}} \quad .$$

Relation (10A.3) shows q^*, the optimal lobbying expenditure, as a function of the coefficient ϵ, which reflects the government's flexibility in the face of pressure and of c, the level of controls. As formulated, the optimal q^* is standardized to equal 1, for $T = 0$, regardless of the elasticity of government response to pressure. Now assume, for instance, that $\epsilon = 1/2$ and increase c. It can be easily seen that q^* reaches a maximum when $c = 1/2$, at which point $q^* = 1/2$. That is, if the elasticity of government response is $1/2$, then the maximum resource waste occurs if restrictions are such that a \$1 expenditure by a lobby is worth only 50¢ to the recipient government official. If such a restriction level is instituted, the optimal lobbying expenditure will be cut by one-half, and half of the expenditure will be wasted, hence resource cost will equal $1/2$. Of course, a higher c would mean a correspondingly higher percentage waste of resources, but a lower waste in absolute terms.

Now repeat this experiment for a "softer" government, one that gives in more easily. Let, for instance $\epsilon = 2/3$. Then maximum waste occurs if $c = 1/3$: at this point optimal $q^* = 4/9$ hence $q^* = 4/27$. With a "softer" government a lower control level resulted in a greater cutback in lobbying and less waste in absolute terms. Here again, a further stiffening of controls (a higher c) would reduce both q^*, the total amount devoted to lobbying and q^*c, the waste.

NOTES TO CHAPTER 10

1. In this formulation, which we used in our earlier papers (Findlay and Wellisz 1982, 1983), voters' preferences are reflected in the "restricting-formation function." Alternately, the voters' preferences may be expressed as arguments of the function, as in Mayer (1983).
2. Large foreign-owned plantations are vulnerable to expropriation; hence they are not likely to play an active political role.
3. In terms of our model it is simplest to think of capitalists as being at the same time importers and manufacturers. In seeking protection, capitalists strive to maximize the sum of rent on capital and of protection-created rent on imports.
4. An illuminating discussion of quota arrangements in Pakistan that illustrates this point is by Naqvi (1964).
5. On this issue, see Gunnar Myrdal (1968: 937–58 and passim).
6. In terms of our earlier treatment, the $R(q)$ function should now be written as $R(z)$ with $z = (1 - c)q$.
7. In terms of Figure 10–1, this can be shown by a clockwise rotation of the $R(q)$ curve and a corresponding clockwise rotation of the $B(q)$ curve.
8. For a discussion of the effect of controls on lobbying on the volume of lobbying and real resource cost under different assumptions concerning the elasticity of response of the government, see Appendix 10A.
9. Such lobbying was explicitly modeled by Pletzman (1976).
10. This could occur for example if licenses for importing an intermediate product were issued as a function of productive capacity. Under competitive conditions the resources used for capaicty overexpansion would be equal in value to the rent on the imported input. In this case, as Krueger demonstrated, the rent measures (shadow-pricing considerations aside) the rent-seeking resource cost.

11 RENT-SEEKING AND THE GROWTH AND FLUCTUATIONS OF NATIONS
Empirical Tests of Some Recent Hypotheses

Frederic L. Pryor

Mancur Olson's 1982 book extends in many different directions the theory of rent-seeking that was presented in the different papers contained in Buchanan, Tollison and Tullock (1980). In this important contribution Olson formulates a series of hypotheses about when and where rent-seeking is found and what is the impact of rent-seeking on important macroeconomic variables. He formulates his theory in a manner such that certain aspects can be relatively easily tested in statistical fashion; the purpose of this chapter is to carry out such a task.

Olson focuses on the income redistributional behavior of private interest organizations that are engaged in rent-seeking or directly unproductive profit-seeking activities. He argues that stable societies with unchanged boundaries tend to accumulate more collusive organizations attempting to collect and increase the available rents and that this rent-seeking behavior in turn has some adverse impact on the performance of the economy unless such groups constitute a significant portion of the economy. This caveat arises because such all-embracing groups must take into account the macroeconomic impact of their activities in trying to maximize the income of their members, and therefore the ill effects of rent-seeking are considerably reduced. In contrast, rent-seeking activity of a small group not only lowers the overall efficiency of the economy but also slows down the economy's capacity to adopt new technologies and to reallocate resources in response to changing conditions. Further, these small rent-seeking groups tend to make decisions more slowly than the individuals and firms they comprise, which lowers still more the adaptability of the economy to changing circumstances. In short, such rent-seeking by small groups reduces economic growth and increases the cyclical behavior of the economy.

155

Olson's approach allows us to isolate three groups of nations: *winners*, countries with relatively little rent-seeking or countries with relatively large rent-seeking groups; *losers*, countries with considerable rent-seeking by small groups; and *others*, countries with characteristics in between those of the other two groups. Comparisons of the growth rates, the rates of growth retardation, and the fluctuations of gross domestic product of the three groups can then be easily made in order to test Olson's ideas.

The tests contained in this chapter represent a development of those presented in an article written a number of years ago (which appeared, after a long delay, in Dennis Mueller, ed. 1983). This earlier paper was, in its turn, a critique of still an earlier version of Mancur Olson's ideas. Since then, both of us have had a chance to reflect and reformulate our ideas. I have also had a chance to obtain some different data and to apply some different kinds of statistical tests. Although I believe that the theoretical objections raised in this earlier essay have not been sufficiently dealt with in Olson's book, I wish to confine myself below strictly to a statistical examination of his hypotheses.

The results of these empirical tests are quite mixed. In certain cases his theory appears more capable of explaining the behavior of the losers than of the winners; in other cases his hypotheses receive absolutely no support at all. In general, however, the tests indicate that Olson's approach does not capture many of the important causal variables underlying growth and fluctuations of nations and that it is more profitable to apply ideas about rent-seeking to lower levels of aggregation of the economy than to the GNP.

THE EMPIRICAL TESTS

The Strategy of the Tests

As I have argued elsewhere (1983a), Mancur Olson does not state his theory with sufficient precision so that it can be tested in an unambiguous fashion. Should we, for instance, focus on growth of gross domestic product, GDP per capita, GDP per economically active (i.e., GDP per member of the labor force), industrial production, or agricultural production? Initially I examine all five of these indicators; thereafter I concentrate on only the first three. Given the manner in which Olson formulated his theory, perhaps the ideal test of his ideas would involve examination of the growth of total factor productivity since this would permit us to hold constant several important sources of economic growth extraneous to his theory. Unfortunately, comparable data on the growth of the capital stock are not available for a sufficient number of nations to make the tests embrace very many countries. The second-best indicator for testing Olson's hypotheses, at least for those dealing with economic growth, is the GDP per economically active; and the higher coefficient of determination of the regressions using this indicator appears to validate this judgment.

The tests presented below are performed on a group of 28 countries that represent all major economically developed and semideveloped nations. The aggregative data that are used for the tests are quite comparable.

As noted previously, we can distinguish three groups of countries: the *winners*, where the ill effects of rent-seeking are lowest; the *losers*, where the ill effects of rent-seeking activities are highest; and the *others*, a group in between. To classify nations into these categories, we must take the following considerations into account.

1. According to Olson, rent-seeking should be relatively lowest in nations that have experienced boundary changes and also destruction of their organizational infrastructure so that their rent-seeking groups were effectively destroyed. World War II provided such circumstances, and Olson notes that nations meeting these criteria of infrastructural destruction or major boundary changes include Germany, Japan, and France. Other nations (not mentioned by Olson) that suffered considerable wartime destruction of their organizational infrastructure or boundary changes include Belgium, East Germany, Italy, and the Netherlands. In contrast, such infrastructural damage was not very great (or, indeed, nil) in nations such as Australia, Canada, Ireland, New Zealand, Portugal, Spain, Sweden, Switzerland, the United Kingdom, and the United States.

2. Nations with all-encompassing interest groups should show fewer ill effects of rent-seeking. As examples of such nations Olson mentions Germany, Norway, Sweden; however, we might add to this list such nations as Japan, the Netherlands, Portugal (at least during the Salazar era), and Spain (at least during the Franco era) plus all of the East European nations that are dominated by a Communist party. In contrast, certain nations appear to have very decentralized interest groups and we might include in these France, Italy, Switzerland, the United Kingdom, and the United States.

Because some nations appear to be winners for one of these two reasons and losers for the other reason, we cannot unambiguously classify them in either group. Eliminating these ambiguous cases, we have eight countries that can be considered as winners: Belgium, East Germany, West Germany, Japan, the Netherlands, Norway, Poland, and the USSR. We also have seven countries that can be classified as losers: Australia, Canada, Ireland, New Zealand, Switzerland, the United Kingdom, and the United States. The remaining 13 countries in the sample fall in the category "other." Since certain commentators on this chapter did not (for reasons that did not appear entirely clear) approve the inclusion of the East European nations in these tests of Olson's hypotheses, I have carried out all tests not only with the total sample of 28 but also with the 21 capitalist, market economies (the "Western sample").

In the tests presented below I include dummy variables corresponding to whether the country is a predicted winner and loser. However, since the grouping of nations into these categories (both my own grouping and that of Olson) is rather subjective, I present the data in a manner so that readers can make their own statistical tests without having to recalculate the regressions. More specifically, I present residuals of regressions calculated without the dummy variables of indicating winners and losers plus data on standard errors of estimate. Such data permit simple statistical tests to be performed with the countries grouped in any manner that the analyst desires.

The Great Growth Rate Contest

In Table 11-1 I present data on the growth rate of five indicators for 28 nations. These growth rates were calculated by fitting exponential curves to the appropriate data for a 30-year period. What variables, other than rent-seeking, might explain the differences?

For economically developed, or semideveloped, nations the level of per capita GDP is often mentioned as an important determinant of the overall growth rate. Justification of such a proposition is usually made by referring to one or more of three relationships: (1) The lower the level of economic development of a nation, the more opportunity it has in raising the level of GNP by shifting workers from low-productivity agriculture to higher productivity industry. Such an opportunity is not open to nations such as the United States, where the economically active in agriculture are only a very small percentage of the total work force. (2) The lower the level of development of a nation, the more opportunity it has for economic growth by inexpensively borrowing technology; the nations with higher levels of economic development must, if they wish to maintain their lead, invest in the development of new technologies, which is very resource consuming. (3) The lower the level of economic development of a nation, the lower is the share of its labor force in services where productivity growth is low. In fact, given the way in which production in some services is measured (namely by inputs), productivity growth in some services appears practically zero.

Another variable that is alleged to play an important role in the rate of economic growth of a nation is the economic system. Although such a relationship can be explained in many ways, it is noteworthy that in almost none of the regression experiments reported below is the calculated coefficient for the systems variable statistically significant. Or, to put the matter more dramatically, *ceteris paribus*, there is no significant difference in growth rates, retardation of growth rates, or fluctuations of aggregate production in capitalist, market economies and socialist, centrally administered economies.

In Tables 11-2 and 11-3 I present the results of regression calculations. Except for agricultural production, we can explain a respectable amount of the variance of the growth rates in both the total sample and the Western sample. It is noteworthy that the explanatory power of these regressions increases as we move from GDP to GDP per capita to GDP per economically active. I tried a number of regression experiments to raise the degree of explanatory power; unfortunately, none of the variables that I tried seemed to work. (The results of similar experiments are reported in Pryor (1985). The general conclusions drawn about these experiments appear quite robust with regard to the form of the regression, and experiments with various transformations of the different variables did not appreciably change the results. Further, it does not appear from a series of F tests on the regressions that the results are influenced by different slope coefficients of the different subgroups, nor did special tests performed to test for heteroskedasticity indicate any problems. In short, these regression experiments appear quite "clean."

For both the total sample and the Western sample, the dummy variable indicating that the country numbered among the predicted winners is not statistically significant. Indeed, for some of the regressions for industrial and agricultural production, the sign is wrong. However, for the GDP per economically active, the dummy variables indicating that the country numbered among the predicted losers is statistically significant, and, indeed, for most of the other indicators the sign is also correct. In short, Olson's thesis appears to work for the losers but not for the winners. Some insight can be gained into such peculiar results by examining the regression residuals in Table 11-4, where the regressions are calculated without the dummy variables for winners and losers.

Among the winners, actual growth appeared much greater than predicted for Japan and Germany, Olson's favorite examples. Among the other winners, however, growth related to the GDP appeared little better (and sometimes worse) than average. The losers all had actual average growth rates considerably lower than predicted. It is noteworthy, however, that six out of the seven losers are English-speaking countries and that most of these seven nations also have many other strong similarities. This raises the serious question as to whether the dummy variable designating the losers is also reflecting some phenomenon other than rent-seeking that is influencing the results.

Unfortunately, there are only three predicted losers for which comparable data on industrial and agricultural production could be found. Given this small sample I have dropped these indicators from further consideration in this chapter.

The Great Growth Retardation Contest

A good argument can be made that it is not growth per se that is reflected by rent-seeking, but rather the retardation of growth. That is, those nations featuring greater rent-seeking behavior should show a greater retardation of growth.

Table 11-1. Average Annual Growth Rates, 1950–1979.ᵃ

Country	Relative per Capita GNP, 1970	Average Annual Growth Rates				
		GDP	GDP per Person	GDP per Economically Active Worker	Industrial Production	Agricultural Production
Predicted "Winners"						
West Germany	78.2	4.85	3.87	4.31	5.55	1.93
Belgium	72.0	4.00	3.51	3.53	5.11	0.61
Netherlands	68.7	4.58	3.39	3.59	5.92	3.18
Norway	68.4	4.15	3.37	3.53	4.88	-0.16
East Germany	63.9	3.77	4.04	3.71	4.68	1.54
Japan	59.2	8.35	7.23	7.06	—	—
USSR	46.9	4.95	3.64	3.62	6.99	3.04
Poland	35.4	4.12	2.98	2.61	6.78	1.56
Predicted "Losers"						
United States	100.0	3.39	2.05	1.67	3.46	1.18
Canada	81.9	4.57	2.69	1.88	5.46	1.49
Switzerland	72.4	3.72	2.52	2.33	—	—
United Kingdom	63.5	2.72	2.29	2.39	2.67	2.17
Australia	69.6	4.54	2.56	2.15	—	—
New Zealand	64.6	3.46	1.78	1.38	—	—
Ireland	40.5	3.45	3.06	3.75	—	—

Other Nations						
Sweden	86.6	3.69	3.08	2.88	4.60	0.22
Denmark	83.3	3.81	3.15	2.97	4.79	0.87
France	73.2	4.86	3.93	4.24	5.84	1.79
Finland	63.1	4.48	3.92	3.95	5.82	1.06
Austria	63.1	4.74	4.38	4.76	5.35	1.82
Czechoslovakia	62.0	3.67	3.02	2.80	4.38	0.62
Italy	49.2	4.92	4.22	4.62	6.71	1.91
Spain	48.9	5.53	4.52	4.86	7.81	2.49
Hungary	42.7	3.64	3.22	2.96	4.81	1.20
Greece	38.7	6.20	5.51	6.40	8.74	2.92
Bulgaria	37.3	5.43	4.69	4.91	9.48	2.51
Romania	31.2	5.81	4.78	4.71	9.45	2.39
Portugal	27.1	5.43	5.07	4.72	7.63	0.86

a. Sources of data and methods of calculations are discussed in Pryor 1985. The choice of winners and losers is discussed in the text.

Table 11-2. Results of Regression Experiments with Average Annual Growth Rates: Total Sample.[a]

Average Annual Growth Rates	Constant	YCAP	SYS	WIN	LOS	R^2	SEE	n
1. GDP	+6.567* (0.782)	−0.0272* (0.0121)	−0.978 (0.496)	+0.324 (0.445)	−0.957 (0.488)	.3681	0.962	28
2. GDP	+6.551* (0.846)	−0.0307* (0.0125)	−0.666 (0.517)	—	—	.1958	1.041	28
3. GDP per person	+6.033* (0.658)	−0.0297* (0.0102)	−0.982 (0.417)	+0.171 (0.375)	−1.519* (0.411)	.5814	0.810	28
4. GDP per person	+6.020* (0.837)	−0.0367* (0.0123)	−0.580 (0.511)	—	—	.2633	1.030	28
5. GDP per economically active	+6.759* (0.702)	−0.0386* (0.0108)	−1.446* (0.445)	+0.159 (0.400)	−1.818* (0.439)	.6472	0.864	28
6. GDP per economically active	+6.745* (0.936)	−0.0471* (0.0138)	−0.977 (0.572)	—	—	.3182	1.153	28
7. Industrial production	+10.207* (1.139)	−0.0642 (0.0178)	−0.488 (0.678)	−0.323 (0.616)	−1.095 (0.908)	.5983	1.251	23
8. Industrial production	+10.558* (1.087)	−0.0737* (0.0156)	−0.541 (0.649)	—	—	.5590	1.235	23
9. Agricultural production	3.004* (0.481)	−0.0252 (0.0126)	−0.139 (0.481)	+0.291 (0.437)	+0.674 (0.644)	.2060	0.887	23
10. Agricultural production	+2.780* (0.766)	−0.0189 (0.0110)	−0.081 (0.457)	—	—	.1520	0.870	23

a. YCAP = per capita GDP.
SYS = 0 if a capitalist, market economy; 1 if a socialist, centrally administered economy.
WIN = 1 if a predicted "winner"; = 0 if otherwise.
LOS = 1 if a predicted "loser"; 0 if otherwise.
R^2 is the coefficient of determination; SEE is the standard error of estimate; n is the number of countries in the sample. The standard errors are placed in parentheses below the calculated coefficients, and an asterisk designates statistical significance at the 0.05 level. The data come from

Table 11-5. Results of Regression Experiments with Average Annual Growth Rates Only Capitalist Market Economies.[a]

Average Annual Growth Rates	Constant	YCAP	WIN	LOS	R^2	SEE	n
11. GDP	+6.319* (0.886)	-0.0248 (0.0138)	+0.584 (0.583)	-0.883 (0.534)	.3921	1.015	21
12. GDP	+6.376* (0.983)	-0.0280 (0.0146)	—	—	.1632	1.126	21
13. GDP per person	+6.119* (0.721)	-0.0324 (0.0112)	+0.402 (0.474)	-1.416* (0.435)	.6427	0.826	21
14. GDP per person	+6.199* (0.964)	-0.0394* (0.0143)	—	—	.2861	1.105	21
15. GDP per economically active	+6.878* (0.740)	-0.0422* (0.0116)	+0.451 (0.487)	-1.687 (0.446)	.7203	0.848	21
16. GDP per economically active	+6.973* (1.067)	-0.0506* (0.0158)	—	—	.3505	1.223	21
17. Industrial production	+9.245* (1.005)	-0.0486 (0.0160)	-0.389 (0.636)	-1.406 (0.761)	.6630	1.005	16
18. Industrial production	+9.803* (1.006)	-0.0624 (0.0146)	—	—	.5668	1.054	16
19. Agricultural production	+2.820* (0.965)	-0.0215 (0.0154)	-0.111 (0.611)	-0.548 (0.731)	.1464	0.965	16
20. Agricultural production	+2.603 (0.873)	-0.0162 (0.0126)	—	—	.1055	0.914	16

a. YCAP = per capita GDP.
   WIN   = 1 if a predicted "winner"; = 0 if otherwise.
   LOS   = 1 if a predicted "loser"; 0 if otherwise.
   R^2 is the coefficient of determination; SEE is the standard error of estimate; n is the number of countries in the sample. The standard errors are placed in parentheses below the calculated coefficients and an asterisk designates statistical significance at the 0.05 level. The data come from Table 11-1.

Table 11-4. Prediction Errors for Growth Rates.[a]

Country		Actual Minus Predicted Average Annual Growth Rates			
	GDP	GDP per Person	GDP per Economically Active	Industrial Production	Agricultural Production
Predicted "Winners"					
West Germany	+0.70%	+0.72%	+1.25%	+0.75%	+0.63%
Belgium	-0.34	+0.13	+0.18	-0.14	-0.81
Netherlands	+0.14	-0.11	+0.08	+0.43	+1.70
Norway	-0.30	-0.14	+0.01	-0.63	-1.65
East Germany	-0.15	+0.94	+0.95	-0.63	+0.05
Japan	+3.62	+3.38	+3.11	—	—
USSR	+0.50	-0.08	+0.06	+0.43	+1.22
Poland	-0.68	-1.16	-1.49	-0.63	-0.47
Predicted "Losers"					
United States	-0.09	-0.30	-0.37	+0.28	+0.29
Canada	+0.53	-0.33	-1.00	+0.94	+0.26
Switzerland	-0.61	-0.84	-1.00	—	—
United Kingdom	-1.88	-1.40	-1.36	-3.21	+0.59
Australia	+0.13	-0.91	-1.31	—	—
New Zealand	-1.11	-1.87	-2.32	—	—
Ireland	-1.86	-1.47	-1.09	—	—

Other Nations					
Sweden	−0.20	+0.24	+0.21	+0.43	−0.92
Denmark	−0.18	+0.18	+0.15	+0.37	−0.34
France	+0.56	+0.59	+0.95	+0.68	+0.39
Finland	−0.13	+0.21	+0.18	−0.08	−0.53
Austria	+0.13	+0.67	+0.99	−0.56	+0.23
Czechoslovakia	−0.31	−0.15	−0.04	−1.07	−0.91
Italy	−0.12	+0.00	+0.19	−0.22	+0.06
Spain	+0.48	+0.29	+0.42	+0.86	+0.64
Hungary	−0.93	−0.65	−0.80	−2.06	−0.69
Greece	+0.84	+0.91	+1.48	+1.04	+0.87
Bulgaria	+0.69	+0.62	+0.90	+2.21	+0.52
Romania	+0.88	+0.48	+0.41	+1.73	+0.28
Portugal	−0.29	+0.04	−0.75	−0.93	−1.41

a. These are the residuals from the regression equations 2, 4, 6, 8, and 10 in Table 11–2.

To explore this idea, I fitted to the data a different kind of regression that would permit exploration of the deceleration of growth, namely

$$\ln Y = a + bt + ct^2 \,,$$

where $\ln Y$ is the logarithm of the series under investigation, t is time, and a, b, and c are the calculated coefficients. Differentiating the equation with respect to t, we can easily determine that the "$2c$" is the coefficient of acceleration (if positive) or retardation (if negative).

The requisite data for the coefficient of growth acceleration (or retardation) are presented in the first three columns in Table 11-5. Looking over these data, it seems quite remarkable that some of the big winners noted in the Great Growth Rate Contest appear to demonstrate the greatest retardation, in particular Germany and Japan. And some of the losers in the contest such as the United Kingdom and Ireland appear to have quite mild growth retardations. (Some nations such as Australia and New Zealand are hopeless on both accounts.)

It could be argued that these results are merely a sign that rent-seeking groups in Germany and Japan have reorganized and are successfully besieging the citadel, while the rent-seeking groups in the United Kingdom and Ireland are being routed by the indignant public, which wants to experience a faster tempo of income growth. Such explanations, however, seem a bit ad hoc.

In order to explain these data in a more systematic fashion, I have selected three possible explanatory variables: the economic system, the level of per capita income, and the average annual growth rate of the series in question. This latter explanatory variable is suggested from the data because it can be argued that those nations experiencing the most rapid economic growth would be using up their growth potential more quickly and would be most likely to experience a regression toward the mean of the growth that corresponds with their per capita income. The results of such regressions are presented in Table 11-6 and the regression residuals (of the regressions excluding the dummy variables for winners and losers) are presented in the last three columns of Table 11-5.

The important results of the tests performed on the winners and losers can be quickly summarized: Neither of these dummy variables is statistically significant for either the total sample or the Western sample. Indeed, at least with regard to the losers, the signs are more often wrong than right. Turning briefly to the other variables, it can be seen that the growth rate variable has the predicted sign and is statistically significant in about half the cases; and that the level of development variable has the right sign in all cases but appeared statistically significant only for the total sample. The regression residuals presented in the last three columns of Table 11-5 give us little additionally useful information.

Given some inverse relationship between the level of economic development and actual growth rates on the one hand and the retardation of growth on the other hand, one important conclusion might be drawn: The results of a growth rate contest in future decades may turn out quite different from the results in the first three postwar decades. (Since Olson is quite ready in his book to explain the differential growth rates of the 1960s in the northern and southern parts of the United States with information about the Civil War a century before, we should be allowed to use information about the growth rates of the period from 1950 to 1980, to say something about the growth rates from 1980 to 2000!)

The Great Fluctuations Contest

In his book Mancur Olson offers some fascinating ideas about the microeconomic foundations of the business cycle, and these can also be tested with the data at hand. Those nations with less rent-seeking should manifest fewer fluctuations from their growth path; the reverse should be true for the losers.

To study production fluctuations I use only the GDP indicator since GDP per economically active is strongly influenced by the degree to which workers are furloughed during cyclical downturns. The statistic by which fluctuations are measured raises some problems and experiments are made with two: The first statistic is simply $(1 - R^2)$, where R^2 is the coefficient of determination of the equations in Table 11-5. This statistic does not turn out to be very satisfactory, for the coefficient of determination is partly a function of the variance of the dependent variable and this variance, in turn, is strongly influenced by the growth rate of the dependent variable. The second measure is the standard error of estimate (SEE) of the same regression equations. Now the SEE is merely the square root of the sum of the squares of the differences between the predicted and actual values of the series under examination, divided by the number of points. Since the predicted variable is in logarithms, the SEE measures something like the geometric average of the ratios of predicted to actual values. Both measures of fluctuations are presented in Table 11-7 in the first two columns.

Again, we are faced with the problem of trying to explain these results. Not having any particular theory about causes of fluctuations, I have selected three possible explanatory variables: the economic system, the level of per capita income (which performed so poorly that the regression was recalculated without it), and the average annual growth of the GDP. This latter variable was selected on the Schumpeterian grounds that growth leads to "creative destruction" and considerable cyclical activity. The requisite regressions are presented in Table 11-8, and the deviations from the trends are shown in the third and fourth columns of Table 11-7.

Although the signs of the calculated coefficients for the dummy variables indicating winners and losers are correct (the winners have lower fluctuations; the losers, greater), they are not statistically significant for either the total sample or the capitalist, market economies. The regression residuals are so mixed as to provide few additional insights.

Table 11-5.   Retardation of Growth, 1950-1979.[a]

Country	Average Annual Change (%)			Prediction Errors (%)		
	GDP	GDP per Person	GDP per Economically Active	GDP	GDP per Person	GDP per Economically Active
Predicted "Winners"						
West Germany	-0.218*	-0.146*	-0.104*	-0.129	-0.083	-0.012
Belgium	+0.038*	+0.057	+0.012	+0.081	+0.092	+0.077
Netherlands	-0.042*	-0.020	-0.001	+0.013	+0.004	+0.060
Norway	+0.048*	+0.065*	-0.039*	+0.088	+0.087	+0.019
East Germany	-0.132*	-0.167*	-0.169*	-0.041	-0.069	-0.050
Japan	-0.199*	-0.216*	-0.149*	-0.039	-0.048	-0.044
USSR	-0.103*	-0.053*	-0.121*	-0.015	-0.006	-0.037
Poland	+0.059*	+0.113*	+0.027	+0.090	+0.109	+0.069
Predicted "Losers"						
United States	-0.005	-0.036*	-0.078*	+0.089	+0.065	+0.009
Canada	+0.036*	+0.116*	-0.017	+0.125	+0.137	+0.037
Switzerland	-0.185*	-0.114*	-0.031*	-0.150	-0.120	+0.012
United Kingdom	-0.028*	-0.010	-0.018	-0.050	-0.043	+0.009
Australia	-0.049*	-0.018	-0.063*	+0.007	-0.028	-0.028
New Zealand	-0.089*	-0.029	-0.089*	-0.083	-0.082	-0.079
Ireland	+0.154*	+0.050*	+0.045*	+0.098	+0.003	+0.051

Other Nations

Sweden	-0.071*	-0.060*	-0.092*	-0.001	-0.014	-0.010
Denmark	-0.055*	-0.042*	-0.115*	+0.010	+0.002	-0.037
France	-0.023	-0.003	-0.070*	+0.043	+0.053	+0.011
Finland	-0.055*	-0.016	-0.026	-0.018	+0.020	+0.030
Austria	-0.070*	-0.071*	-0.106*	-0.024	-0.016	-0.036
Czechoslovakia	-0.104*	-0.080*	-0.096*	-0.021	-0.029	+0.003
Italy	-0.124*	-0.122*	-0.138*	-0.107	-0.102	-0.098
Spain	+0.006	-0.007	+0.019	+0.043	+0.025	+0.063
Hungary	-0.099*	-0.088*	-0.093*	-0.066	-0.066	-0.029
Greece	-0.022	-0.009	+0.024	+0.012	+0.045	+0.077
Bulgaria	-0.124*	-0.102*	-0.154*	-0.044	-0.029	-0.065
Romania	+0.021	+0.027	+0.036	+0.098	+0.092	+0.109
Portugal	+0.014	-0.009	-0.110*	-0.008	+0.004	-0.112

a. The asterisks designate that the calculated coefficient of average annual change (acceleration if positive; retardation if negative) is statistically significant at the 0.05 level. The prediction errors are based on the regression equations 2, 4, and 6 in Table 11–6. The data come from Pryor 1983b.

Table 11-6. Results of Regression Experiments with Retardation Rates.[a]

Retardation Rate	Constant	YCAP	SYS	Growth Rate	WIN	LOS	R^2	SEE	n
Total Sample									
1. GDP	+0.271* (0.131)	-.00263* (.00111)	-.0758 (.0445)	-.0332 (.0173)	+.0118 (.0374)	+.0130 (.0438)	.2659	.0799	28
2. GDP	+0.277* (0.114)	-.00255* (.00102)	-.0761 (.0392)	-.0342* (.0147)	–	–	.2638	.0765	28
3. GDP per person	+0.339* (0.124)	-.00263* (.00104)	-.0779 (.0405)	-.0527* (.0182)	+.0174 (.0328)	-.0321 (.0452)	.3443	.0705	28
4. GDP per person	+0.257* (0.101)	-.00199 (.00098)	-.0561 (.0360)	-.0425* (.0137)	–	–	.3022	.0707	28
5. GDP per economically active	+0.141 (0.112)	-.00210* (.00096)	-.0689 (.0382)	-.0180 (.0148)	+.0188 (.0285)	+.0116 (.0411)	.2371	.0613	28
6. GDP per economically active	+0.144 (0.085)	-.00199* (.00082)	-.0674* (.0312)	-.0186 (.0103)	–	–	.2209	.0595	28

Only Capitalist Market Economies

							SEE	R^2	
7. GDP	+0.265 (0.147)	-.00217 (.00125)	—	-.0373 (.0201)	+.00411 (.04976)	+.00159 (.04773)	.2618	.0842	21
8. GDP	+0.263* (0.124)	-.00213 (.00112)	'—	-.0370* (.0162)	—	—	.2615	.0794	21
9. GDP per person	+0.269 (0.141)	-.00181 (.00118)	—	-.0474* (.0208)	+.00750 (.04148)	-.0323 (.0474)	.2952	.0707	21
10. GDP per person	+0.202 (0.106)	-.00154 (.00104)	—	-.0363* (.0141)	—	—	.2699	.0679	21
11. GDP per economically active	+0.0558 (0.1251)	-.00137 (.00106)	—	-.00986 (.01663)	+.0260 (.0342)	+.0263 (.0415)	.1585	.0582	21
12. GDP per economically active	+0.0789 (0.0885)	-.00130 (.00090)	—	-.0133 (.0106)	—	—	.1142	.0562	21

a. The abbreviations of the variables are the same as in Tables 11–2 and 11–3. The "growth rate" variables correspond to the variable whose retardation is being studied; thus for equations 1 and 2 the GDP growth rate is used. R^2 is the coefficient of determination; SEE is the standard error of estimate; the standard errors are placed in parentheses below the calculated coefficients and an asterisk designates statistical significance at the 0.05 level. The data come from Table 11–5.

Table 11-7. Fluctuations in Production, 1950-1979.[a]

Country	GDP Fluctuations		Prediction Errors	
	$1 - R^2$	S	$1 - R^2$	S
Predicted "Winners"				
West Germany	.0030	.0245	−.00457	−.01180
Belgium	.0082	.0332	−.00004	+.00173
Netherlands	.0060	.0325	−.00179	−.00227
Norway	.0024	.0187	−.00573	−.01360
East Germany	.0080	.0311	+.00134	+.00392
Japan	.0078	.0637	+.00301	+.00728
USSR	.0018	.0192	−.00392	−.01480
Poland	.0093	.0364	+.00293	+.00723
Predicted "Losers"				
United States	.0099	.0309	+.00117	+.00302
Canada	.0057	.0317	−.00209	−.00303
Switzerland	.0166	.0449	+.00813	+.01510
United Kingdom	.0050	.0176	−.00427	−.00647
Australia	.0076	.0352	−.00021	+.00060
New Zealand	.0180	.0375	+.00933	+.00916
Ireland	.0082	.0291	−.00048	+.00084
Other Nations				
Sweden	.0088	.0319	+.00031	+.00224
Denmark	.0117	.0378	+.00330	+.00748
France	.0039	.0275	−.00366	−.00891
Finland	.0084	.0376	+.00053	+.00344
Austria	.0038	.0268	−.00386	−.00888
Czechoslovakia	.0060	.0283	−.00073	+.00165
Italy	.0034	.0262	−.00412	−.01050
Spain	.0128	.0575	+.00577	+.01730
Hungary	.0049	.0235	−.00186	−.00299
Greece	.0045	.0382	−.00200	−.00585
Bulgaria	.0079	.0442	+.00256	+.00750
Romania	.0047	.0364	−.00033	−.00253
Portugal	.0084	.0428	+.00129	+.00315

a. $(1 - R^2)$ is one minus the coefficient of determination of the time series regressions of the logarithms of the specified dependent variable; S is the standard error of estimate of the same regression. The choice of these statistics for measuring fluctuations is explained in the text. The prediction errors are calculated from the regressions reported in Table 11-8, equations 2 and 4. The data come from Pryor 1983b.

Results with Standard Error of Estimate Measure of Fluctuations

Fluctuations Variable	Constant	GDP Growth	SYS	WIN	LOS	R^2	SEE	n
				Total Sample				
1.	+.00326 (.00861)	+.00674* (.00166)	-.0008 (.0040)	-.00323 (.00381)	+.00424 (.00463)	.4451	.00846	28
2.	+.00847 (.00690)	+.00574* (.00146)	-.00291 (.00371)	–	–	.3927	.00849	28
				Only Capitalist, Market Economies				
3.	+.00001 (.00958)	+.00747* (.00189)	–	-.00424 (.00484)	+.00481 (.00485)	.4935	.00860	21
4.	+.00728 (.00761)	+.00600* (.00162)	–	–	–	.4188	.00870	21

Results with $(1 - R^2)$ Measure of Fluctuations

Fluctuations Variable	Constant	GDP Growth	SYS	WIN	LOS	R^2	SEE	n
				Total Sample				
5.	+.00805 (.00387)	+.00021 (.00077)	-.00060 (.00180)	-.00100 (.00172)	+.00287 (.00208)	.1914	.00380	28
6.	+.0114* (.0031)	-.00079 (.00067)	-.0018 (.00016)	–	–	.0896	.00387	28
				Only Capitalist, Market Economies				
7.	+.00739 (.00460)	-.00002 (.00090)	–	-.00181 (.00232)	+.00282 (.00233)	.1892	.00413	21
8.	+.0115* (.0037)	-.000805 (.000787)	–	–	–	.0522	.00422	21

a.   The abbreviations of the variables are the same as in Table 11–2. R^2 is the coefficient of determination; SEE is the standard error of estimate; the standard error are placed in parentheses below the calculated coefficients and an asterisk designates statistical significance at the 0.05 level. The data come from Table 11–7.

SOME BRIEF REFLECTIONS

Mancur Olson's theory of rent-seeking allows us to classify nations as to whether they will be winners or losers in growth rate, growth retardation, and production fluctuation contests. For the most part the calculated coefficients for the dummy variables indicating whether the nation is a winner or loser do not turn out to be statistically significant when these contests are run. Further, in those few cases where the results are encouraging to Olson, his theory seems to work only for the losers. As I suggested previously, the dummy variable for the losers may be picking up other causal factors, especially since six of the seven losers are English-speaking nations. In sum, although the results are somewhat mixed, they do not provide for much confidence in Olson's approach.

If my tests are appropriate for Olson's theory, what is wrong? Part of the problem may lie in the nature of the tests themselves. Although Mancur Olson told the reader that other causal factors might also play a role in determining the macroeconomic success of particular nations, he stressed primarily the role of rent-seeking. Although I have tried to hold constant some of the other major causal variables, the percentage of unexplained variance is uncomfortably high. It is certainly possible that Olson's approach permits an explanation of some of these differences in growth rates and fluctuations of nations; unfortunately, the impact of rent-seeking is masked by a number of other important causal elements.

Part of the problem may also lie in the theoretical foundations of Olson's approach. Other chapters in this book and also the book edited by Mueller (1983) discuss some possible shortcomings, such as a lack of proper attention to the role of the state, or to the constellation of events other than wars that act to reduce the influence of rent-seeking groups, or to the interaction of rent-seeking with other variables influencing economic growth and fluctuations. Some have claimed that Olson has also overemphasized the performance potential of nations with minimal governmental roles in the economy and few opportunities for rent-seeking in contrast to nations whose governments have intelligently attempted to assist economic growth and to combat production fluctuations (activities that give rise to rent-seeking) so that the empirical tests would not support Olson's ideas. It might also be argued that Olson's theory is formulated in a manner still too general to prove successful in the empirical tests and that more intervening variables need to be specified.

Although the title of Olson's book refers to the aggregative economic behavior of nations, I believe that his approach might be most fruitful in understanding economic behavior at a lower level of aggregation than the GDP. One highly interesting direction to take is provided by Peter Murrell's comparison (Mueller 1983) of differential sector growth rates in West Germany and the United Kingdom. By showing that "new" industries (which presumably feature relatively little rent-seeking in either country) are much more similar in the two countries than "old" industries (where rent-seeking is more advanced in the United Kingdom), Murrell provides some useful positive evidence for Olson's approach. A related avenue of research would focus on the cyclical behavior of industries in different countries that are characterized by differential degrees of rent-seeking.

Most of the discussion in the literature on rent-seeking has been on a micro-economic level; Olson's approach is unique in focusing on important economic aggregates. However, my results (as well as Murrell's) suggest that the major area of empirical application of Olson's approach ought not to be on the most macroeconomic level, but rather at some level in between the most aggregative level and the micro level—that is, that his insights be applied to more modest problems than those to which they were originally addressed.

The rent-seeking approach offers an exciting new method with which to analyze economic reality. If it is to become more widely used, it is imperative to move from theorical to empirical analysis. But in making that important step, let us not throttle research by claiming too much for it or by making its area of application too cosmic.

NOTE TO CHAPTER 11

1. All data used in the tables are drawn from Pryor (1985). The data for Eastern Europe are all Western recalculations; the data for the capitalist, market economies are from the Organization for Economic Cooperation and Development. The data on per capita GDP are calculated on the basis of weighting quantity data for each country with the same set of prices.

12 THE INVISIBLE FOOT AND THE WASTE OF NATIONS
Redistribution and Economic Growth

William A. Brock and Stephen P. Magee

Adam Smith's invisible hand symbolizes the unseen benefits which economic competition confers on the coordination of economic activity. We see a contrasting image in Mancur Olson's *The Rise and Decline of Nations* (1982), which we shall call the "invisible foot." The invisible foot symbolizes the welfare-reducing effects of political competition over redistribution. The adjective in the label emphasizes the difficulties of observation, quantification, and measurement. In general, we agree with Olson's view that redistributive lobbying leads to institutional sclerosis and economic waste. However, the economic effects of redistributive activity are more complicated than he envisioned. The effects depend, in part, on whether redistributive activity is directed toward income or wealth. We investigate *wealth redistribution* in Model 1 and *income redistribution* in Models 2 and 3. This paper extends earlier theoretical work on the Olson hypothesis (see Hicks, 1983). For several papers on the hypothesis, see Mueller (1983).

We demonstrate the difficulty of observing invisible foot behavior by providing theoretical examples of economies with an Olson scenario but with opposite effects; e.g., in Model 1 we find that increases in labor devoted to *wealth redistribution* can increase (rather than decrease) GNP and GNP growth. An example of this phenomenon is an attorney who is paid a contingency fee of, say, one-third of the wealth which he successfully transfers from one individual to another. The attorney's fee is a transformation of wealth into income and if this fee exceeds what the attorney would have earned in nonredistributive activities, his predatory behavior increases measured GNP in the short run. Successful quantification of this effect would require better measurements of wealth than we now have.

Model 2 analyzes *income redistribution in a static world* while Model 3 analyzes *income redistribution in a dynamic framework.* Both of these models are formalizations of an Olson approach: in some cases they reinforce his points while in others, they conflict with his views. There are four major results in Model 2. First, as in Model 1, large and positive growth rates of GNP are compatible with growth of redistributive activity. Second, the growth rates of productive and redistributive activity converge in the long run. Third, a negative association between growth rates of GNP and growth in redistributive activity is most likely early in the redistributive process rather than later. This conflicts with both Olson's view that negative correlation occurs in older economies and with Model 1 in which negative correlation occurs in "middle-aged" economies. Fourth, Model 2 is consistent with countercyclicity of redistributive activity in the business cycle.

Model 3 explores income redistribution in an intertemporal model. First, we find that the more wealthy an economy, the more resources will be devoted to redistribution. Our result may be difficult to separate empirically from Olson's thesis that redistributive battles increase with the age of the economy. In our model, the result comes from the first-order condition showing that more labor will be devoted to redistribution the higher the capital stock. In other words, redistributive conflict over shares increases with the size of the pie (to the extent that the larger pie is caused by a higher capital stock). This emerges despite our behavioral specification that redistributive activity was directed at income rather than capital. As an aside, we speculate that some care will have to be exercised in empirical work to disentangle this effect on GNP from the normal diminishing returns to capital. As with the Olson effect, diminishing returns to capital can slow the growth of GNP as an economy ages.

Second, the intertemporal equilibrium demonstrates clearly our assumption of arbitrage between productive and redistributive activity. In equilibrium, identical workers will be indifferent between devoting their efforts to productive vs. redistributive activities. This causes the equilibrium proportion of the labor force devoted to redistribution to be inversely related to the wage rate.

A third and unexpected result of dynamic income redistribution is that the equilibrium capital/labor ratio is independent of the level of redistributive activity. This occurs because redistribution reduces GNP, the capital stock, and the labor force by the same proportion in the long run in Model 3; thus, the ratios of any two of the three variables are unaffected. The result implies that if we attempted to correlate some independent measure of redistribution with capital/labor ratios across economies, we should find no relationship. Fourth, as in the previous models, there is no association between growth rates of economic variables and redistributive waste in the long run.

In summary, all three models suggest no stable relationship between GNP growth rates and redistributive activity. We are not surprised at Pryor's (1983a, 1983b) empirical rejections of the Olson growth rate hypothesis. GNP growth rates are probably uncorrelated with economic hardening of the arteries, lobbying and the pursuit of redistributive perversities.

MODEL 1: WEALTH REDISTRIBUTION

Olson argues that over time GNP growth will fall for two reasons in invisible foot economies: because resources are being removed from productive activity and because perverse policies lead to economic sclerosis and inefficiency. However, the perverse economic effects of redistribution can be harder to detect than Olson imagined. In some cases, increased redistributive action can lead to an increase in the level of GNP and in a country's growth rate.

To see this, let us first assume that redistributive activity is directed at wealth rather than income. Assume that the total labor supply, T, follows one of two activities: L is engaged in productive activity while R pursues redistributive activity.

$$T = L + R \qquad (12.1)$$

Productive labor helps produce economic income, whereas redistributive labor relabels wealth, transferring it from one member of society to another. This process is determined by an exogenous social technology of law, accounting, economics, criminal tendencies, and tradition. We also assume that all redistributed wealth is converted to income. The division of this income into consumption and savings is not important for the points we wish to make here. Total income, Y, in the invisible foot economy comes from two sources: economic income, F, and redistributive income, Kr:

$$Y = F(K,L) + Kr(R) \qquad (12.2)$$

where

$\quad K, L$ = capital and labor in production;

$\quad r$ = fraction of capital that is redistributed each period and converted to income;

$\quad R$ = labor engaged in redistributing capital.

In contrast, total income in the invisible hand economy can be written

$$Y = F(K,T) \ . \qquad (12.3)$$

Assume that the two economies have identical labor forces and identical capital stocks. From Eqs. (12.2) and (12.3) it is clear that the hand economy will have more economic income because $T > L$, but the foot economy will have redistribution income if $r > 0$ because redistribution converts parts of the capital stock back into income each period. *GNP and GNP per capita can be higher in the invisible foot economy.* This should be true if r is sufficiently high and early in the redistribution phase. This can be seen by transferring one unit of labor from economic activity to redistributive activity in equation (12.2), starting at a low R. The labor would not have made the transition voluntarily unless the income it received from redistribution, Kr', exceeded the foregone wage, F_L. But this is the very condition that guarantees that the transfer to redistribution increases GNP: i.e., $(Kr' - F_L) > 0$. This result ignores defensive actions by the redistributees to prevent the transfer. These may or may not provide an offset to the income-increasing effect. If people finance their defenses out of wealth rather than income, this too increases measured GNP, at the expense of wealth (e.g., the income of locksmiths and defense attorneys appears in national income).

Another result that emerges from this simple framework is that early in the redistribution period, *wages are higher and returns to capital are lower in the invisible foot economy* (when compared to an invisible hand economy with an identical capital stock and total labor force). Since there is less labor in economic production, the capital/labor ratio is higher, the marginal product of capital is lower, and the marginal product of labor is higher in the foot economy. Thus, any economy with increasing redistributive activity should show a rise in wages relative to rentals and *factors market pressures for labor immigration and capital emigration.*

To determine the effects of redistribution on growth, we differentiate (12.2) totally (all derivatives are with respect to time):

$$dY = F_K \, dK + F_L (dT - dR) + rdK + Kr_R \, dR$$

$$= \left\{ F_K \, dK + F_L \, dT \right\} + \left\{ rdK + (Kr_R - F_L) dR \right\}$$

$$(12.4)$$

Consider the growth rates of income in two economies, each starting with identical stocks of K and T with identical production and redistribution technologies. Let the invisible foot economy be initially at $R = 0$ and not in redistribution equilibrium. This will be the case if the marginal payoff to increasing redistribution (Kr_R) exceeds the cost of one less laborer in production (F_L), by the earlier discussion. The second brace in equation (12.4) indicates that *invisible foot economies entering periods of wasteful redistribution will have unambiguously higher growth rates of GNP than invisible hand economies.* The reason for this is simple: collectors of GNP statistics value all services at the amount the wage earner receives. They do not ask redistributors whether their services were socially productive and they do not inquire whether wealth was extinguished to pay them. In the United States, it is illegal for lawyers and criminals not to report their successful redistributive ventures as taxable income. (We do not know the extent to which transfers of wealth into criminal income are counted in U.S. GNP.)

Early in invisible foot economies, GNP growth rates will be higher the more rapid the growth of labor in the redistributive sector; that is, so long as the economy's redistribution equilibrium in labor markets has not yet been reached. Since $(Kr_R - F_L)$ is positive, the redistributive growth term in equation (12.4) increases with dR. In the earliest phases of redistribution, dR will be large simply because R is near zero. Also, note in (12.4) that the marginal payoff to entering redistribution will also increase with the capital stock if $(r_R - F_{LK}) > 0$. If this is the case, initially, *capital-abundant economies will demonstrate more rapid growth with increasing redistribution than labor-abundant economies.*

Once R has grown sufficiently in the invisible foot economy, diminishing returns will lead to a redistribution equilibrium in labor markets. The marginal returns from redistributive activities will equal those in economic activities and no more labor will wish to move from economic to redistributive activity. I.e., the salaries of marginal lawyers will equal those of marginal engineers, causing $(Kr_R - F_L) = 0$. In this medium-run phase of the redistributive process, GNP growth can be written as

$$dY = F_K\,dK + F_L\,dT + r\,dK$$
$$= (F_K + r)dK + F_L\,dT \tag{12.5}$$

In (12.5), the growth of the foot economy compared to the hand economy is harder to determine. Even with identical K and T, the results are ambiguous: r is greater for the foot economy, but F_K and probably dK are lower. Parenthetically, the change in capital will be

$$dK = (I/K - e - r)K \tag{12.6}$$

I/K = gross investment/capital ratio

e = depreciation rate of capital

r = redistribution rate for capital

which should yield a lower dK because of a lower K and a positive r. Nevertheless, it appears possible from (12.5) that invisible foot economies could grow faster than invisible hand economies, even in the medium run.

MODEL 2: STATIC INCOME REDISTRIBUTION

Let there be $N(t)$ people at date t who own one unit of labor each. Suppose that one unit of labor produces $w(t)$ units of final goods output using a single-input, constant-returns technology. Then each individual j solves the following problem (we suppress t until it is needed):

$$\text{Maximize } wL_j \, \Phi(R_j, R_{-j}) \quad \text{s.t. } L_j + R_j = 1 \qquad (12.7)$$

where L_j denotes productive labor; R_j denotes labor devoted in redistribution; $R_{-j} = (R_1, \ldots, R_{j-1}, R_{j+1}, \ldots, R_N)$ = the vector of redistributive inputs by everyone but j; and Φ denotes the impact of redistribution upon j's income as a function of all redistributive activity in society. We shall assume that Φ increases in R_j, decreases in R_{-j}, and is the same function for everybody. (The assumption of homogeneous individuals will be made throughout.)

The interpretation of Φ is the following: If j increases R_j enough, he will obtain more than perfectly competitive earnings, wL_j, from his labor. But large enough inputs R_{-j} of his $N-1$ rivals will make $\Phi < 1$, so that he gets less than his perfectly competitive earnings. We shall assume $\Phi(R_j, R_{-j}) = 1$ where $R_1 = R_2 \ldots = R_N$ to dramatize the zero-sum nature of noncooperative equilibrium. The situation here is analogous to an arms race or a prisoners' dilemma (see Young and Magee 1982 for prisoners' dilemma outcomes in lobbying equilibria over tariff setting).

In order to derive some specific illustrative results, consider the following special case for Φ.

$$\Phi(R_j, R_{-j}) \equiv R_j^\alpha \left(\sum_{k \neq j} R_k^{-\alpha}/(N-1) \right), \quad \alpha > 0 \qquad (12.8)$$

The solution of (12.7) must satisfy the first-order necessary conditions

$$\partial \Phi_j / \partial R_j = \Phi/L_j \qquad (12.9)$$

from which we obtain from (12.8)

$$R_j \equiv R = \alpha L_j \equiv \alpha L, \quad L = \frac{1}{1+\alpha}, \quad R = \frac{\alpha}{1+\alpha} \qquad (12.10)$$

Let Y denote observable GNP. Since all income earned by labor (whether wasteful or not) is recorded in GNP accounts, we put, by definition,

$$Y \equiv wN \qquad (12.11)$$

The reader may be uneasy about (12.11) because each j is using his own labor to redistribute. But that labor, through (12.8), is valued at w for each unit. In a model where there were specialists who were better at redistribution than j, the equilibrium would be for j to sell R_j units at w and purchase R_j units from someone else. In this model all redistributive labor income would show up in GNP accounts. The analysis of this more elaborate model would be straightforward but more complicated. Therefore we stick with (12.11).

Let Y = GNP; X = value of final goods production; and Z = total value of resources in redistribution. From (12.10) we have

$$Y = wN, \quad X = (1 - r)\,Y, \quad Z = rY, \quad r = \frac{\alpha}{1 + \alpha} \qquad (12.12)$$

Using (12.12) to calculate rates of growth, and letting α vary over time

$$g_Y = g_w + g_N \;, \qquad (12.13a)$$

$$g_Z = g_r + g_Y = \frac{g_\alpha}{(1 + \alpha)} + g_Y \;, \qquad (12.13b)$$

$$g_X = \frac{-\alpha g_\alpha}{(1 + \alpha)} + g_Y \;, \qquad (12.13c)$$

$$g_Y = \frac{\alpha g_Z}{(1 + \alpha)} + \frac{g_X}{(1 + \alpha)} \qquad (12.14)$$

The quantity $\alpha(t)$ determines the share of resources diverted to redistribution and must be less than unity in order for our model to be sensibly posed. The rate of growth of α can be anything over short periods of time.

We make four points. First, in the short run just about any patterns of rates of growth of real output are possible. As in the first model, large positive rates of growth of GNP are compatible with large positive rates of growth of both productive activity and redistributive activity.

Second, an important case is where $g_\alpha \to 0$ as $t \to \infty$. In this case, the share of GNP going to redistribution settles down in the long run. Then, under modest regularity of the function $\alpha(t)$ we have

$$\alpha(t) \to \overline{\alpha} \;, \quad t \to \infty \;. \qquad (12.15)$$

Hence the growth rates of Y, X, and Z converge.

Third, as indicated by (12.13), the negative association, if any, between rates of growth of redistribution and rates of growth of GNP is more likely to show up in *young* countries: This contrasts with the results in Model 1, and it is the reverse of Olson's view.

Fourth, this model is consistent with the stylized fact of the countercyclicity of redistribution. As an economy falls into recession, the most likely values are for g_w to be negative and g_α to be positive. Therefore $g_Z = g_Y + g_\alpha/(1 + \alpha) > g_Y$ when falling into a trough. On the rise out of the trough it is natural to expect that $g_\alpha < 0$ and $g_w > 0$. Therefore on the upswing we should expect that $g_Z = g_Y + g_\alpha/(1 + \alpha) < g_Y$. While these results depend on our specific functional forms, we suspect that similar results will turn up in more general models that capture the decline in the rewards of production relative to redistribution in the business cycle. For theoretical and empirical development of the negative covariation of political and economic returns in a general equilibrium international trade model with redistribution, see Magee, Brock and Young (1983).

MODEL 3: DYNAMIC INCOME REDISTRIBUTION

We explore next the economic impact of income redistribution in an intertemporal model. We assume that N homogeneous individual households maximize their life-cycle utility. We will not derive the explicit optimization in what follows. The budget of household h is

$$C_h + dK_h/dt = (rK_h + wL_h + d_h \pi) \Phi (R_h, R_{-h}), \quad K_h(0) = K_{h0} \quad (12.16)$$

where C_h is consumption by h, K_h is capital owned by h, r is the rental rate on capital, w is the wage rate on labor L_h, π is corporate profits (which are assumed to be redistributed lump sum in fraction d_h, à la Arrow and Debreu), and Φ is the impact of redistribution on income, which is increasing in own redistribution labor R_h and decreasing in the others R_{-h}.

Assume that the households are homogeneous and have time-stationary preferences

$$\int_0^\infty e^{-\rho t} U(C_h(t)) dt. \quad (12.17)$$

where ρ is the subjective rate of time preference. The variables ρ, r and C_h are related by Irving Fisher's equation,

$$\rho = (dU_h'/dt)/U_h' = r \Phi \quad (12.18)$$

where U_h' is the marginal utility of consumption. The constant-returns productive sector is given at date t by

$$Y = F(K,L,t) = rK + wL \quad \pi \equiv F(K,L,t) - rK - wL = 0 \quad (12.19)$$

Each household has one unit of labor to allocate each period. Therefore the household solves (since $\pi = 0$ in equilibrium)

$$\underset{0 \leqslant L_h \leqslant 1}{\text{Maximize}} \quad (rK_h + wL_h) \Phi (1 - L_h, R_{-h}) \quad (12.20)$$

Using the function developed in Model 2, we find

$$L_h = \frac{1}{1 + \alpha} \left(1 - \frac{\alpha r K_h}{w} \right) \quad R_h = \frac{1}{1 + \alpha} \left(\alpha + \frac{\alpha r K_h}{w} \right) \quad (12.21)$$

Notice that all other things equal, *the more wealthy an economy, the more resources are used in protecting wealth from redistribution* (since R_h increases with K_h). Competitive markets require

$$r = F_K(K, L, t) = F_K(K/L, 1, t) \quad w = F_L(K/L, 1, t) \tag{12.22}$$

where subscripted symbols denote partial derivatives and the equalities follow from constant returns. Since we are not focusing on population growth in this model, we put $N = 1$ for convenience.

Suppose that there is no technical progress so that F is independent of t. Then, in steady state $dU_h'/dt = 0$ so that

$$\rho = r = F_K(K/L, 1) \tag{12.23}$$

Let $k(\rho)$ solve (12.23); $k(\rho)$ falls in ρ since F is concave.

Notice that $k(\rho)$, *the capital labor ratio, is independent of redistributive activity.* This is partially an artifact of the assumed absence of redistributive activity by firms. Substitute $k(\rho) = K/L$ into (12.21), to obtain

$$L_h = \frac{1}{1 + \alpha\tau(\rho)} \quad R_h = \frac{\alpha\tau(\rho)}{1 + \alpha\tau(\rho)} \quad \tau(\rho) \equiv 1 + \frac{\rho k(\rho)}{w(\rho)} \tag{12.24}$$

$$K = k(\rho)L = \frac{k(\rho)}{1 + \alpha\tau(\rho)} \quad, \quad X \equiv F(K, L) = LF(k(\rho), 1) = \frac{F(k(\rho), 1)}{1 + \alpha\tau(\rho)}$$

$$\tag{12.25}$$

We draw three main conclusions. First, while the national capital stock and national output are smaller with redistribution, ($\alpha > 0$), *the fraction of redistributive waste is the same for national output and the national capital stock.*

Second, *economies with higher ratios of capital income, ρK, to labor income in the productive sector, wL, have higher propensities to redistribute.* Thus, a high-capital-income economy has to invest more to protect its capital. And thus, waste and wealth should be positively correlated, giving an alternative explanation to Olson's for greater redistribution in wealthier economies. *The larger the pie, the larger the fraction of labor devoted to fighting over shares of the pie.*

Third, in the steady state all growth rates will be the same. Hence *there is no association between growth rates of economic variables and redistributive waste in the long run.* We suspect also that no clear relation may exist between short-run growth rates and redistribution in a model of this type.

CONCLUSION

Each of these models demonstrates a different part of the redistributive process. As one can easily see, the expected empirical result can be quite complicated, even in these elementary models. They demonstrate that one must be careful about drawing simple conclusions.

13 A RENT-SEEKING EXPLANATION OF THE BRITISH FACTORY ACTS

Gary M. Anderson and Robert D. Tollison

The British Factory Acts enacted over the period 1833-1850 placed restrictions of gradually increasing severity on the employment of children, adolescents, and adult women in the textile industry.[1] Later legislation extended similar restrictions to other industries. For at least a century opinion among historians has been virtually unanimous to the effect that the early British legislation, ostensibly designed to protect women and children from labor market exploitation, was paradigmatic of enlightened intervention by the state. Even a writer usually identified with extreme laissez faire, George Howell, wrote in 1891 that the Factory Acts "have for their object the *protection* of women and children, who were, and still are . . . unable to protect themselves" (1891: 150). In this evaluation he shares the same bed as Engels, the Webbs, and most recent writers.

Over the past century a handful of writers—including Hutt (1954) and Mises (1966)—have chosen to lock horns with the conventional wisdom regarding the Factory Acts. These critiques have basically constituted jabs at the orthodoxy rather than frontal assaults. However, more recently, Marvel (1977) and (arguing in a different vein) Nardinelli (1980) have mounted empirically based challenges to fundamental elements in the received view. Marvel claims that the first effective Factory Act—Althorp's Bill of 1833—represented a successful attempt by a clearly defined industry group to establish a cartel in the textile industry. Nardinelli, approaching the problem from a different perspective, attempts to

We are grateful to Robert McCormick and to participants in the Middlebury Conference on Rent-Seeking and Appropriability, especially Douglass North, Frederic Pryor, and Gordon Tullock, for helpful comments. The usual disclaimer about responsibility for errors applies.

establish that the Factory Acts were actually beside the point. In reality they only served to speed up a movement away from child labor that was already taking place as a result of rising real income and technological change.

Our position is that while the conventional wisdom with respect to the Factory Acts amounts to nothing more than apologetics for government intervention, Marvel and Nardinelli do not provide fully satisfactory alternative explanations of this legislation. In each case the Factory Movement—which even a cursory examination of the history of the legislation will reveal as having played an important role—is allowed to remain exogenous. Any convincing challenge to the conventional wisdom must explain the role of the so-called Ten Hours Movement in economic terms.

Our purpose is to outline what we think is a convincing alternative to the conventional wisdom in this case. This alternative can be summarized succinctly. The Factory Acts represented the mechanism by which skilled male operatives (especially at first in the cotton textile industry) attempted to limit competition from alternative labor suppliers (children, adolescents, and adult women), who were becoming increasingly close substitutes as the nineteenth century progressed. We believe that we can demonstrate that the Factory Movement was motivated not by righteous outrage at social injustice, but by the rents available to skilled adult male laborers (the core of the Factory Movement) resulting from parliamentary intervention in the labor market.

The chapter proceeds as follows. After describing previous approaches to explaining the Factory Acts, we outline an alternative model of the Factory Acts involving rent-seeking by skilled male operatives. The point is to demonstrate the clear incentives of the operatives to limit competing labor suppliers. We then examine the political influence of the operatives, showing that the operatives possessed an effective supply of votes and attended important legislative hearings to press their cause. We conclude with a summary assessment of the available evidence pertinent to our explanation.

PREVIOUS APPROACHES TO THE PROBLEM

Consensus among historians is unusual, but the causes and consequences of factory legislation is one of the few issues on which writers as diverse as Ashton (1967: 96-97) and the Webbs (1920) and practically everyone in between essentially agree. It is generally agreed that the Factory Acts represented humanitarian regulation that increased the welfare of women, children, and workers by putting a stop to abuses of the factory system.

There are various problems with this conventional wisdom, but the basic problem is that it is not a satisfactory explanation of the legislation. It rests more on the rhetoric of those who lobbied for the legislation than on the underlying motivations and effects of the legislation. A handful of historians and economists in this century have proposed alternatives to the conventional wisdom.

Two prominent writers—Hutt (1954) and Mises (1966)—challenged the contention that the Factory Acts improved the welfare of those they allegedly protected. Essentially, both argue that the Factory Act regulations decreased the welfare of those they were ostensibly designed to promote and that the factory system substantially increased per capita income among the poor. While we agree with the basic thrust of both arguments, these writers do not offer an alternative explanation for the Factory Acts, but leave the legislation exogenous and focus on its effects.[2]

Nardinelli (1980) offers a similar argument contending that the legislation was largely irrelevant. According to him, the available evidence "implies that the Factory Acts only speeded up a movement which was already taking place. Rising real income and technological change were the main causes of the decline of child labor" (p. 739). While Nardinelli makes an important point about child labor, it must be kept in mind that the Factory Acts were later extended to adolescents and adult women. Moreover, some of Nardinelli's empirics are inclusive. For example, he employs an apparently useful proxy in the form of data on children's employment in nontextile industries (free of legislative restrictions until the 1860s and 1870s) to suggest that the Factory Acts had little impact on levels of child employment in the textile industry (pp. 752–53). But he indicates the dubious nature of the proxy by explaining that the textile industry employed a higher proportion of child labor than nontextiles (in general) as late as 1851, and most certainly over earlier periods (p. 753). For these types of reasons we feel that Nardinelli's position that factory legislation only codified underlying trends in the economy is not conclusive.

The conventional wisdom, specifically with respect to the Factory Act of 1833, has been strongly challenged by Marvel (1977). Arguing that the public interest explanation offered by historians is implausible and unmotivated, Marvel maintains that the 1833 Act was designed in the interest of leading English textile manufacturers to restrict output, raise textile prices, and increase quasi-rents to those manufacturers whose operations were least affected by the bill's provisions. His central thesis is that the legislation was designed to place a differential burden on a subset of textile manufacturers, namely those whose mills were water- rather than steam-powered. In effect, Marvel argues that legislation restricting the employment of children would have tended to raise the costs and decrease the output of water-driven producers correspondingly more than it did for their steam-powered competitors.

Marvel's approach to the problem of the Factory Acts is innovative. He claims to have established by use of empirical techniques the approximate magnitude of the net wealth transfer (quasi-rents) to the proponents of the 1833 Bill as a result of the selective regulatory burden on water-powered mills (92,000 pounds sterling in 1833, p. 392). Moreover, using multiple regression techniques, Marvel claims to have established a statistically significant correlation between the burden due to enforcement activity and the size of the mills. In other words, although all textile mills faced positive costs of regulation, regulatory enforcement was selective, imposing a significantly larger burden on the water-powered mills, which were generally rural and smaller.

Marvel has offered the best-motivated explanation of the process leading to Althorp's Bill. His industry interest-group theory is straightforward and appears to be corroborated by his econometric evidence. However, Marvel's analysis is not without problems.

First, Marvel does not offer a single name of a mill owner in England who supported (and presumably lobbied for) Althorp's Bill, restricting child labor. This is not surprising; the historical sources agree that supporters of Althorp's Bill among manufacturers were a *small* minority. Perusal of Ward's definitive *Factory Movement* (a source sympathetic to the reforms) yields six or seven names of declared supporters of the bill at a time when this was a tiny percentage of English mill owners. Marvel offers only one example (1977: 388, n. 34) of a mill owner involved in the controversy, and in this case he (Ashworth) was an "implacable opponent."[3]

Further, there is evidence that the consensus among historians that the owners were in general opposed to the bill represents a fairly accurate assessment. The Royal Commission of 1833, which proved highly sympathetic to the legislation in the end, called a group of manufacturers (mostly from Lancashire) as witnesses who were overwhelmingly opposed to the proposed regulations.[4] (We shall have more to say about who showed up to testify and what they said.)

There are also problems with Marvel's differential burden argument, the linchpin of his model from a factual standpoint. His argument assumes that the cotton textile industry in 1833 was bifurcated into two readily distinguishable segments—the large urban steam-powered mills, which employed relatively few children, and the small rural water-powered mills, which employed relatively many children. This situation provided the foundation for the differential burden resulting from the legislation because when the rural water-powered mill lost production due to drought, the only feasible means available for making up for lost output was working extra hours. But plants could not operate without child labor, and children could no longer legally work overtime.[5] Generally, Marvel's argument is that the smaller, rural mills were the marginal producers in the textile industry, and that they incurred differentially higher costs as a result of the 1833 Factory Act.

Marvel's technological bifurcation assumption overemphasizes the importance of weather conditions and underestimates the adaptability of profit-maximizing mill owners. Not all streams utilized to provide water power to cotton mills were subject to drought; many represented consistent and reliable power sources. Moreover, there is abundant evidence that indicates that as early as 1820 water-powered mills subject to periodic droughts were rarely if ever forced to close or even reduce their output as a result of these meteorological shocks. Records show that mill owners affected by these problems invested in steam-powered back-up systems that allowed them to maintain steady rates of output even though droughts.[6] By 1830, it was unusual for a predominantly water-powered textile firm to lose significant amounts of time to drought due to the relatively high elasticity of substitution between the alternative energy inputs of water and steam. This is not to imply that mills did not occasionally shut down temporarily. However, such instances were typically in response to changes in market rather than weather conditions (such as a shift in the demand for textiles or a temporary cotton shortage), and were evidently uncorrelated with firm size and/ or power source.[7]

In sum, Marvel seems to chase a largely hypothetical interest group to explain the 1833 bill while largely ignoring an undeniably real interest group that loudly clamored for the 1833 bill and continuing factory acts into the 1850s—the Ten Hours Movement. Of course, we recognize that both of us can be right. Recent contributions to the positive theory of regulation emphasize the transmission mechanism by which interest groups obtain wealth transfers through the political process (Peltzman 1976; Moore 1978; Landes 1980). In these approaches both capital and labor supply inputs (money and votes) to vote-maximizing politicians, who in turn supply transfers to both types of inputs. Marvel stresses the benefits from factory legislation that accrued to a subset of capital owners in the textile industry; we stress the benefits that went to skilled male workers in the industry. Our effort in this chapter is to complete the analysis begun by Marvel by spelling out and amplifying the role of the skilled textile operatives in the transmission mechanism that produced Althorp's Bill and, more important, later factory legislation aimed at restricting labor market competition from adolescents and women.

THE TEN HOURS MOVEMENT

Our goals in this section are two. First, we provide an account of the Ten Hours Movement that places it in what we believe to be the correct historical context. Second, we show why the Ten Hours Movement acted as the mechanism that achieved quasi-rents for its members—skilled adult male operatives in the cotton textile industry—by restricting employment opportunities for children and women.

The Ten Hours Movement in Historical Perspective

The primary interest group, at least in terms of size and visibility, behind the passage of Althorp's Bill (as well as later, more comprehensive factory legislation) was the Ten Hours Movement. Members of this movement were almost exclusively adult men, most of whom were operatives in the textile industry. The usual account of the goals of this group maintains that relief of the worst abuses of child labor were foremost in their minds (e.g., Ward 1962: 33ff). Even Marvel seems to accept this view (1977: 382). We agree that the Ten Hours Movement played an important role in the passage of Althorp's Bill; however, we think that its behavior can be explained without recourse to altruistic motives.

The Ten Hours Movement is normally depicted by historians as appearing in 1830 (e.g., Ward 1962: 33). While literally true, this claim is misleading. The main stated goal of the Movement—limiting the hours of labor of children and later of adult women—has a long history. Ashton explains that the apprenticeship clauses of the Statute of Artificers (1563) originated from the attempt of adult male workers to limit the field of competition for employment. Efforts to maintain and extend such restrictions continued throughout the eighteenth century (1977: 223-24). In fact, some of the earliest trade unions arose in the later eighteenth century expressly in order to restrict competition from children (Brentano 1870: 117, 120).

There was also a lengthy record of activities among male workers aimed at restricting the entry of competing women into the textile industry. Ashton reports (1977: 223) that as early as 1769 there was agitation in the industry to exclude women from various jobs (e.g., operating knitting frames). In 1818, women were excluded from both the Manchester Spinners and the Manchester Small Weavers' Societies (Neff 1929: 32). By 1829, at a meeting of the cotton spinners of the United Kingdom in Manchester (an early attempt to organize a national rather than a local union), the spinners laid down the rule "that the union shall include only male spinners and piecers" (ibid.).

After the formal repeal of the anticombinations law in 1824, "one of the major tasks undertaken by [the new] unions was to try to control entry" of new workers (Fraser 1970: 97). In fact, both of the national conferences of cotton spinners, held on the Isle of Man in 1829 and at Manchester in 1830, were primarily concerned with the need to restrict entry by new workers. While such efforts were aimed at restricting entry by immigrant adult male labor (especially immigrants from Ireland) as well as by women and children, the new workers of principal concern were children and young women.

Our point is that the Ten Hours Movement, rather than suddenly arising in 1830 like some humanitarian phoenix in response to the social injustice of the time, was in reality the consistent extension of efforts in the textile industry by skilled adult male labor to quash competition in the labor market. The most significant difference between these earlier and largely unsuccessful attempts and the Ten Hours Movement is that the latter successful restrictionist efforts were cloaked in moralistic rhetoric whereas the earlier attempts were generally quite frank concerning their actual purpose.

Another important difference between the Ten Hours Movement and the earlier agitation involves the tactics chosen to achieve a closed labor market. Action prior to 1830 tended usually to have a local emphasis (leading to strikes and riots), whereas the Ten Hours Movement concentrated its energies on influencing Parliament to provide an effective legislative remedy. While there were attempts to achieve labor market restrictions by legislative means prior to 1830 in the textile industry—for example, there was agitation as early as 1806–7 among cotton workers for a Parliamentary Minimum Wage Bill, which would have tended to price children out of this market (Wood and Wilmore 1927: 148)—much effort was dissipated in generally ineffective local action.

Children and Women as Competing Labor Suppliers

The conventional view among historians has been that children were complementary labor inputs to adult male operatives in the textile production process. This claim seems plausible; small children were almost exclusively employed as piecers in cotton mills and performed odd jobs and janitorial chores and in general assisted the machine operators. Because of the training and physical strength required to operate machinery, especially the cotton-spinning mules, children under 12 were not substitutes for adult labor.

Typically, historians have extended this contention, arguing that adolescents and women were not competitive with adult males. This seems less obvious; a 15-year-old boy or a woman would seem as capable of operating any machine as adult males. However, in the conventional explanation an additional assumption is made that evades this problem and seemingly serves to explain why the potential substitutes did not become actual competitors. This is the assumption that women and children in textile mills were wives and children of adult male operatives in the same mills. Obviously, in such a circumstance family as opposed to individual (male) income was being maximized, and restrictive legislation would tend to have "the immediate effect ... [of a] reduction in real income per family" (Blaug 1958: 225). Rational male operatives would not have pursued legislative restrictions as an attempt at wealth maximization in this case. This reasoning will not stand up to close examination. The argument involves three major fallacies.

First, abundant evidence indicates that older children, adolescents, and adult women were close substitutes for adult male labor in the cotton textile industry. This became increasingly true as the nineteenth century progressed, as a direct result of technological progress. Even Gaskell, who enthusiastically supported legislation restricting women's employment in factories, acknowledged that increasing mechanization was rapidly eliminating by the 1830s what comparative advantage adult males had previously enjoyed (Gaskell 1968: 146). By 1832, "women were to be found in almost every department of the cotton factories"; until the passage of legislation restricting the employment of women in 1844, women were even mule spinners – the elite among skilled cotton workers (Neff 1929: 24).

It has been maintained by Neff, by Pinchbeck (1969: 186–97) and others, that replacement of adult men by women on the larger mules was usually impossible due to the great physical strength required to operate these machines. This was probably true but beside the point. There is no question that women could operate smaller mules and that the elasticity of technical substitution between larger and smaller mules was quite high. It remained feasible – prior to the Factory Acts – for women to undercut the wages of men by performing basically identical work on smaller mules. Similar employment opportunities existed for adolescents of both sexes except in the most highly skilled positions.

Second, the assumption that child labor was a necessary complement to the labor of adult males (and hence in no way represented a competing labor supply) is fallacious on two counts. Children performed no function in the production process that could not have been performed by adults; it was technically feasible to replace children in the mills with adults. In fact, increasing restrictions on the employment of children in the textile mills tended to lead to their replacement by women and later by adult men. The Factory Act of 1833 led to a gradual replacement of children by women in the mills (Pinchbeck 1969: 198). The Factory Acts of 1844 and 1847 led to replacement of children and women by men in unskilled positions. Neff reports: "By 1844 the spectacle of men doing nothing or doing the work of children excited the indignation of the factory inspectors" (1929: 51).

But more obviously, small children do not remain small children forever. Even if, say, 10-year-olds were not close substitutes for 20-year-olds, they would tend to become substitutes as they grew older. Moreover, there is considerable evidence indicating that employers in the textile industry preferred to hire future adult workers as children. According to the testimony of Edward Brown (a Manchester mill owner) before the Parliamentary Children's Employment Commission in 1833; "Those employed from infancy are always the best hands" (British Parliamentary Papers 1968: *Industrial Revolution*, vol. 3, p. 167).

This helps to explain why the Ten Hours Movement focused its attention on obtaining legislation restricting the employment of children, and was evidently not concerned with competition from adult males in other trades or immigrants. A 35-year-old man was commonly considered to be too old to learn a trade (British Parliamentary Papers 1968: *Industrial Revolution*, vol. 7, p. 16). Ure maintained in 1835 that: "it is found nearly impossible to convert persons past the age of puberty, whether drawn from rural or from handicraft occupations, into useful factory hands" (1967: 15). In short, skilled male operatives in the textile industry did not face significant competition from unskilled men. By contrast, children, over the relevant time span, were significant competitors.

Finally, the family joint-income maximization claim is based on a false assumption. Neither the children nor the women working the mills were usually related to the male operatives. This is another example of an intuitively plausible claim that just happens to be wrong. A survey was taken in 1833 of 1,833 Sunday School children, of whom 426 boys and 823 girls were employed in factories in 1833. Of these, 40 percent of the boys and 50 percent of the girls stated that they were unaware that either of their parents had ever worked in a factory; of the rest, in only a few cases did the children report that one or both parents worked in the same factory as they (Edwards and Lloyd-Jones 1973: 313).

Most women in the cotton mills were unmarried. Neff maintains that mill owners and some factory inspectors stated that married women were seldom employed in factories (1929: 40). More substantially, Hewitt concludes from an analysis of 1851 Lancashire census data that only about 26 percent of the total female labor force in the cotton mills were either married or widowed; earlier, this percentage was probably smaller (1958: 11).

Of course, restrictions on competition from children and women would be irrelevant if the supply of other adult males who were substitutes for the skilled male operatives was perfectly elastic. Any rents created by restricting entry of children and women would then have been rapidly dissipated by the entry of other adult men. However, it is apparent that the supply curve of adult male skilled cotton operatives was not highly elastic. Only the subset of potential adult male employees with a history of factory employment would be considered for employment in the industry (due to concern with discipline problems), and training in the necessary skills was costly and time-consuming. But most important, the fact that the Ten Hours Movement continued its restrictionist efforts over a period of almost 20 years suggests that a perfectly elastic supply of adult male skilled operatives was not serving to dissipate rents, unless we assume that the members of the Ten Hours Movement were irrationally investing in political action.

The core of our argument thus far is that skilled male textile workers had a clear economic incentive to seek legislated restrictions on labor market competition from children, adolescents, and women.[8]

THE POLITICAL POWER OF THE OPERATIVES

Even if a convincing argument can be made that the male operatives were primarily motivated by the desire to restrict the supply of competing labor, a mechanism remains to be identified through which they were able to influence the political process. According to Marvel, "the franchise did not extend to the operatives" (1977: 382). Notwithstanding this comment, a good case can be made that the skilled operatives could vote. Indeed, considerable numbers of adult male operatives were probably eligible to vote in the parliamentary election of December 1832.

Prior to 1832, the franchise in England was basically restricted to the middle- and upper income brackets. Voting qualifications varied considerably between boroughs and districts, but their impact was fairly uniform. Working people (e.g., cotton spinners) did not have an income high enough to qualify to vote.

The Reform Act of 1832 changed this situation. The franchise in England was extended to adult males who owned or rented homes worth £10 or more per annum (Halevy 1950: 36). While the qualifications varied across districts, the requirements were fairly uniform in practice. Still, £10 was a considerable sum to spend on housing in the 1830s, and many working people probably had incomes insufficient to qualify them to vote. Thus, their interests could be ignored by Parliament at relatively low cost. But was this true of the textile operatives?

The prime movers in the Ten Hours Movement were the skilled cotton operatives. More specifically, Ward (1962: 52–53) makes clear that the centers of the movement were Lancashire and to a lesser extent Yorkshire and neighboring Cheshire. According to data derived from the *Supplementary Report from the Factory Commissioners* of March 1834 (Wing 1967: clxxxvi), the average annual income of male cotton mill employees in Lancashire between the ages of 21 and 51 was £50.27. At this income the average Lancashire operative spending 20 percent of his income on housing would have spent just over £10 per annum on rent, making him eligible to vote.[9]

These figures are biased downward because the wages of male spinners are averaged in with the lower wages of male piecers, warpers, and weavers. Collier (1974: 69) cites another official report from which it can be deduced that the average annual earnings for adult male cotton spinners in Lancashire and Cheshire amounted to £66.04. The implied housing expenditure in this case is £13.2 per annum. But apparently the wages in some cotton mills were higher still for spinners. Collier (1964: 17) reports data that suggest that spinners employed in 1833 in Thomas Houldworth's mill were earning between £86.84 and £110.37 per annum. These spinners could easily have spent £10 a year on housing.

It is undoubtedly true that the majority of male operatives could not vote, even after 1832, because their annual incomes were not high enough to generate the required housing expenditure. But a large minority, including most cotton spinners, could have voted after 1832. Halevy cites a speech given by Lord John Russell before the House of Commons in December 1831 in which it was claimed that in a fairly typical Manchester cotton mill, 31 of 108 householders were eligible to vote (1950: 35–36, n. 3). Such evidence suggests that the textile operatives constituted a significant voting bloc.

Furthermore, the writing was on the wall with regard to franchise reform as early as the beginning of 1831 (Halevy 1950: 22), which makes the rapid growth of the operatives' movement after 1830 understandable. By February 1832, the £10 qualification had been officially approved in committee. The operatives, especially the cotton spinners, would have been rational to expect that the increased political clout provided by the franchise would extend to them in the near future.

This helps explain the events surrounding the Sadler Committee Hearings. Michael Sadler of Leeds was the spokesman for the operatives' movement in Parliament. In December 1831, he introduced a bill to limit the working day (of everyone) to 10 hours (Marvel 1977: 382). The bill seems to have been a stalking horse for restrictions on the employment of children and adolescents. This is apparent when the minutes of evidence of the Select Committee appointed to study the bill are examined (Wing 1967). The witnesses were exclusively questioned about the conditions for children and young people working in textile mills, and they provide a uniformly dismal view of the conditions.

The committee was run by Sadler and basically represented the views of the operatives' movement. The composition of the group called to testify is instructive. The hearings were divided into three parts. Sixty witnesses were called before the Committee in "Class I" (Wing 1967: 1–92). Of this group 58 were males. The average age of males testifying was 33.5 years. No one under 14 testified, although two 14-year olds appeared. Of the total of 60 witnesses, 54 men identified themselves as cotton industry operatives. About two-thirds of these were spinners, and the rest were overlookers (supervisors) whose wages usually exceeded those of the spinners (Collier 1964: 69).

The composition of the two additional groups of witnesses was also predictable. "Class II" basically included Oastler, founder of the Ten Hours Movement in 1830, and written testimony by 14 ministers and three school teachers (Wing 1967: 93–110). This testimony emphasized the necessity for getting children out of factories and into school (during this period most ministers operated schools of some sort).[10]

"Class III" was composed of 20 physicians who offered a unanimous portrayal of the medical horrors resulting from the labor of children in mills (Wing 1967: 111–255). The Althorp Act was good to physicians, considerable numbers of whom were employed as factory health inspectors. As enacted, the law required textile mill owners to obtain certificates from physicians certifying both the age and the health status of their nonadult employees (Chapman 1904: 92).

Of course, Marvel (1977: 382–83) and most other writers maintain that Sadler's committee, while responsible for bringing the horrors of child labor to public attention, did not itself lead directly to the Althorp Bill of 1833. They argue that the Royal Commission of 1833 (which included Chadwick, Smith, and Tooke as commissioners) was the more important influence on the passage of the legislation.

Our view is that the Sadler committee is important, not because it led directly to the 1833 Factory Act but, rather, because it serves as a convenient showcase for the composition and motivations of the Ten Hours Movement. But a close examination of the Royal Commission is also consistent with our theory. Manufacturers from Lancashire and elsewhere testified virtually unanimously that they opposed the proposed regulations on the hours of children in the textile industry. Operatives, again principally male and older, testified overwhelmingly in favor of restrictions on the hours of children (British Parliamentary Papers 1968: *Industrial Revolution*, vol. 3).[11]

The December election of 1832, which preceded the passage of the 1833 Act, resulted in an overwhelmingly Whig victory (with 500 of 658 members of the new Parliament being Whigs; Halevy 1950: 61). The number of radicals, who were supporters of Althorp's Act, increased dramatically. Most of these men were from Lancashire and other large textile districts (Halevy 1950: 64). The link between the Reform Act of 1832 and Althorp's Bill appears to have been important.

Although there was sporadic parliamentary debate concerning the details of the later Factory Acts, formal testimony was not taken again from interested parties until the 1870s. It appears that once the wedge in the form of the 1833 act was achieved, the passage of later legislation was achieved at significantly reduced cost to proponents.

CONCLUSION

The conventional wisdom among historians has long held that the Factory Acts represented the legislative response to a sudden and dramatic upswell of protest against the inhumanities of child labor. We have also seen that recent attempts by economists to displace the conventional wisdom are fraught with problems. Our explanation—that the Factory Acts represented an attempt by skilled male operatives to restrict competition from children, adolescents, and adult women— is a strong alternate hypothesis, simple in design and in accord with the historical evidence we have been able to gather.[12]

Perhaps the most significant evidence in this regard is that those supposedly helped by the legislation perceived its effects differently. Adult women fought the restrictive regulations affecting them vehemently. As early as 1832, when the proposal that "females of any age" be excluded from "manufactories" began to be discussed, female operatives in Todmorden organized in opposition (Pinchbeck 1969: 199-200). Women opposed labor unions in the textile industry well into the 1850s (Neff 1929: 34). The organized opposition of women to the Factory Acts—which by 1874 had extended beyond the textile industry—became increasingly vocal by the 1870s. The Short-Time Bill of 1873 "encountered great opposition from the female organizations," which the Webbs found ironic in view of the bill's alleged purpose of relieving the suffering of women and children (1920: 311). In the 1870s and 1880s women were excluded from the annual Trades Union Congresses (Pelling 1963: 80-81). The Factory Acts Commission of 1876 took evidence from a number of working class women who came to protest legislative interference with adult female labor; the Working Women's Provident League resolved almost unanimously to urge Commissioners "in the direction of repeal rather than of further restrictions" (Hutchins and Harrison 1966: 189-90). Organized opposition among women to the Factory Acts continued without much result for the rest of the century (ibid.: 185-89).

Finally, we have been able to identify the political mechanism through which male laborers were able to influence Parliament; after 1832, cotton spinners (the core of the Ten Hours Movement) apparently had the vote and constituted a sizeable, cohesive, and active voting bloc. There is also the possibility that other interest groups may have benefited as a result of the Factory Acts. Beginning with the 1833 Act, medical inspection of factories was mandated, increasing the demand for physicians. Education clauses in the Factory Acts increased the demand for teachers. Reductions in job opportunities for children and women in textile mills may have reduced wages for farm help, thereby profiting landowners. Households may have enjoyed an expanded supply of maids, who would otherwise have been employed in factories. Additional research on the role of these potential supplementary interest groups could prove fruitful.

NOTES TO CHAPTER 13

1. The first important Factory Act was Althorp's Bill, passed in 1833. This legislation prohibited factory labor by children under age 9, and placed various restrictions on the length of the work day for children and adolescents. The 1844 Act extended legal restrictions on the length of the workday to women. The 1847 and 1850 bills reduced hours of women and children still further. For a more detailed discussion, see *Palgrave's Dictionary of Political Economy* (Higgs 1925: vol. 2, pp. 4-8).

2. For Mises's discussion see Mises 1966: 612-23. In reference to the Factory Acts he writes: "They delayed the accumulation of capital, thus slowing down the tendency toward a rise in the marginal productivity of labor and in wage rates. *They conferred privileges on some groups of wage earners at the expense of other groups*" (p. 622, emphasis added).

3. Ashworth's opposition to the Althorp Bill is not consistent with Marvel's model. Boyson reports that "[Ashworth family] had never run their mills for more than 69 hours a week and as they employed no children below the age of nine, they were unaffected by the legislation" (1970: 160). Furthermore, it is apparent that Ashworth basically favored the Althorp Bill. In fact, he proposed a mandatory 6-hour limitation to the workday for children under 12, and stated that he believed in compulsory full-time education for children in this age group. He evidently objected only to the Althorp Bill's provisions for Home Office as opposed to local enforcement and other practical details (ibid., pp. 159-160).

4. This is one of the clear conclusions drawn in the Royal Commission's First Report (British Parliamentary Papers 1968: *Industrial Revolution*, vol. 3, p. 34).

5. Other weather-related problems for water-powered mills included floods (which could have the effect of "drowning" the wheel causing a stoppage) and (especially in northeast Scotland) ice; losses from freezing were rare elsewhere in the United Kingdom. But drought was by far the most serious problem. (See Tunzelman 1978: 170–71.)

6. According to Farnie, "[Steam power's] main advantage in the elimination of any natural restrictions upon the production of power increased when factory legislation from 1819 limited the 'making up' of time lost during summer droughts" (1979: 52). From 1820, it became increasingly common for water-powered mills located on less dependable streams to invest in supplementary steam-power in the form of an auxiliary steam engine. By the 1830s, this solution was "widespread" (Tunzelman 1978: 171). The same author reports that by 1833 most firms outside the immediate Pennine valleys of Derbyshire, Nottinghamshire, Lancashire, Yorkshire, and Cheshire had adopted auxiliary steam power (ibid.).

7. The empirical part of Marvel's paper also has problems. Marvel's "rough estimate of the magnitude of these quasi-rents" (the net wealth transfer effected by the 1833 Act) is not measured directly, but indirectly, employing a proxy in the form of the average annual percentage of days lost to water-powered mills as a result of adverse weather conditions. The data on which he bases his calculations are derived from a survey of water-powered mill owners taken after the passage of the 1833 Act. These men maintained that the irregularity of their water supplies would cause them to lose a substantial percentage of their annual output without "make-up time" provisions. In other words, Marvel bases his calculation of the approximate magnitude of quasi-rents on statements of interested parties who had a clear incentive to overreport downtime. A common complaint among factory inspectors throughout the 1830s and 1840s concerned mills that were partially water-powered using the "make-up time" provisions of the 1833 Bill to evade the regulations (making phoney claims of time lost during droughts). For example, see the testimony of J. J. Howell (British Parliamentary Papers 1968: *Industrial Revolution*, vol. 7, p. 3).

8. We also note that the view that the Ten Hours Movement was aimed not at restricting the competition of women and children but at achieving a 10-hour day for all workers is not a very strong argument. There is no good reason to think that the labor market of the time would not have accommodated a demand by workers for a 10-hour day.

9. The Royal Commission on the Housing of the Working Class reported in 1884–85 that 88 percent of members of the working classes spent over 20 percent of their annual incomes on housing (British Parliamentary Papers 1970: vol. 2, p. 29).

10. According to Ward (1962), the demands for education clauses in the various factory acts came primarily from teachers. To other groups education clauses were of minor importance at best (p. 151).

11. This evidence is even more interesting when placed in proper context. The commission regarded the voluntary testimony of operatives as reliable and honest, and the legally compulsory testimony of factory masters as sus-

pect. Legally, the commission was empowered to "reexamine" masters as often as it liked, suggesting possible harrassment of more hostile employers. The instructions to the commissioners include the following statement: "You will in general take the evidence of the employers of labourers the last; you will however, should any material contradiction be made to the evidence of the preceding witnesses, re-examine them, or give them an opportunity of answering any new allegations made in evidence" (British Parliamentary Papers 1968: *Revolution*, vol. 3, p. 4).

12.   Legislative restrictions on competition from children and women were achieved by interest groups of nontextile male workers as well. Adult male mineworkers were the principal influence on Parliament for controls in the mining industry, and in 1842, Parliament passed an act that prohibited employment in mines of women and of males under age 10 and restricted the use of adolescents to unskilled positions.

V POSSIBILITIES OF REFORM

14 TAMING THE RENT-SEEKER

Kenneth J. Koford and David C. Colander

The analysis of rent-seeking, cartelization, or DUP activities has been rather like the analysis of the weather: much discussion and complaining, but few suggestions for improvement. This chapter attempts to alleviate that failing. It addresses the policy problem rent-seeking poses for economics and examines a menu of policies that society might use to reduce the harm it causes.

The first question that must be addressed is What is rent-seeking? In their critique Warren Samuels and Nicholas Mercuro (Chapter 4) argue that the analysis of rent-seeking is merely an attempt to institute a conservative bias favoring status quo institutions. They argue that since attempts to change the rules are an important tool for redistribution, rent-seeking's focus on output and efficiency reducing activities is merely a way of classifying all attempts to redistribute income as bad and to create an implicit bias against political action. Although we agree that rent-seeking could be used in such a fashion, it need not be. In our view, *output* and *efficiency* in the rent-seeking literature are used as shorthand notation for social utility. Thus, the term *waste* is used as a proxy for those situations in which there will be a reduction in social welfare.

To make this analysis clear, the underlying social welfare function must be specified. As mentioned in the introduction and spelled out more carefully in Colander (1983), we believe that this implicit function is a Kantian one (one in which individuals judge an issue in reflective equilibrium considering general distributional consequences but not any specific distributional effects on themselves). Thus, an attempt to lobby, say, for a program favoring the poor, would not be classified as rent-seeking. Moreover, for many policy questions, the distributional effects are unclear. In such cases what happens to total output is a reasonable proxy for what happens to social welfare. These qualifications add a subjective element to the concept of rent-seeking. Nonetheless, we believe there is a relatively large set of activities that almost all economists would agree can be described as rent-seeking. In this category we include attempts to monopolize (via restrictive trade practices such as Tullock's egg cartel example), lobbying for quotas and tariffs, and attempts to prevent entry into labor and product markets.

Our purpose in this chapter is not to determine which activities qualify as rent-seeking, but to provide a menu of policies that might be used to reduce the amount of those activities that individuals agree are rent-seeking activities. Thus, while we would be willing to defend the proposition that many particular activities deserve to be called rent-seeking, we do not do so here.

The available policy menu is diverse, ranging from conservative policies of limiting governmental collective action to liberal incomes policies. We consider such diverse policies to emphasize that neoclassical political economics is inherently neither liberal nor conservative. It is, rather, an approach that recognizes that self-seeking individuals attempt to influence policies to benefit themselves and that such actions have a predictable effect on the policies actually chosen. Any policy proposal must take these actions into account.

We present our policy menu in the optimistic spirit that ideas make a difference. Unlike Professor Stigler (1982a, b), we do not propose these ideas merely to increase our potential marketability, although we do not oppose such an outcome; we believe economists make a difference and that the current balance of forces can be changed by economists. In our view, new ideas, like other innovations, play a role in policymaking and in the evolution of institutions. We see economists' role as that of institutional entrepreneurs, suggesting institutional changes and explaining their consequences. Fortunately for us, but unfortunately for society, in this field there is little competition.[1]

The problem of taming rent-seekers can alternatively be expressed as a problem of devising institutions that can change rent-seeking into profit-seeking. As the previous chapters of this book show, distinguishing between the two is not easy and requires a value judgment as to whether the new institutional arrangement is superior to the old.[2] The question is complicated because almost all activities include both types of seeking behavior; profit-seeking is merely self-seeking activity that generates sufficient positive externalities (along with the negative externalities) for us to consider the outcome socially superior.

The question we address is this: What can be done to reduce the success of such rent-seeking activities? The menu of policy proposals we consider is the following.

1. Provide information on the existence of rent-seeking activity.
2. Create a climate of moral attitude or an ideology opposed to rent-seeking.
3. Improve the process of adjusting property rights.
4. Create sunset provisions so that undesirable institutional restrictions created by rent-seeking naturally erode.

5. Buy out monopoly positions.
6. Change the institutional framework so that all rent-seeking is more difficult—for example, by establishing demand-revealing mechanisms.
7. Tax specific rent-seeking activities and subsidize rent-destroying and anti-
   rent-seeking activities.

PROVIDE INFORMATION IN
RENT-SEEKING ACTIVITIES

If there were perfect information about peoples' intentions, rent-seeking
would be significantly reduced. If a group has to say, "this tariff will increase
my wealth at another group's expense," they are less likely to win its approval
than if they argue that they want it for humanitarian reasons. Economists play
an important role in limiting such activities by providing a second opinion of the
underlying reasons for policy proposals.

An example of the type of information we have in mind was recently reported in *Fortune*.[3] It seems that a strong lobbying effort was made to change
building codes to prohibit polyvinyl chloride (PVC) pipes, ostensibly because of
the fire hazard associated with them.[4] We do not know the merits of the case,
but the article pointed out that the leader of the lobbying was a steel company
whose share of the conduit market had fallen from 50 percent to 32 percent,
largely because of competition from PVC pipes. That information was sufficient
for us and, we suspect, the editors of *Fortune*, to question the arguments against
PVC. Without that information, the stated fire hazard argument for change
would have seemed more persuasive. Thus, the very analysis of rent-seeking reduces its quantity, especially if there is a broad consensus among economists
that it is a rent-seeking activity.

CREATE AN IDEOLOGY OR A CLIMATE OF MORAL
ATTITUDES OPPOSED TO RENT-SEEKING

When individuals believe that the society's rules are fair and just, they are more
likely to play within the existing set of rules. Fair and just rules are likely to
limit rent-seeking behavior. McPherson (Chapter 5) points out that most people
prefer cooperative solutions to ones involving conflict because they consider
them fairer. Both he and North (Chapter 2) point out that the very operation of
the market requires cooperative attitudes, which limit individuals' self-seeking.
Thus, contrary to Milton Friedman and many libertarians, we do not see calls
for businesses and individuals to do good as fundamentally misguided. The difficulty with action based upon cooperation is that it may be unstable. When cooperation succeeds, a society is far more efficient, but as soon as even one individ-

ual takes advantage of the system, the cooperative effort is likely to give way to a free for all. Thus cooperation must be, in large part, self-enforcing.

Social attitudes or ideologies are one important means of enforcing cooperation. To return to our previous example, an ideology that presumes that private firms' lobbying efforts are socially harmful will make such efforts less likely to be attempted. An ideology that approves of action based upon a perception of society's interests will reinforce such action.

While some actions for the "public interest" are efforts of people to work out personal problems by acting them out in society, and virtually all actions combine self-interest with public interest, we believe that, on average, public spirited actions in which the individual has no specific interest are less likely to be rent-seeking activities. Society might properly favor nonprofit organizations and encourage the education of youth by such organizations. We would emphasize, however, that desire to "do good" absent of information of *how to accomplish that goal*, can easily do harm. Better information is a prerequisite for the creation of better attitudes.

IMPROVE THE PROCESS OF ADJUSTING PROPERTY RIGHTS

In order to operate effectively a society must have a set of rules as James Buchanan and Gordon Tullock (1962) and Richard Posner (1973) have argued in their analysis of the role of the constitution and law. However, they both skirt the difficult question of how, as societies evolve, that set of rules and hence property rights are supposed to change. Clearly, rules cannot be changed instantaneously in response to evolving problems; if they were they would no longer be rules. But neither can they remain unchanged indefinitely.[5] Thus there is a constant tension between the need for change and the need for rules, a tension with which economists have not come to grips.

Technical change provides an example of the type of changes that require an evolving or changing institutional structure. Gains from innovation occur in a variety of ways. Some make property rights boundaries that were once clear, indistinct, in a way that allows the entrepreneur to appropriate some other's property. Others create new areas of property rights. Ideally, the property rights structure would be set up so that innovators and entrepreneurs profit by actions that are socially beneficial and do not profit from ones that are not. But under private rent-seeking, this is often not the case. For example, a product might increase social welfare, but not have a value that can be readily captured by the firm or individual who creates the product.[6] These are goods that are not defined as such; we might think of a book, film, or recording whose value is reduced by illegal but unpreventable copying.

On the other side are innovations that allow the appropriation of others' property, for example video tape recorders that allow the unauthorized taping of films. Such recording increases households' convenience of viewing of films shown on television but also allows households to appropriate films without paying the producer for them. The recorder has value partly because of its convenience—which increases social welfare—and partly because it allows users to take others' property without paying for it. In the short run such actions may increase social welfare, but in the long run they may not because the expectations of future appropriation will prevent the initial development of that and similar goods.

The policy problem in these examples occurs because property rights are public goods. For these rights to be developed (say, by general laws governing the use of land, fisheries, airwaves, or the "normal use" of consumer products in warranties), it must be in some party's interest to expend substantial resources to find a new definition of rights. But by the nature of the case, since we are talking about a new right, there is insufficient incentive for every affected party to worry about the right. So the most interested party has a strong incentive to act, and the structure of rights that develops is most likely to reflect narrow individual interests rather than the social interest.

This evolution of property rights raises complicated issues. Property rights are partly a matter of custom and partly a matter of contract; hence, if one party can be the "first mover," it can establish the custom in a way that maximizes its returns. The example of the video tape recorders indicates that the first mover can also set up a pattern of custom and contract that imposes costs upon others and thus become a subtle form of rent-seeker. To meet this problem, society needs not only a set of rules governing property rights; it also needs a set of rules governing how property rights change.[7]

At present there are two forms of rules governing evolving property rights; one has been fairly successful, while the other has largely failed. The relatively successful model is that of the patent office. Patents are awarded partly to encourage innovation and partly to encourage innovators to make their innovation public. In a sense, the patent office creates new property rights according to a general rule. But while the innovator gains monopoly profits from an innovation, those gains are only temporary, according to a fixed rule.

The relatively unsuccessful model is of the more traditional areas of regulation, which were developed because of property rights problems in areas of technical innovation. Often parties claimed "predation" and "chaos," using that claim to demand governmental action. Regulation was adopted to create a system of property rights for the new industry. For example, the FCC was created because no idea of how to create private property rights in airwaves existed when radio was developed. In railroads and airlines, a rationale for regulation existed because a transport system was a public good to the industry as a whole. Each railroad attempted to impose control over its competitors via the need for some organization of the industry.

This history suggests a model for future areas of new technology, where property rights are not well-established. The model follows from the observation that initially, economists often have little idea of desirable property rights or a reasonable organization of industry but that, over time, economists generally develop concepts of property rights that would allow the industry to operate more competitively. The model would be to set up an agency that would establish a procedural structure of property rights for a decade or two that gives the innovator high profits but no right to impose costs upon others. The agency might, while designing a new property rights structure, find one that would automatically be turned over to the private market after a decade or two. Thus, in areas such as recorded performances (movies and video) and other forms of intellectual property, such an agency would attempt to devise a more appropriate means of maintaining property rights than that for publishing, which has so clearly broken down.

In areas such as computer software, new life forms, and product liability, which are not easily defined as either books or gadgets, the property rules are currently in total disarray, and the industries reflect it. An agency such as that proposed would determine an appropriate property rights form, endow the industry with it, and then after monitoring the system for some years, would withdraw automatically from any further role in the development of the industry. The industry would enter into new rules of this sort upon request from either the courts, the executive branch, or members of some industry, who could correctly point to rent-seeking behavior because of some absence of established property rights.

CREATE SUNSET PROVISIONS

A key aspect of the foregoing discussion of rules governing evolving property rights is that it reflects the reality that special interests initially dominate the political process but then, over time, the general interest becomes better known. Sunset provisions in all laws allow for change in as orderly a fashion as possible, in a manner recognizing the simultaneous need for rules and change.

In the early development of the United States, one could even make an argument for having established limits on ownership rights to land, say 150-year leases, after which time ownership of the land reverts back to the government. Had the federal government done so with its initial land grants, it is likely that much of the private incentive to settle and develop the land could have been maintained, but the general increase in value would not have stayed with private individuals, but could have gone to the state, reducing the need for income taxes. Henry George's dream could have come true.[8] Hong Kong has, roughly, such a system.

The argument that sunset provisions will have few negative incentive effects relies on a difference between the acquisition of knowledge by special interests and by the general public. The special interests that demand some new statute or regulation are usually the only sources of "expertise" to cope with the new "problem." If a solution is to be found, it will reflect their interests. After some years of experience with their solution it is at least a fair probability that others will understand the problem too. At that point the special interests will not be anxious to give up laws or regulations in their favor. A sunset provision automatically requires that they do so. To reinstate the law, the special interests would have to persuade the now better informed majority that the law was really in their interest.[9]

BUYING OUT MONOPOLY POSITIONS

Despite the best efforts of institutional entrepreneurs, rent-seeking will occur, leaving undesirable rules and restrictions in its wake. One would think that these rules could merely be eliminated; unfortunately they cannot. Gordon Tullock (1975) has neatly captured the problem in his discussion of the transitional gains trap. Individuals, in capturing short-run gains, leave behind a myriad of trade restrictions and limitations that serve no purpose.[10] But the rents have already been captured as the original owners have sold out to others. Thus, it would be unfair merely to reverse the process if the present owners had a legitimate right to expect the regulation to continue.

Sunset provisions remove some of the problem because they remove the legitimacy from the expectations and reduce the value of any monopoly right, but they will not remove it completely. There is one aspect of such rent-seeking that offers a potential solution, however. Even in the absence of sunset provisions the value of those restrictions is unlikely to be equal to the maximum value a monopoly could extract. As Tullock argues, establishing the restrictions is likely to be difficult. They will be set once and left. If one chooses the correct historical moment when the value of those restrictions to the monopolists is low, in some instances it may be possible to reverse the process, via government buy-outs of monopoly positions with lump-sum payments.[11] Societies often bribe past rent-seekers to accept change by grandfathering, the practice of exempting existing individuals from a rule change. Buyouts are what might be called super-grandfathering, whereby individuals maintain not just a monopoly but a contractual right to the value of their monopoly position in exchange for reducing the restrictions on future producers. A highly visible example of the negative effects of past rent-seeking is the American steel industry. Some initial calculations suggest that $30 billion would be sufficient to bribe the workers in the steel industry to lower their wages to a level equal to those of steel workers in Japan.[12] At that wage it would be worthwhile for firms to invest and modernize and our steel industry could be competitive.

The serious problem with buyouts as a permanent aspect of government policy is that the possibility of buyouts increases the value of the monopoly restrictions and thus engenders more of the various activities it is designed to eliminate. Thus, a buyout policy clearly should not become a permanent weapon in government's anti-rent-seeking arsenal. However, used as a once and for all policy at the correct historical moment it may be appropriate.[13]

CHANGE THE INSTITUTIONAL FRAMEWORK SO THAT RENT-SEEKING IS MORE DIFFICULT

Self-seeking individuals inevitably seek rents through political action. Such rent-seeking may be reduced by changing the political system to reduce the returns to those seeking political rents. Currently, accommodating rent-seeking appears to be a major activity of U.S. legislatures. William Riker (1962, 1982) has argued that under a simple-majority decision rule, minimum-winning coalitions will continually form, win, and then be succeeded by further minimum-winning coalitions. Each coalition gains by dispossessing the losers; the ultimate result is that everyone has victimized everyone else, and everyone is probably worse off. While Riker's model is a substantial simplification of the political process, we believe that it captures an essential property of the system: A majority can appropriate a minority's property without compensation.[14]

There are two solutions to this problem: Either limit specific activities that are likely to lend themselves to rent-seeking, or establish policies that change the basic structure of political decisionmaking. One example of the first is a constitutional restriction upon activities likely to involve rent-seeking. Such activities include trade tariffs and quotas, specific price ceilings and supports, and subsidies to specific producer or consumer groups. In addition, budget deficits can be the result of rent-seeking raids upon the federal budget and the federal tax system and might also be constitutionally restricted.

In practice, however, constitutional limitations are only a partial solution: Rent-seekers can mobilize to oppose the constitutional limitations and can undermine them either by subtle reinterpretation of the rules or by repeal. Bennett and Di Lorenzo (Chapter 15) show how state constitutional limitations on spending have been evaded. Ultimately, a balance of power favoring the constitutional rule must be maintained or it will be gradually nullified.

Despite the limitations of constitutional restrictions, the current balanced budget amendment probably improves on the current situation, because it does not actually prohibit deficits but, rather, requires an increased majority to obtain passage of budget bills when the budget is in deficit. That increases the power of anti-rent-seeking forces somewhat, although at the cost of limiting potentially worthwhile government projects. An alternative that might also limit rent-seeking might be a permanent increased majority for spending legislation (55 percent of those present and voting).[15] Other constitutional rules that would reduce rent-seeking include, in the broadest form, a ban on restrictions upon private agreements that do not hurt third parties, a guarantee of the free operation of private markets (including free international trade with friendly countries), and a ban on regulation or government taking without compensation. However, each of these raises important and difficult equity concerns.

An alternative approach would be to alter the nature of the voting structure of democratic societies.[16] The argument for such a change is that our political system still seems modeled after the old policy of the German tribes, of counting spears, and letting the more numerous side win (quite reasonably since that side could defeat the other in battle). We have added onto this some of the Roman Republican system, particularly ordeal by committee and debate plus a long gauntlet of potential vetoes.

A voting scheme that would involve less rent-seeking would be a political analog of a competitive market.[17] Rather than our present system, a system of allocating legislators some additional votes, which they could cast on the issues about which they were most concerned, would move closer to a true competitive market. So too would allowing legislators to commit their vote(s) on a particular decision in advance—assuring that vote-trading deals were made, kept, and public. Alternatively it might be possible to move to a full demand-revealing system of votes in Congress, using a vote-unit as the unit of account, and providing each legislator with the same endowment of votes (see Coleman 1983).

Changing voting procedure within government is one approach to reducing political rent-seeking. It is even more crucial to internalize externalities between individual citizens and their representatives, or between individual citizen preferences and state action. Direct voting using demand-revealing mechanisms might do that on issues that are not too technical for ordinary citizens to understand. Or a group of citizens could appeal the laws passed by Congress to a direct popular vote that would use the demand-revealing mechanism. One difficulty with demand-revealing mechanisms in citizens' voting is that they permit inequality, with wealthier citizens having more power over decisionmaking than the less wealthy. A voting scheme with relatively equal endowments seems essential, although a mechanism by which relatively concerned citizens could invest their resources in greater political power has merits as well. Continual citizen voting for legislators, which Tullock (1967) has discussed, would also increase the connection between legislators and the public. In Tullock's mechanism, citizens choose a representative as their own but may freely change their representative at any time. Each representative casts the total number of votes he or she currently represents.

The "approval voting" scheme of Brams and Fishburn (1978) provides an intermediate policy. It moves toward an intensity-measuring system for voters, while not increasing the administrative complexity of elections. Each voter casts a vote for every citizen of whom he or she approves. By reducing the ability of a small, intense minority to gain power over the possibly intense opposition of the majority, it reduces the opportunity for rent-seeking in elections. Incentive payment schemes (such as Clarke taxes), by which voters choose public goods, are a means of providing goods that currently are chosen by governments. For example, consumers value product information, but that information is a public good. A demand-revealing mechanism could have consumers place a value upon the information they might obtain, and then pay for it through that mechanism.

TAX RENT-SEEKING ACTIVITIES AND SUBSIDIZE ANTI-RENT-SEEKING ACTIVITIES

One of the more novel approaches to the problem of rent-seeking is the tax-subsidy approach. Rent-seeking is essentially the process of monopolization. If you want to discourage it, why not tax it? In Chapter 8 Olson and Colander argue that market and tax-based incomes policies (TIPs) do precisely that. Under these policies everyone begins with a certain right to a price per unit of factor inputs he supplies. Any increase in that price per unit involves monopolization (increasing the price per unit of input). A TIP taxes raising one's price or monopolization and subsidizes reducing one's price.

Monopolization occurs for many reasons; some involve entrepreneurial activity such as finding a better way to build a mousetrap; some involve pure luck — demand for one's product could unexpectedly increase; others involve building up monopolies through government. Most economists would agree that it would be beneficial to reduce the building up of monopolies through government. Thus, those aspects of TIPs are positive. However, to determine a TIP's net effect we need to consider the first two. One of the reasons people invest and undertake new activities is that they hope to be lucky. Taxing profits due to luck will therefore reduce some forms of entrepreneurial effort.

While the TIP plans do tax profits, they also subsidize losses, so the net effect of the plans on monopolies that develop from luck is merely a decrease in the variance of entrepreneurial profits, not the overall level. When the projects involve pure rents to monopolistic positions (such as differences in innate abilities), those rents are taxed and this tax seems as close an approximation to a pure tax on rents as one can get. The plans discourage entrepreneurial activity only to the degree that it is not measured as an input; the question is whether this problem outweighs the gain in discouraging rent-seeking. For instance, in the mousetrap example, if the initial research is measured as an input, then the firm receives a subsidy for the initial development and is taxed after the traps are sold. Only if that initial entrepreneurial effort cannot be measured is mousetrap research discouraged.

CONCLUSION

A contradiction is inherent in all the policies we have discussed. The primary way to reduce rent-seeking is to establish collective rules either socially or through government. But the very attempt to limit rent-seeking through government creates new possibilities for rent-seeking. The additional rent-seeking created by policy initiatives could more than offset the reduction in rent-seeking the policy achieves. Thus care must be taken in establishing any new policy.[18] We should also caution that many of these initiatives tend to maintain the status quo distribution of income, which is not necessarily the most just distribution. Thus, one must always keep the distributional issues in mind when finally judging any new proposal.

Although we are enthusiastic about the proposals suggested here we are not optimistic that many of them will be adopted. Our current political system is so based on rent-seeking that establishing policies in the general interest is unlikely. We are, however, not totally without hope. There is a widespread dissatisfaction with the ineffectiveness and shortsightedness of our current institutions. If institutional changes can be shown to remedy those defects, those changes could become extremely popular and widely supported, just as, occasionally, other reforms have been demanded and adopted. Over the long run good institutions eventually will drive out bad ones; if the economy gets bad enough, major institutional changes will be forthcoming. It is in bad economic times such as now that the return to institutional entrepreneurship is highest.

NOTES TO CHAPTER 14

1. The concept of institutional entrepreneur is developed more fully in Lerner and Colander (1983). Economic theory predicts that private organizational entrepreneurs should far outnumber public organizational entrepreneurs because public organization is a public good.

2. The formal specification of a rent-seeking activity is the following: If $a_1 \ldots a_n$ is the set of activities available to be undertaken, and $Sj (a_1 \ldots a_n)$ is individual j's social welfare function, with members of society $j = 1, \ldots J$ we classify an activity a_i as rent-seeking or profit-seeking by the sign of the vector $\partial S/\partial a_i$, defined as $[\partial S_1/\partial a_i, \partial S_2/a_i, \ldots \partial SJ/\partial a_i]$, with $\partial Sj/\partial a_i$ defined as the effect of an increase in activity i on individual j's social welfare function. Those activities for which all individuals agree social welfare is reduced, $\partial S/\partial a_i < 0$, are rent-seeking. Those activities upon which all individuals agree social welfare is increased, $\partial S/\partial a_i > 0$, are true profit-seeking. Those activities in between are ambiguous. These "acitvities" are considered in a long run or constitutional context and are judged by individuals behind a veil of ignorance.

   Because within a social welfare context most activities fall into the ambiguous category, in practice rent-seeking is generally defined as activities that reduce aggregate output, and profit-seeking is defined as activities that increase aggregate output with the proviso kept in the back of one's mind that one is actually concerned with social welfare.

3. *Fortune*, February 7, 1983. Other examples are given by Tullock in Chapter 16 of this book.

4. In a fire, PVC pipes burn, creating black smoke and giving off hydrogen chloride, a corrosive gas that can kill in high concentrations.
5. For a further discussion of this point, see Lerner and Colander 1983.
6. Scherer (1982) argues that a high but variable proportion of the gains from innovation cannot be appropriated by an entrepreneur.
7. The argument can be carried to higher and higher levels.
8. Taxes are, of course, merely a form of governmental partial expropriation of property rights. Had government maintained partial title to begin with, no taxes would be necessary.
9. Another argument that supports sunset provisions concerns the difference between the collective time preference and private time preference. Society is, or should be, concerned about its long-term success, while individual members, on average, may be less concerned. The continuation of society is a public good, and hence gains can exist through collective action. The problem is that in a democracy, the political expression of that social interest on specific issues is more concerned with the short run than the long run. Sunset provisions provide a limit on the political process.
10. Olson (1965, 1982) describes numerous examples of private rent-seeking of this sort.
11. Japan did this to the Samurai during the Meiji restoration.
12. The calculations were made by Brian Napack.
13. It is of course difficult to prevent a one-time policy from being built into expectations for a later time.
14. The traditional political science solution to political rent-seeking has been the creation of "responsible parties," the political parties, which are unwilling to dissipate their capital stock of credibility with voters by favoring special interests. Riker's model shows that our primary system allows candidates to capture the title "Democrat" or "Republican," thereby allowing them a free ride on whatever credibility those titles may retain. Parties then lose most of their meaning, and as primaries have spread, responsible parties have disappeared.
15. Koford (1982a) shows how to calculate optimal majority rules.
16. Proposals along these lines include demand-revealing mechanisms, Tullock's point-voting schemes, and Brams and Fishburn's approval voting scheme. Public Choice, vol. 29, no. 2 (1977) is devoted to a discussion of demand-revealing techniques.
17. While Koford (1982b) argues that centralized vote-trading in legislatures is a fairly close analog to a competitive market, it makes actions efficient only from the legislature's point of view and this legislative market has serious imperfections in any case.
18. In judging the relative degrees of rent-seeking of laissez faire and activist positions, one must remember that new policies initially entail far more opportunities for rent-seeking than do old established policies. But most of the proposals we have discussed are long-run institutional changes and the rent-seeking they initially create is merely part of the set-up costs to be amortized over the life of the policy, when rent-seeking will be reduced.

15 POLITICAL ENTREPRENEURSHIP AND REFORM OF THE RENT-SEEKING SOCIETY

James T. Bennett and Thomas J. DiLorenzo

The problem of reforming the rent-seeking society is widely perceived to be the adoption of an appropriate set of rules to limit the powers of government. The power of the state and its burden on the private sector have been associated with public sector expenditure and employment, both of which have increased dramatically over the past decades in both the United States and the rest of the industrialized world. Thus, reform has centered on efforts, particularly in the United States, to restrict by constitutional amendment the ability of government to borrow, tax, and spend. Revenue is regarded as the lifeblood of the public sector, so that, if public sector income is limited, the intrusiveness and burden of government can be controlled, and the negative-sum game of rent-seeking contained.

Although such a prescription may be appealing, there is ample evidence that statutory and even constitutional limitations on the fisc will, at best, be only a temporary and partially effective restraint. Certainly, it will by no means be a panacea. There is no self-enforcing constitution, and every rule requires interpretation and implementation. Rent-seeking entrepreneurs have every incentive to subvert any limitations on their freedom of action and, as shown below, in the United States and elsewhere these entrepreneurs have found ways to bypass constitutional and statutory constraints on a wide scale. In other words, in response to limitations imposed on their abilities to accumulate power, wealth, and tenure by dispensing the fruits of rent-seeking, politicians have themselves actively engaged in rent-seeking behavior at yet another level, which may be described as

Research support provided by the Sarah Scaife Foundation and the Earhart Foundation is gratefully acknowledged.

217

the avoidance of rent destruction. Elected officials do not passively accept citizen demands for fiscal restraint, but merely exploit loopholes in order to disguise taxes, expenditure, and debt. In effect, there is a public sector underground that is the direct counterpart of the underground private economy. Constraints on budgets and borrowing have been systematically subverted by redefining the budget so that much of the public sector's activity is moved off-budget, beyond the control and scrutiny of the taxpayer. The use by rent-seeking political entrepreneurs of off-budget devices to create an underground government is the focus of this chapter. The discussion proceeds as follows: First, the political motivation for public expenditure and debt is briefly explored. Second, a historical perspective on constitutional constraints on fiscal activities of state and local governments in the United States is provided to show that such limitations have existed for more than a century. Third, a survey is given of off-budget activities at the local, state, and federal levels of government in the United States. Finally, some implications of the analysis for reform of the rent-seeking society are drawn.

THE POLITICAL ECONOMY OF THE POLITICIAN: PUBLIC EXPENDITURE AND DEBT

One of the principal actors in the drama of the rent-seeking society is the politician, whose motivations and political objectives play a major role in shaping public policy. For the politician, income, prestige, power, and perquisites are derived from only one source: tenure in public office. This observation has two important implications. First, a major goal of politicians is to remain in office, and second, the planning and performance of the politician are geared primarily to success in the next election contest—hence, there is an innate bias toward a *short-term time horizon.* The ultimate success or failure of elected public officials is determined in the political arena (at the ballot box), rather than in the marketplace. To remain in office, the politician must appear to satisfy the needs of his or her constituents by providing benefits that are concentrated among supporters while the costs are widely dispersed among all taxpayers and, preferably, deferred in time. Politicians are very well aware of voter/taxpayer attitudes toward government, which may be best described as a love-hate relationship: The public loves the services provided, but hates to pay for them via taxes. National surveys of citizens have repeatedly shown that Americans are strongly in favor of reductions in taxes but at the same time support existing welfare-transfer programs and even the extension of these programs, particularly in the area of health care.[1] Apparently, taxpayers are strong believers in the free lunch (if attitude surveys are taken seriously), and politicians who appear to be able to provide something for nothing are likely to be highly successful at the ballot box.

Every candidate in an election has a strong incentive to appeal to the voters' craving for a free lunch; campaign promises proliferate in every contest, and most are inevitably broken—a fact that has contributed significantly to the distrust and suspicion now directed toward government programs and public institutions. One promise that is rarely made (by a victorious candidate) is that taxes will be raised substantially in order to pay for benefits provided. Once in office, however, the public official must deliver in some way on pledges made during the campaign or risk being discredited by an opponent in the next election. At this point the ideal politician becomes a magician who is able to produce something from nothing: namely, increases in the quantity or quality of public services without corresponding increases in taxes can be achieved by borrowing.[2] Debt is a politician's delight, for it permits large amounts of spending to occur immediately (during the politician's current term of office) with the problems associated with repayment spread over a long period in the future (perhaps even when someone else is in office). Additionally, deferred payments are always attractive to elected officials; witness the fact that pension plans in the public sector are typically far more generous than in the private sector. The budgetary impact of increased pension benefits for current employees does not fully occur until many years in the future; an outright wage increase for public employees produces an immediate effect on government outlays.[3] There is, then, a strong political rationale for substituting improved pension benefits for higher wages and salaries. Expenditure financed by debt provides an ideal strategy for ambitious politicians and has been a principal source of public sector profligacy.

THE LEGACY OF POLITICAL PROFLIGACY: LIMITATIONS ON DEBT AND EXPENDITURE

Constitutional and statutory restrictions on expenditures, taxation, and debt are by no means new or innovative, despite the highly publicized endorsement of a constitutional amendment requiring a balanced federal government budget in the United States. In the 1820s, a great drive was undertaken to provide internal improvements to the economic infrastructure of the states by building roads and canals and by establishing banks. State governments took a very active role in financing these projects by issuing mammoth amounts of debt; indeed, public sector involvement in private sector activities was mandated or encouraged by the state constitutions adopted in the 1820s, for these directed or permitted the legislature to take an active role in furthering internal improvements. The debt was to be repaid from investment income; but mismanagement, fraud, and abuse were common, so that many investments were unprofitable. The borrowing bubble burst in the panic of 1837; many states defaulted and others simply repudiated their debts. Concern about the profligate borrowing by state governments was deep among investors both at home and abroad, not to mention the taxpayers whose taxes were raised dramatically. To avoid future excesses and soothe tax-payer frustrations and to restore investors' confidence in their bonds, constitu-tional limits on debt were imposed at the state level. As new states were formed, debt limits were also incorporated in their constitutions so that the bond offer-ings of these new entities would not be at a competitive disadvantage in the capi-tal markets (Taylor 1951: 373; Bogart 1936).

As a result of this experience, stringent limitations on borrowing still exist that appear to be more than adequate to prevent politicians from plundering the taxpayer's purse. Moreover, there are constitutional as well as statutory bounds on operating deficits—more than half the states have legal provisions that re-quire spending reductions if there is a shortfall in revenue; at least seven states go even further and constitutionally mandate that taxes must be increased to offset any operating deficit.

A similar scenario was replayed during the 1860s and the 1870s when a boom in railroad construction occurred. Because state governments were prohibited from involvement in such ventures, local government politicians undertook mas-sive borrowing to finance the ventures because they deemed the existence of rail service essential to the economic vitality of their communities. Again, much of the expenditure was squandered, and widespread default and repudiation of municipal debt resulted in the 1870s. State legislatures, aroused by irate taxpay-ers, placed stringent restrictions on local government borrowing, authority to tax, and even the terms under which approved debt can be issued (Fishlow 1965: 190; Kirkland 1951: 277).[4]

These restrictions still exist at the state and local levels of government in the United States. Thus, it would appear that various checks have long existed to assure the taxpayer that there is no cause whatever for concern about the abuse of public financing. However, the taxpayer who sleeps soundly because of the security provided by constitutional and statutory protections on public debt is profoundly naïve about the wiles of politicians. Politicians and public employ-ees are adept at developing and exploiting loopholes in the law and, despite the explicit checks and balances that have existed for decades, have found little diffi-culty in overcoming constitutional constraints and statutory restrictions on spending and borrowing.[5]

THE LIMITATIONS OF FISCAL LIMITATIONS: OFF-BUDGET FINANCE

On the surface, it would seem that tax revolts and fiscal constraints in the form of statutory or constitutional restrictions on taxation, spending, or debt pose major problems for ambitious politicians. After all, fiscal limitations of any sort restrict the freedom of action of policymakers in the public sector to pursue their own political goals. When public opinion supports constitutional or statutory limits on taxes, expenditures, and borrowing by government, the politician who ignores the will of the voter does so at his own peril. Elected officials are also aware that a favorable impression can be made on voters by advocating the reduction in the size and scope of government and the improvement in the efficiency of the public sector.

For elected officials, however, continued expansion of the public sector and the associated patronage that can be dispensed to supporters are key elements of success. Ideally, the politician would like to preach fiscal conservatism to his constituents while simultaneously increasing the size and scope of the public sector. Off-budget enterprises, as will be explained, permit politicians to perform this feat. Spending limitations can be avoided by redefining categories of expenditure, and tax limitations can be avoided by the expedient of user fees. The avoidance of restrictions on public debt is more difficult to accomplish and requires a more novel approach than is the case with taxes and expenditures. But politicians are crafty and resourceful in their own interest and the solution they developed was disarmingly simple: Separate corporate entities were created by state and local governments, which could issue bonds that were not subject to the legal restrictions on public debt. These entities masquerade under a variety of guises; they are called districts, boards, authorities, agencies, commissions, corporations, and trusts. Regardless of their title, an essential feature of all these organizations is that their financial activities do not appear in the budget of the governmental unit or units that created them. Thus, politicians have been able to make part of the public sector disappear simply by forming separate entities— off-budget enterprises (OBEs)—to conduct borrowing and spending activities.

The historical roots of off-budget organizations can be traced back at least as far as early eighteenth-century England, where toll bridges were financed by revenue bonds. Bonds were issued to pay for the construction of toll bridges, and toll revenues were pledged to repay the principal and interest on the bonds. One distinguishing characteristic of OBEs is that their operations, at least in theory, are not financed from taxes, but from revenues generated by their activities. The facts differ greatly from the theory. Because the taxpayer is not deemed to be liable for the financial obligations of OBEs, voter approval is not required for the debt issued by such organizations and, more importantly, debt restrictions do not apply. The first American OBE obtained judicial approval from the Supreme Court of Maine in 1899 and, as the political maxim contends, "As Maine goes, so goes the nation" (Morris 1958).[6]

The prototype for off-budget authorities in the U.S. is the Port Authority of New York and New Jersey (modeled after the Port of London Authority) created by Congress in 1921. The widespread adoption of the concept did not occur until the 1930s, when the federal government actively encouraged all units of government to go off-budget on an unprecedented scale. Since then, federal sponsorship of off-budget activity has continued, prodded by the promise of various forms of largesse from the national Treasury in the form of grants-in-aid and subsidies.

Unfortunately, it is simply impossible to obtain accurate data on the number of OBEs that exist or on their activities. Most states do not keep statistics on the number of corporations established by local governments. Indeed, for politicians, an important part of the intrinsic appeal of the OBE device is that its operations are not publicized. One thing is known with certainty: There are thousands of OBEs throughout the nation engaging in a bewildering variety of activities. In the state of Pennsylvania alone there were 2,456 municipal OBEs in operation as of July 1976, and, collectively, these OBEs had almost $5 billion in debt outstanding (Schlosser 1977).

Some statistics are collected by the U.S. Bureau of the Census and, although these are known to be incomplete, the data indicate that almost 26,000 off-budget enterprises were operating nationwide in 1977. This number exceeds the number of on-budget, general purpose units of government in existence.[7] One measure of the scope of off-budget activity is the debt issued by these entities. General purpose (or "on-budget") governments issue only "full faith and credit" debt, which has been approved by the voters in a referendum, with repayment guaranteed by the power to levy taxes. OBEs issue nonguaranteed debt, which has not been approved by voters. By 1978 the amount of outstanding long-term nonguaranteed state debt issued by OBEs stood at $61.1 billion, whereas voter-approved state debt was only $48.3 billion. At the local level of government, nonguaranteed OBE debt outstanding was $85.8 billion in 1978, and the comparable figure for voter-approved debt was $97.1 billion.[8] Thus, the underground government rivals the on-budget public sector in size, at least in terms of debt —government has gone off-budget in wholesale fashion in response to fiscal constraints.

Even if debt restrictions did not exist, politicians would benefit from off-budget activities. The public sector is constrained by numerous regulations designed to protect the public interest. Virtually none of these applies to any OBE. For example, civil service regulations do not apply, so that it is easier for politicians to create patronage jobs off-budget; there are no requirements for competitive bidding procedures on contracts, so that campaign contributions can be obtained and loyal supporters can be rewarded; the members of the boards of directors of every OBE are political appointees, not elected or responsible to voters, so that the will of politicians cannot easily be frustrated by a recalcitrant bureaucracy. OBEs are given wide powers by law: They are granted monopoly franchises, may have powers of eminent domain, can override zoning ordinances, are exempt from regulations and paperwork that strangle private firms, have no legal restrictions on collective bargaining agreements, and are often specifically exempted from antitrust laws regarding price fixing.

The creation of an off-budget entity automatically generates a number of special-interest groups who lobby for the expansion of its activities: The employees, suppliers, contractors (and their unions), and those who participate in marketing the entity's debt such as bond underwriters, banks that act as trustees, and bond attorneys. In each case the individuals in these interest groups are concerned with their private self-interest first and foremost.

The public interest is a phrase that is difficult to define. Although OBEs are touted as existing to further the public interest, such as assertion still does not explain why the public interest should be fostered off-budget where voters do not elect the directors of the enterprise and have no control over the issuance of debt or the rate of spending. The array of activities undertaken by OBEs is nothing short of amazing, including the financing of school buildings, airports, parking lots, recreation centers, courthouses, marketing, shipping and transportation terminals, subways, bridges, tunnels, highways, parks and playgrounds, lakes, sewer systems, landfills, steam heating plants, flood control projects, hospitals and health care centers, industrial development subsidies, water supply systems, sports arenas, electric utilities, and housing, to name a few. Indeed, many of the activities undertaken off-budget by government compete directly with taxpaying private firms. The question is then not so much should these activities be conducted off-budget, as should they be conducted by the public sector at all.

The myth that off-budget finance should not require voter approval because the projects are self-supporting has been shattered by the fact that billions of tax dollars are used to subsidize and support OBE activity. The taxpayer, in reality, is carrying the burden of off-budget operations while the politicians reap the political benefits, as shown by the following examples.

UNDERGROUND GOVERNMENT
IN THE UNITED STATES

As governor of New York, Nelson Rockefeller orchestrated off-budget finance like a maestro during his terms of office between 1959 and 1974. The state constitution contains strict limitations on the issuance of debt; since 1846, a referendum requirement had mandated voter approval of state borrowing. Rockefeller raised taxes rapidly (at an annual rate of 12.6 percent during his first term), but the revenues were hardly sufficient to support his grandiose spending schemes. Voters frequently turned down bond referenda, but opposition to Rockefeller's spending plans was repeatedly ignored by the governor throughout his tenure by simply financing various projects through off-budget enterprises. For example, after 1956 voters had rejected a $100 million housing bond issue for the third time, Governor Rockefeller created the Housing Finance Authority, which issued massive amounts of nonguaranteed debt, at one point in excess of the entire guaranteed debt of New York State. In 1961, voters rejected a $500 million higher education bond issue for the fourth time; the governor created the off-budget State University Construction Fund. In 1965 the voters rejected, for the fifth time, a housing bond issue; the Governor created the Urban Development Corporation. In 1962, Rockefeller's fourth year as governor, there were 125 OBEs in New York State, 26 of them statewide, with a total outstanding debt of $3.3 billion. By the time he resigned from office in 1974, fourteen months before the state faced default and bankruptcy, OBE debt had quadrupled. At $13.3 billion, the OBE debt was approximately four times the amount of guaranteed, voter-approved borrowing, and the debt of the Housing Finance Authority alone exceeded the entire guaranteed debt of the state by about 50 percent! The constitutionally imposed referendum requirement for the issuance of state debt obviously placed no effective constraint whatever on the ambitious spending plans of Rockefeller and other state politicians.

One would be hard pressed to assert that the debt and expenditures were undertaken in the public interest, unless one is willing to assert that the dictates of the voters expressed at the ballot box are irrelevant in determining what is best for society. Repeated attempts by taxpayers to seek redress through the courts have only met with failure. Eventually, so much nonguaranteed debt was issued that investors became suspicious and refused to purchase it. These suspicions were allayed when the "moral obligation" bond was invented; although the legislature was not *legally* bound to repay principal and interest on nonguaranteed debt, it was *morally* obligated to do so under the indentures of moral obligation bonds. Thus, the pyramid of debt continued to grow and the taxpayers have been left on the hook.

As the tax revolt progressed through the 1970s, OBEs proliferated at the state level of government, as did their borrowing and spending. A rough approximation indicates that off-budget enterprises at the state level spent about $106 billion in 1980, whereas on-budget state governments expended about $143 billion in that year. Make no mistake, the rent-seeking politician is alive and well—and thriving off-budget as well as on-budget.

New York's neighbor Pennsylvania is one of the states where OBEs proliferate at the local level of government. The Pennsylvania legislature had imposed constitutional restrictions on municipal borrowing by limiting it to 7 percent of assessed property valuation. However, in 1935 the state legislature enacted the Municipal Authorities Act, which exempted "municipal corporations" from municipal debt restrictions. Numerous OBEs were created to finance the building of schools, airports, parking lots, recreation centers, as well as other facilities.

In the late 1940s, Pennsylvania voters began pressuring their state representatives for limits on local property taxes, much in the spirit of the tax revolt of the 1970s. As a result, in 1949 statutory property tax rate limits were enacted that applied to cities, boroughs, townships, and school districts. Local politicians responded by rapidly increasing the use of the off-budget mechanisms. The number of municipal corporations created tripled in 1950, and the amount of nonguaranteed bonds issued increased by 465 percent, from $11.5 million to

$65 million in that year. Thirty-four school building authorities alone were formed in 1950, compared to a total of fourteen in the preceding fifteen years, and the amount of nonguaranteed debt issued by school building authorities increased by 583 percent, from $2 million to $11.8 million, in 1950 alone. By 1975 the number of OBEs in Pennsylvania had risen to 2,456, with $4.8 billion in debt outstanding compared to $2 billion in voter-approved "full faith and credit" local debt outstanding. As of 1975, 71 percent of total local debt outstanding in Pennsylvania was therefore not approved by taxpayers. In response to every fiscal limitation, politicians at the local level of government immediately responded by moving activities off-budget. Neither expansion of the public sector nor its appetite for resources was reduced; only the form was altered.

The off-budget enterprise that vividly illustrates the runaway nature of OBEs is the Washington Public Power Supply System (WPPSS), aptly pronounced "Whoops." WPPSS is an off-budget organization of 23 publicly owned utilities in the state of Washington that joined together to build five nuclear power plants. By any standard, this OBE is a financial disaster. The plants are now five years behind schedule, two plants have been canceled, more than $7 billion in debt has already been issued, and cost *overruns* are 500 percent more than the original cost estimate (and still rising rapidly). In two years, electric power rates have increased by 120 percent and will continue to rise, and their recent default will be in the courts for years. Enraged by the fraud, mismanagement, and corruption that sent electricity rates soaring, voters passed a referendum requiring that additional debt issues be approved by the voters. The matter is now in the courts, with the federal government claiming that the voter initiative interferes with congressional policy and asking that voter approval of additional debt be set aside. The will of the voters, who eventually pay the freight, must not be allowed to hinder those in the public sector who seek their own goals at the taxpayers' expense, so it seems.

Although widespread at the state and local levels of government, off-budget borrowing and expenditure has, in the past, played a relatively minor role at the federal level. Federal politicians have not been constrained by constitutional or effective statutory limitations on borrowing, and the federal government has virtually unlimited access to credit markets. Prior to 1973, none of the activities of federal agencies was conducted off-budget. The Congressional Budget and Impoundment Control Act of 1974, which created a budget committee for each house responsible for setting targets for total expenditures, revenues, and the resultant deficit (or surplus), has induced federal politicians to place outlays off-budget. Off-budget federal outlays increased from $100 million in 1973 to about $32.2 billion in 1981—an increase of more than 32,000 percent in less than one decade.

There are three basic ways in which, through the credit markets, federal spending is hidden and kept off the budget. First, numerous agencies have simply been deleted from the budget. Second, government control over resource allocation is extended by guaranteeing loans made to specially privileged individuals, businesses, and governments. Third, there are many privately owned, but federally sponsored and controlled, enterprises such as the Federal National Mortgage Association that are also off-the-books borrowers. In addition to manipulating credit market activities, federal politicians have increasingly recognized that, in principle, anything that can be accomplished through taxing and spending can also be accomplished by regulation. All of these activities must be taken into account to assess accurately the role of the federal government in the economy.

The list of federal agencies involved in off-budget activities is long and varied. It is sufficient to note here that the scope of federal actions is far greater than indicated by federal expenditures and employment, the traditional measures used as indicators of the size of government. The move toward "back door" spending appears to have universal appeal: It was the Reagan administration that placed the Strategic Petroleum Reserve off-budget. As pressures build for fiscal responsibility, such as the current drive for a balanced budget amendment to the constitution, the historical record indicates that further budgetary machinations are to be expected.

THE IMPLICATIONS FOR REFORM

The problem of reform of the rent-seeking society has often been viewed as the specification of appropriate constitutional constraints to control public sector expenditure, debt, and the burden of taxation. The record shows, however, that constitutional restraint has been tried as a reform device without great success. The rent-seeking society has continued to burgeon, but off-budget rather than on-budget. Little has changed except that the public sector has altered its form in order to subvert the fiscal limitations. The off-budget operations of government are deeply disturbing, for the voter has little control of much of its fiscal activity, and the directors and managers of off-budget enterprises are not directly responsible to the electorate they purport to serve. Unless we recognize the limitations of constitutional provisions for reforming the rent-seeking society, the prospects of reform by instituting fiscal restraints on politicians are by no means propitious. The specification of new rules is no panacea, but only a short-term palliative.[9]

History has shown that public sector entrepreneurs seek out legal loopholes and develop imaginative techniques to subvert constraints imposed on their actions. A statutory or constitutional limit is likely to produce modified behavior toward reform only so long as it is not nullified by such maneuvers. No constitution can be effective without the support of at least a majority of the electorate. In light of this, one role of the economist is to "do well by doing good," as Gordon Tullock suggests, by devoting more time to informing the general public of the activities of the government sector, both on-budget and off.

NOTES TO CHAPTER 15

1. Seymour Martin Lipset and William Schneider (1981: 89–94) present a discussion and summary of such surveys.
2. It is also possible, though highly unlikely, that the governmental entity could have a budget surplus so that the same level of taxation could provide more or better services. Budget surpluses are rare—every politician has an incentive to spend as much as possible to court votes—and dangerous as well. The Proposition 13 movement in California was undoubtedly fueled by the existence of a large surplus (about $5 billion) at the state level, which some individuals had proposed using for rather dubious purposes, such as a state space program.
3. The chickens do, eventually, come home to roost. The pension plans of New York City had become so overly generous in the extreme that the city was (and, many would argue, still is) on the verge of financial collapse. See, for example, Robertson, "Going Broke the New York Way," (1975: 144–49, 212–14).
4. Additional information relating to this fiscal fiasco may be found in Ratchford (1941: chs, 4, 5) and in Moak and Hillhouse (1975: 262). Further, see Hillhouse (1936, esp. ch. 7).
5. This should come as no surprise to the student of constitutional law. Bernard Siegan, in his book *Economic Liberties and the Constitution* (1980), documents how for decades legislatures have passed laws that effectively abolish many of the economic liberties embodied in the federal constitution. And, as Siegan illustrates, the Supreme Court has upheld most of these changes since the mid-1930s.
6. For a detailed discussion of the underground government, see Bennett and Dilorenzo 1983.
7. See U.S. Department of Commerce, Bureau of the Census, *Census of Governments*, various issues.
8. These data are taken from *Facts and Figures on Government Finance* (Washington, D.C.: Tax Foundation, 1979), pp. 221 and 253.
9. Indeed, new rules may be totally ignored. In 1978 and again in 1979, Congress passed laws mandating a balanced federal budget in fiscal year 1981. No enforcement powers were included in the laws and Congress has failed to abide by its own dictate, a bad omen for the future of government reform efforts.

16 HOW TO DO WELL WHILE DOING GOOD!

Gordon Tullock

Economic research always has the potential of contributing to public welfare since improved knowledge can have an effect on the world that is desirable and is unlikely to have an effect that is undesirable. Nevertheless, I would estimate that the average article in economic journals these days has very little prospect of contributing to the well-being of the world. Most economists know this and worry more about publication and tenure than about the contribution their research will make to public welfare. The argument of this chapter is that virtue does not have to be its own reward. The average economist can benefit his career while simultaneously making a contribution to the public welfare.

Consider, for example, the case of the dissolution of the Civil Aeronautics Board (C.A.B.). In 1937, Congress cartelized the U.S. air transport industry, establishing a government agency, the C.A.B., to supervise and control the cartel. As a result, in the United States air transportation prices were held well above their equilibrium, even though they were lower than the prices charged internationally and in Europe.[1]

In 1984, the C.A.B. was abolished, and it is clear that economists played a major part in its destruction. A group of economists (Jim Miller is the one that I know best) devoted a great deal of time and effort to economic research in connection with the airline industry and to what we may call public relations activities in connection with it. They formed an improbable political alliance between the American Enterprise Institute and Senator Kennedy for the purpose of bringing the control device to an early grave. Further, they were able to convince some of the airlines that they would gain from the elimination of the C.A.B.

As far as I can see, when these economists began their campaign there was substantially no public interest in the matter at all; most people and politicians would have argued that the C.A.B. was necessary in order to prevent the airlines from exploiting the passengers. It is also true that most of the economists who looked at the problem had approved the regulation. It should be said that a good many of the economists that looked at it were members of that small subset of the profession who were professional public utility economists and whose own personal income depends very heavily on the continued existence of these boards for which they can give expert testimony. Miller could have joined this small group but chose the other side, and in view of his subsequent career, it is hard to argue that he was not right, both from the standpoint of the public interest and his own career.

I do not want to, indeed am not competent to, go into the detailed history of this successful campaign, but I should like to point out two important factors: the first is that the average citizen, if he or she had known the truth about the C.A.B., would always have been opposed to it. This is one of the reasons why you can argue that it was in the public interest. The second is that it was not too hard to get the actual story out. The problem was mainly that of explaining the matter to the politician and the media. This is not necessarily easy since neither of these groups have any particular motive to think hard about the true public interest. They are both much more interested in the image of public interest currently in the minds of the citizenry. But to say that it is not easy, is not to say that it is impossible, and here we have a clear-cut case where it was accomplished. The theme of this sermon is "Go Thou and Do Likewise."

The C.A.B. is not by any means the only example. Banking regulation has to a large extent collapsed in recent years. This was to a considerable extent the result of technological developments, but the existence of a vigorous group of economic critics of the regulations was no doubt important. After all, the regulators could have just changed their regulations to take in the new technology. The fact that they did not was certainly, to some extent, the result of the work of the antiregulation economists in this area. The partial deregulation of the trucking industry is almost entirely the result of economic activity and, indeed, during the latter part of the Carter administration an economist was acting chairman of the ICC.[2]

In all of the cases originally the majority of the economic profession was on the wrong side, *favoring* regulation. This is one of the problems we face when we talk about economists having a good effect on policy. We must admit that in the past economists have frequently had a bad effect. Good economists have always had a good effect, however, and those who had a bad effect were bad economists. This is not just an ad hoc argument; I believe that one can look into the matter and discover that the people who favored such agencies as the ICC at the time they were set up were markedly poorer economists than the ones who objected to it.

There are other striking examples. In 1929 the United States was probably the world's highest tariff nation. It is true that during the intervening years we have developed a habit of setting up quotas and voluntary agreements, but even if you add those on, we still are a very low trade barrier nation. This change seems to be almost entirely an outcome of steady economic criticism. Certainly, it is very hard to put your finger on any other reason for the change.

Once again however, the history is not clear. The protective tariff, of course, has long been a bête noire of the economists, but a review of the advanced theoretical literature over the last years shows far more discussion of optimal tariffs than of the desirability of getting rid of tariffs. This is particularly surprising because the articles dealing with optimal tariffs rarely, if ever, point out that their optimality is a rather special one and that, in any event, it would be impossible to calculate an optimal tariff in the real world.[3] Still, the majority of economic opinion was always against protective tariffs even if this point of view did not get much attention in the technical journals. In a way the success of the tariff-lowering movement depended a great deal on the fact that the secretary of state for some twelve years was a former southern congressman who had learned free trade in his youth and stuck with it. Cordell Hull, of course, has been dead for many years, but the trend that he started continued. Certainly, the general favorable economic climate for such cuts was important there.

What can we do now and, more specifically, what can readers do that is good but will also help them in their careers? My argument is that there are numerous instances that almost all economists can agree are rent-seeking and detract from general welfare. In such cases virtue need not be its own reward.

AN EXAMPLE OF AN ANTI-RENT-SEEKING ARGUMENT

Let me begin with an example on which almost all economists would agree. There are about 300 British Columbian egg producers, and some time ago it occurred to them that they were not as wealthy as they would like to be. They pressed the British Columbia government into setting up the British Columbia Egg Control Board, a cartel in which the government not only fixed prices but actually engaged in civil service employing operations. Specifically, the Egg Control Board purchased the eggs from the owners of egg factories and then sold them to the public.

The original arguments for this program (other than that it would make the egg producers wealthy), were that they would stabilize prices and protect the "family farm." They have stabilized prices. If you compare prices in British Columbia to those in Washington State, which has roughly the same conditions, it is clear they fluctuate more in Washington State. However, they have stabilized prices primarily by preventing the falls in price that periodically cause so much distress for producers of eggs in Washington. Whether this particular kind of stability is admired by the housewife, as opposed to the egg producer, is not pelucidly clear. As for protecting the "family farmer," I doubt that these enterprises really should be referred to as family farms, but it is true that there is some evidence that the average size is possibly slightly suboptimal in British Columbia.

In order to charge a monopoly price it is, of course, necessary to prevent entry into the business. This is done by the traditional grandfather clause, so that those who are producing eggs in British Columbia when the scheme started are the only ones who are permitted to do so. As a result, the wealth of the farmers has increased very greatly because the permits to produce eggs are now valuable. Indeed, for the average egg producer, the permit is more than half his total capitalization.

It should be pointed out, however, that in addition to the egg producers there is one other beneficiary of this scheme. The egg producers produce more eggs than can be sold in British Columbia at what the British Columbia Egg Marketing Board thinks is a stable price. The additional eggs are sold on the international market for conversion to things like dried eggs at whatever the market will bring.

How do I know all of this about the British Columbia Egg Marketing Board? The answer is simple. Two economists decided that it would be a worthwhile study and the Fraser Institute published it in the form of a small booklet.[4] Borcherding and Dorosh thus acquired a reasonably good publication, probably quite easily. It is no criticism of the pamphlet to say that it involves no particular economic sophistication or advanced techniques. It may have been a little difficult, because I presume the Egg Board was not exactly enthusiastic about cooperating with them. Nevertheless, I would imagine that the cost/benefit analysis of this pamphlet, in terms of getting a publication and the effort put into it, was very exceptionally favorable. Further, the pamphlet itself certainly will make the survival of the Egg Board, at least, a little less certain, a result most economists believe would be beneficial.

Of course I hope that more is done here. The pamphlet was published by the Fraser Institute, which exists essentially for the purpose of doing this kind of thing and attempting to influence public policy by its research. The head of the Fraser Institute frequently appears on television. I would think that the prospects for the Egg Board are clearly worse than they were before all of this started. I hope that Borcherding and Dorosh follow up on this, not so much by further research although that of course probably can be done, as by trying to get other publications in the local media.

Here, I am going to suggest that they do something unprofessional; I believe economists should make an active effort to interest the local newspaper and other media in such issues. Stories of a small entrenched interest robbing the general public are the kind of story that does go well once you sell a reporter. Further, they are not particularly complicated.

Such activities are not the ones economists normally engage in; moreover, it will be a little difficult to interest newspaper reporters. Newspaper reporters tend simply to say what other newspaper reporters have said.[5] Granted that reporters behave this way, they are nonetheless normally looking for a scandal which they can make headlines about, and there are innumerable examples. The licensing of private yacht salesmen in California is my favorite case of the public being protected against low commission rates, but I am sure most economists can think of a half dozen more. But let us defer further discussion of general publicity for now.

We can roughly divide various rent-seeking activities for which there is likely a consensus among economists that they are indeed rent-seeking into three categories: those that involve spending money in a way that in the standpoint of the average taxpayer is foolish but that benefits a particular group, those that involve fixing prices above equilibrium, and those that involve obtaining cartel profits by restricting entry into a business.[6]

Economists have not been very successful in their efforts to stop federal government expenditures resulting from rent-seeking. Jack Hirshleifer, for example, devoted a good deal of time and energy, together with a number of experts in the field, in attempting to prevent the Feather River Project from being built in California. It has not been completed yet, but, on the whole, their efforts cannot be said to have made a major impact. I do not know why it is harder to stop government expenditures of this sort than the other kinds of government activity, but I suspect the problem is simply that from the standpoint of the citizens of California, the project is in fact a good one.[7] Their efforts were very largely concentrated in California. The cost, on the other hand, was very largely borne outside of California. There has been relatively little in the way of efforts on the part of economists to stop locally financed expenditures where I think they could have more impact. In making attacks on local expenditures, I think it is wise to keep in mind that in many cases the money actually is federal. It is not unwise of the local government to accept a gift from the national government even if the gift is not in optimal form. The conclusion that can be drawn is that rent-seeking can most often be stopped if the groups that are bearing the cost can be informed.

Turning to the other two categories, entry restriction and price control, most of these are state and local regulations, although there are, of course, federal examples. At these lower levels of government the beneficiaries and the injured groups are somewhat closer together and informing the injured group is somewhat easier. Further, an individual's activities are more likely to have effect in such a restricted area, and last but not least, most of these projects are fairly simple. Thus, it seems better to concentrate anti-rent-seeking activities in these areas.

Let us begin with the cases in which the prices are fixed by some government board, with a maximum and minimum price. This is essentially the British Columbia Egg Board, and there is a simple argument to be used against it, which is that there should be no minimum price. Consumers can hardly be protected by a minimum price. If you can get the minimum price out, the pressure group that set the thing up in the first place will probably see to it that the maximum price is eliminated.

At this point, I should perhaps mention the standard rationalization,[8] that advocates of the minimum price will almost certainly use. They will allege that if the minimum price is not imposed then some company with a lot of money will cut prices, drive the competition out of business, and then exploit its monopoly. This argument is eliminated by not arguing against the maximum price, and instead leaving that to the regular political process. The lesson here is a simple one: the best economic reasoning is not always (indeed, it is generally not) the best politics. Policy economists must formulate arguments that are most liable to lead to the desired outcome, not that are most elegant.

Restrictions on entry are subject to a variety of forms of arguments. The formal rationalization—that is, that they make certain that the service provided is on a certain level of quality—can be countered by Milton Friedman's "certification," which is that the state or local government could provide certificates of competence to anyone who passed their regulations, but not prohibit people who do not have such certificates from practicing provided that there was no fraud. In other words, the person without a certificate would not tell people who solicited his services that he had one. This procedure would probably eliminate most of the monopoly gains and convert the present arrangements into something that might even be socially desirable.

The usual argument against this, of course, is that people are not bright enough even to look at the certificate. (Why people who argue this way think that people are bright enough to vote, I don't know, but they do.) To counter this argument one can move to a second line of defense, by pointing out that these regulations are not and, in fact, make very little effort to pretend to be, efforts to raise the quality of services.

Uniformly, when such restrictions are put on, everyone now in the trade is grandfathered in. Indeed, that is the reason they are put on—the current people in the trade want to have their lifetime income raised by reducing competition. Clearly, if everybody now in the trade is competent without investigation of any sort, it is unlikely that an investigation is of any use. Thus, all new proposals of this sort can be opposed quite readily.

If we turn to the older ones, there may well be an examination, usually an irrelevant examination, but the examination is given only to new entrants. The appropriate argument here is simply that it is possible for a person practicing, whether as a doctor or as a plumber, to fail to keep up with new developments, forget old developments, or, for that matter, become a dipsomaniac. It would be desirable, therefore, that everyone in the trade not only be examined when he enters but be reexamined from time to time. It is hard to think of any argument against this, but it clearly would eliminate the political pressure for the restriction if the restriction had to take the form of continuing examinations.

Finally, there is a constitutional argument. The Supreme Court has held that requiring a waiting period for a new entrant into a state before he can go on relief violates his constitutional rights to travel freely. Prohibiting him from practicing his trade as a carpenter would also do so. Of course, if the restriction were literally evenhanded—that is, if the New York restriction on carpentry is the same for New Yorkers as for Californians who want to migrate to New York, then this constitutional argument would not exist. Such a restriction, however, would imply that if all people who are practicing carpentry in New York at the time the law was passed are admitted without examination, people who are practicing carpentry in other states at that time should also be admitted without examination. If we could get the Supreme Court to hold that this is what the Constitution said, we could feel confident that there would be absolutely no political effort to establish new restrictions on entry in the states and local governments throughout the United States.

If an examination for carpenters has been in existence for a long time so that there are not very many carpenters from other states who were carpenters at the time that the original carpenters were grandfathered in, there is a somewhat more difficult constitutional problem. Here, however, an argument would be needed that the examination is not really intended to certify people's ability as carpenters but to prevent migration from other states. It seems to me that the simple fact that the examination is not given regularly to people who are already practicing in order to make certain that they are retaining their skills, and not becoming dipsomaniacs, would be adequate here. Such constitutional arguments may or may not be successful in the courts. I recommend its use in economic arguments, even though it is not strictly relevant, simply because I think it will have a persuasive effect on the average voter.

In making any anti-rent-seeking argument, one should always point out that the data are inadequate (one can also imply in a tactful manner, that the reason that the data are inadequate is that the guilty are concealing or keeping secret evidence of their guilt). More data are always needed and generally the pressure group is to some extent unwilling to provide data because it fears strengthening your argument. Mainly, however, this argument places you in a very good position for rebuttal. Almost certainly, the pressure group representatives will argue that you are simply ignorant in their field. A response in which you say that your ignorance is partly because they are keeping secrets and ask them to provide further information generally would be helpful. In the unlikely event that they do provide additional information, of course, you have opportunity for further and better research.

A second argument that inevitably can be made is that the pressure group has something material to gain from its activities. Although we, as economists, do not regard this as in any way discreditable, the average person does. In fact, the pressure group will normally be arguing that its existence benefits people it in fact injures, but they will normally not deny that its own members are gaining, too. You will thus merely be giving strong emphasis to something the pressure group tends to pass over lightly.

If individual economists would select some blatantly undesirable activity, preferably of a state or local government, and become a modest expert on it, it is my contention that the economy would improve. Doing so does not involve a major investment. In general, these programs are not complicated, but nevertheless becoming an expert will involve some work. After becoming an expert, the economist should attempt to get media publicity for the position with the result first, of certainly attracting the attention of the pressure group, which may or may not be useful, and, second, if the economist pushes hard enough and is persistent, he probably will have at least some effect on the activity of the pressure group.

Here, I should emphasize that though I am suggesting this as an individual effort, there is no reason why small collectives of economists should not be involved, and there is certainly no reason why you should not seek out the support of other groups. The League of Women Voters, for example, tends to go about looking for good causes and you may be able to improve their taste. There are also various business groups, Rotary Clubs, and so on that are always on the lookout for a lecturer and that would give you an opportunity to provide some influence.

Persistence will, however, be necessary. The pressure group will continue and a mere couple of months' noise about it is helpful but unlikely to accomplish a great deal. Persistence is not difficult, however. Once you have passed the threshold of knowing enough about the organization so that you can regard yourself as a modest expert, it is very easy to keep up with further developments and incorporate additional data into your analyses. Further, your contacts with the media are apt to be self-reinforcing. After you have convinced people that you know a great deal about, let us say, controls on egg production, you are likely to find television program directors asking you questions about all economic matters. You should answer them, of course, to the best of your ability, and this will not only, we hope, contribute to the economic information of the public but also give media representatives an idea of your expertise so that when you bring up the subject of eggs or whatever it is, they are likely to pay attention.

Most economists only occasionally give lectures to something like the Rotary Club. I am suggesting that this aspect of professional life be sharply increased. Furthermore, I am suggesting that you become an expert on some rather obscure topic instead of giving your lecture to the Rotary Club on what is right or what is wrong with Reaganomics. This is indeed a change from the normal academic life but not a gigantic one. I am not suggesting that you devote immense amounts of time to these joint projects, merely that you do indeed devote some time to them. In a way it may be a pleasant change from the more profound and difficult work that I am sure mainly occupies your time.

So far I have been telling you how you can do good and have not explained why I think you can also do well. The first thing to be said is that of course the kind of research I am proposing does have some potential for publication in the regular economic literature. *The Journal of Law and Economics, The Journal of Political Economy, Public Policy*, and others all are interested in such articles. I would also suggest that the political science journals would be interested, although it would be necessary to make a few changes in your approach if you submitted articles to them.

But while all of these people would be interested and, I think, the prospects for publication are quite good, it has to be said that if a great many economists began working in this area it would rapidly exhaust the desire for such articles in these journals. After awhile, only the very best of such articles could be published there. Further, in this case "best" would not refer entirely to the quality of the work but also to the importance of the subject matter. A new twist in cartel economics would, for example, probably be publishable when hundreds of studies of specific cartels would not.

So far, of course, the tolerance of these journals for this kind of article has by no means been exhausted and those of you who get in first could no doubt take advantage of that tolerance. Once we turn from this kind of journal publication, however, there are a number of other places with gradually decreasing prestige where you can get published. There is now a chain of economic institutes who are in general interested in studies of this kind of cartel.[9] The Borcherding and Dorosh pamphlet is a good example. Clearly this is a perfectly suitable publication to put on your vitae even if it does not carry quite so much weight as publication in *The Journal of Political Economy*. I, as a matter of fact, have three such things on my own vitae. Indeed, I would imagine that in cost/benefit terms these things are considerably more highly paying than JPE articles because although the payoff is not as high, the cost of producing them is also low.

Below that level there is the possibility of fairly widespread publication in such things as articles in local newspapers, letters to the editor, and so on. These are not great publications and you might want to indicate on your bibliography that you think they are not. For example, you could have a separate section for newspaper articles and letters to the editor. You might even mention your appearances on TV in this separate section.

With respect to these less important articles, speeches, and the like, the payoff in academic life is, of course, quite low per unit. Most universities, however, regard activity in the public arena as meritorious and pay it off in higher wages. It also carries with it the advertising value that an article in *The Journal of Political Economy* carries, although, once again, at a lower level.

But although these are less important publications, their cost is also quite low. Once you have become an expert in this area you could grind them out practically at will, producing a letter to the editor, for example, in a half hour. Thus, once again, the cost-benefit analysis from a pure career standpoint seems to be positive.

But this may immediately raise a question in your mind. How do I know that better information is likely to cause the end of these special-interest arrangements? After all, they have been in existence a long time and most economists know about them in general even if the public does not. They do not seem to be very secretive. I believe that they depend on either ignorance or misinformation on the part of the public. My reasons for believing so are two: first, if you discuss any of them with average voters it will turn out that they have never heard of them, or if they have heard of them, they are badly misinformed about them. In the case of the British Columbia Egg Board, the average voter probably does not know that there is such an organization. The voter who does probably has bought the argument that the organization stabilizes prices and protects the family farm.

But in addition to this informal public opinion poll, there is another and, in my opinion, more important reason. If we think of the British Columbia Egg Board, any economist could quickly arrange a set of taxes on eggs together with direct subsidies to the people who were in the business of producing eggs[10] that would make both the customers and the producers of the eggs better off. We do not see this direct subsidy being used. Why do pressure groups not simply aim at a low tax on the entire population that is used to pay a direct sum of money to them rather than these clearly non-Pareto-optimal arrangements that we in fact observe? I think the only available explanation for this is that they know that a certain amount of confusion and misdirection is necessary. A direct cash transfer, a tax of $10 per family in British Columbia for the purpose of paying a pension to the 300 people who happen to own egg factories at the time the program was put into effect, would never go through because it is too blatant and obvious. It is necessary that these things be covered by some kind of deception. Granted that I am right about this — that these programs require that the people be misinformed — informing them is likely to terminate the program. No politician is going to tax all of his constituents a small sum of money in order to give a large sum of money to a small group no matter how well organized that small group is if everyone knows that is what he is doing. Economists can see to it that they do know.

Note here, also, that the nature of the mass media is on your side. The mass media all aim at large audiences. The small pressure group does not have much chance of getting the attention of the mass media except, possibly, unfavorable attention. The small pressure group very likely has its own journal, which it uses for internal communication, but the owner of a TV station or a newspaper will tend to come down for his customers en masse, not a tiny minority of his customers. Thus, not only is secrecy and deception necessary here but the nature of the mass media means that unmasking of these villains is likely to be popular with those who want to make money in the media business.

I am sure all of this sounds rather wild to most of you. I gave an earlier version of this paper at my own university and a young ABD, who had been listening and apparently could not believe his ears came up afterward and asked me whether it was really true that I was suggesting that he not only study up on some local government-managed cartel but seek publication in places other than the JPE. I assured him that was my objective. He went away looking astounded, not, I think, at the brilliance of my ideas, but at the eccentricity.

This particular young man will, I think, have great difficulty getting any publications ever in the JPE. Competition is stiff (even to this day I have about half of my submissions turned down[11]), and most economists will never get a single article published in a leading journal. Still, I assume all of you are members of that small minority who do occasionally break into print in such places as JPE, the AER, and the QJE.

Turning to the problem of the man who does have great difficulty getting anything published, something on his vita is better than nothing, and the proposal that I am making is a way in which he can pretty much guarantee he will have at least something on his vita. For the more productive economist, who does currently produce articles for the leading journals, it is still helpful to add additional items even if these additional items are not of Nobel Prize quality. Once again, the cost of producing these things is comparatively low, so you make a good deal per unit of effort.

Even if there were no beneficial impact on your career, nevertheless, I would urge it on you. All of us are, to some minor extent, charitable and this is a particularly convenient way for economists to work out their charitable feelings. Getting rid of the British Columbia Egg Board might not impress you as a major accomplishment, but individuals can expect to have only small impacts on the massive structure that we call modern society. It is likely that you will do more good for the world by concentrating on abolishing some such organization in your locality than the average person does—indeed, very much more. It is an unusual form of charity, but a form in which the payoff would be high. But although such work falls squarely in the path of virtue, it also has positive payoffs. You can, to repeat my title, do well while you are doing good.

NOTES TO CHAPTER 16

1. The apparent reason that American airlines' prices were lower than those in Europe was not that our airlines were any less monopolistic but that they were more efficient, with the result that the optimum monopoly price for them was lower than the optimum monopoly price for such monsters of inefficiency as Air France or Japan Airlines.
2. Unfortunately, this partial deregulation seems to have stopped. (I hope temporarily.) Once again, it is encouraging that most economists were opposed to this regulation.
3. It is not that the optimal tariff literature is wrong. It is that it can be misused and that economists are more likely to have a positive effect on pub-

lic policy because rent-seeking forces will be pushing for a tariff that is far beyond any optimal tariff.

4. The booklet is *The Egg Marketing Board, A Case Study of Monopoly and Its Social Costs*, by Thomas Borcherding and Gary W. Dorosh (Vancouver: The Fraser Institute, 1981).

5. The "deregulation" that has been so successful in recent years in the United States is an example. It has become more or less a fad with most of the correspondents for *The Washington Post* who were in favor of it without having any clear idea why.

6. I leave aside here those cases in which if we look only at the short run, as unfortunately the voter does, the beneficiaries outnumber the people who pay. Price controls on gas are a current example.

7. Ignoring, of course, those particular farmers who will be damaged by the canal across the delta.

8. I encountered it in high school.

9. The bulk of them owe their origin to the energies of Antony Fisher.

10. Some of these might, of course, decide to stop producing eggs and move to Hawaii on the subsidy.

11. I have a large collection of unpublished articles.

BIBLIOGRAPHY

Abraham, Katherine. 1983. "Structural/Frictional vs. Deficient Demand Unemployment: Some New Evidence." *American Economic Review* 73 (September): 708–24.

Alchian, Armen A. 1965. "Some Economics of Property Rights. *El Politico* 30, no. 4: 816–29.

Alchian, Armen A., William R. Allen, and others. 1973. *The Economics of Charity*. London: Institute of Economic Affairs.

Alchian, Armen A., and Harold Demsetz. 1972. "Production, Information Costs, and Economic Organization." *The American Economic Review* 62, no. 5 (December): 777–95.

Anam, Mahmudul. 1982. "Distortion-Triggered Lobbying and Welfare: A Contribution to the Theory of Directly-Unproductive Profit-Seeking Activities." *Journal of International Economics* 13, nos. 1–2 (August): 15–32.

Anderson, Terry L., and Peter J. Hill. 1980. *The Birth of a Transfer Society*. Stanford, Calif.: Hoover Institution Press.

Arnot, R.P. 1966. *The Miners: Years of Struggle*, vol. 1. New York: Augustus M. Kelley.

Arrow, Kenneth J. 1963. "Uncertainty and the Economics of Medical Care." *American Economic Review* 53 (December): 941–73.

Arrow, Kenneth J. 1972. "Gifts and Exchanges." *Philosophy and Public Affairs* 1, no. 4 (Summer): 343–62.

Arrow, Kenneth J. 1973. "Social Responsibility and Economic Efficiency." *Public Policy* 21 (Summer): 343–62.

Arrow, Kenneth J. 1974. *The Limits of Organization.* New York: W.W. Norton.

Ashton, T.S. 1967. *The Industrial Revolution: 1760–1830.* London: Oxford Univ. Press.

Ashton, T.S. 1977. *An Economic History of England: The 18th Century.* London: Methuen.

241

Balassa, B. 1971. *The Structure of Protection in Developing Countries.* Baltimore: The Johns Hopkins Press.

Baldwin, Robert. 1976. "The Political Economy of U.S. Trade Policy." *The Bulletin* 1976-4. Center for Study of Financial Institutions, Graduate School of Business Administration, New York University, New York.

Baldwin, Robert. 1982. "The Political Economy of Protectionism." In *Import Competition and Response*, edited by J.N. Bhagwati, pp. 263-86. Chicago: Univ. of Chicago Press.

Barro, Robert. 1979. "An Appraisal of the Non-Market Clearing Paradigm." *American Economic Review* 69 (May): 54-59.

Barzel, Yoram. 1980. "Measurement and the Organization of Markets." University of Washington (April). Mimeo.

Bates, R.H. 1981. *Markets and States in Tropical Africa.* Berkeley: Univ. of California Press.

Bauer, P.T. 1976. *Dissent and Development.* Cambridge, Mass.: Harvard Univ. Press.

Baysinger, Barry; R. Ekelund; and R. Tollison. 1980. "Mercantilism as a Rent-Seeking Society." In *Toward a Theory of the Rent-Seeking Society*, edited by James Buchanan, Robert Tollison and Gordon Tullock, pp. 235-68. College Station: Texas A&M Univ. Press.

Becker, Gary S. 1983. "A Theory of Competition among Pressure Groups for Political Influence." *Quarterly Journal of Economics* 93 (August): 371-400.

Bennett, James T., and Thomas J. DiLorenzo. 1983. *Underground Government: The Off-Budget Public Sector.* Washington, D.C.: Cato Institute.

Bhagwati, Jagdish N. 1971. "The Generalized Theory of Distortions and Welfare." *Trade Balance of Payments and Growth: Papers in International Economics in Honor of Charles P. Kindleberger*, edited by J.N. Bhagwati et al. Amsterdam: North Holland, 69-90.

Bhagwati, Jagdish N., ed. 1974. *Illegal Transactions in International Trade: Theory and Policy.* Series in International Economics, vol. 1. Amsterdam: North Holland.

Bhagwati, Jagdish N. 1978. *Anatomy and Consequences of Exchange Control Regimes.* New York: National Bureau of Economic Research.

Bhagwati, Jagdish N. 1980. "Lobbying and Welfare." *Journal of Public Economics* 14 (December): 355-63.

Bhagwati, Jagdish N. 1982a. "Shifting Comparative Advantage, Protectionist Demands, and Policy Response." *Import Competition and Response*, edited by J.N. Bhagwati. Chicago: Univ. of Chicago Press.

Bhagwati, Jagdish N. 1982b. "Lobbying, DUP Activities and Welfare: A Response to Tullock." *Journal of Public Economics* 14 (December): 395-98.

Bhagwati, Jagdish N. 1982c. "Directly Unproductive, Profit-Seeking (DUP) Activities." *Journal of Political Economy* 90 (October): 988-1002.

Bhagwati, Jagdish N. 1983. "DUP Activities and Rent Seeking." *Kyklos* 36: 634-37.

Bhagwati, Jagdish N.; A. Brecher; and T. Hatta. Forthcoming. "The Generalized Theory of Transfers and Welfare, II: Exogenous (Policy-imposed) and Endogenous (Transfer-induced) Distortions." *Quarterly Journal of Economics.*

Bhagwati, Jagdish N., and Bent Hansen. 1973. "A Theoretical Analysis of Smuggling." *Quarterly Journal of Economics* 87 (May): 172–87.

Bhagwati, Jagdish N., and T.N. Srinivasan. 1973. "Smuggling and Trade Policy." *Journal of Public Economics* 2 (November): 377–89; also in *Illegal Transactions in International Trade*, edited by J.N. Bhagwati, Amsterdam: North Holland, 1974, pp. 27–38.

Bhagwati, Jagdish N., and T.N. Srinivasan. 1980. "Revenue Seeking: A Generalization of the Theory of Tariffs." *Journal of Political Economy* 88 (December): 1069–87.

Bhagwati, Jagdish N., and T.N. Srinivasan. 1982. "The Welfare Consequences of Directly-Unproductive Profit-Seeking (DUP) Lobbying Activities: Prices versus Quantity Distortions." *Journal of International Economics* 13: 33–44.

Blaug, M. 1958. "The Classical Economists and the Factory Acts: A Reexamination." *Quarterly Journal of Economics* 73 (May): 211–26.

Bogart, Ernest Ludlow. 1936. *Economic History of the American People.* New York: Longmans, Green.

Borcherding, Thomas, and Gary W. Dorosh. 1981. *The Egg Marketing Board: A Case Study of Monopoly and Its Social Costs.* Vancouver: The Fraser Institute.

Bowles, S., and H. Gintis. 1976. *Schooling in Capitalist America: Educational Reform and the Contradictions of Economic Life.* New York: Basic Books.

Boyson, Rhodes. 1970. *The Ashworth Cotton Enterprise: The Rise and Fall of a Family Firm 1818–1880.* Oxford: Clarendon Press.

Brams, Steven J., and Peter Fishburn. 1978. "Approval Voting." *American Political Science Review* 72, no. 3 (September): 831–47.

Brecher, Richard A. 1982. "Comment." In *Import Competition and Response*, edited by Jagdish N. Bhagwati. Chicago: Univ. of Chicago Press, 234–38.

Brennan, G., and J.M. Buchanan. 1980. *The Power to Tax.* Cambridge: Cambridge Univ. Press.

Brentano, Lujo. 1870. *On the History and Development of Guilds and the Origin of Trade Unions.* London: Trubner.

Breton, A. 1964. "The Economics of Nationalism." *Journal of Political Economy* 26 (August): 376–86.

British Parliamentary Papers. 1968. *Industrial Revolution: Factories*, vol. 1. Shannon, Ireland: Irish Univ. Press.

British Parliamentary Papers. 1968. *Industrial Revolution: Children's Employment*, vol. 3. Shannon, Ireland: Irish Univ. Press.

British Parliamentary Papers. 1968. *Industrial Revolution: Industrial Relations*, vol. 7. Shannon, Ireland: Irish Univ. Press.

British Parliamentary Papers. 1970. *Urban Areas: Housing*, vol. 2. Shannon, Ireland: Irish Univ. Press.

Brock, William A., and Stephen P. Magee. 1975. "The Economics of Pork-Barrel Politics." Report 7511, Center for Mathematical Studies in Business and Economics, University of Chicago (February).

Brock, William A., and Stephen P. Magee. 1978. "The Economics of Special Interest Politics: The Case of the Tariff." *American Economic Review* 68 (May): 246–50.

Brock, William A., and Stephen P. Magee. 1980. "Tariff Formation in a Democracy." In *Current Issues in Commercial Policy and Diplomacy*, edited by John Black and Brian Hindley. New York: St. Martin's Press: 1-9.

Buchanan, James M. 1964. "What Should Economists Do?" *Southern Economic Journal* 30 (January): 213-22.

Buchanan, James M. 1972. *Explorations in the Theory of Anarchy*. Blacksburg, Va.: Center for the Study of Public Choice.

Buchanan, James M. 1977. "Law and the Invisible Hand." In *The Interaction of Economics and The Law*, edited by Bernard H. Siegen, pp. 127-38. Lexington: Lexington Books.

Buchanan, James M. 1980a. "Rent Seeking and Profit Seeking." In *Toward a General Theory of the Rent-Seeking Society*, edited by James M. Buchanan, Robert Tollison, and Gordon Tullock, pp. 3-15. College Station: Texas A&M Univ. Press.

Buchanan, James M. 1980b. "Reform in the Rent-Seeking Society." In *Toward a Theory of the Rent-Seeking Society*, edited by James M. Buchanan, Robert Tollison, and Gordon Tullock, pp. 359-67. College Station: Texas A&M Univ. Press.

Buchanan, James M.; R. Tollison; and G. Tullock, eds. 1980. *Toward a Theory of the Rent-Seeking Society*. College Station: Texas A&M Univ. Press.

Buchanan, James M., and Gordon Tullock. 1962. *The Calculus of Consent*. Ann Arbor: Univ. of Michigan Press.

Cagan, Phillip. 1979. *Persistent Inflation*. New York: Columbia Univ. Press.

Chamberlain, Edward H. 1933. *The Theory of Monopolistic Competition*. Cambridge: Harvard Univ. Press.

Chapman, S.J. 1904. *The Lancashire Cotton Industry*. Manchester, England: Manchester Univ. Press.

Choi, Kwang. 1983. "A Statistical Test of Olson's Model." In *The Political Economy of Growth*, edited by Dennis Mueller, pp. 57-78. New Haven, Conn.: Yale Univ. Press.

Clower, Robert. 1965. "The Keynesian Counterrevolution: A Theoretical Appraisal." In *The Theory of Interest Rates*, edited by F.H. Hahn and F.P.R. Brechling. London: MacMillian.

Coase, Ronald. 1937. "The Nature of the Firm." *Economica* 4, no. 16 (November): 386-405.

Coase, Ronald. 1960. "The Problem of Social Cost." *Journal of Law and Economics* 3 (October): 1-44.

Colander, David. 1982. "Stagflation and Competition." *Journal of Post Keynesian Economics* 5 (1) (Fall): 17-33.

Colander, David. 1983. "The Institutionalist Critique of Rent-Seeking." Middlebury College. Mimeo.

Coleman, James. 1983. "Social Choice with Discounted Point Voting." Public Choice Annual meeting. Mimeo (March).

Collier, Frances. 1964. *The Family Economy of the Working Classes in the Cotton Industry 1784-1833*. Manchester, England: Manchester Univ. Press.

Congleton, Roger. 1980. "Competitive Process, Competitive Waste, and Institutions." In *Toward a Theory of the Rent-Seeking Society*, edited by

James M. Buchanan, Robert D. Tollison, and Gordon Tullock, pp. 153–79. College Station: Texas A&M Univ. Press.

Davis, Lance, and Douglass C. North. 1971. *Institutional Change and American Economic Growth*. Cambridge, England: Cambridge Univ. Press.

Demsetz, Harold. 1964. "The Exchange and Enforcement of Property Rights." *Journal of Law and Economics* (October): 11–26.

Demsetz, Harold. 1967. "Towards a Theory of Property Rights." *American Economics Review* 57, no. 2 (May): 347–59.

Demsetz, Harold. 1968. "Why Regulate Utilities." *Journal of Law and Economics* 55 (October).

Dinopoulos, Elias. 1983. "Import Competition, International Factor Mobility and Lobbying Responses: The Schumpeterian Industry." *Journal of International Economics* 14 (May): 395–410.

Dworkin, Ronald. 1980. "Is Wealth a Value?" *Journal of Legal Studies* 9: 191–226.

Edwards, M.M., and R. Lloyd–Jones. 1973. "N.J. Smelser and the Cotton Factory Family: A Reassessment." In *Textile History and Economic History*, edited by N.B. Harte and K.G. Ponting. Manchester, England: Manchester Univ. Press.

Edwards, Richard. 1979. *Contested Terrain*. New York: Basic Books, Inc.

Ekelund, Robert B., and Robert D. Tollison. 1981. *Mercantilism as a Rent-Seeking Society*. College Station: Texas A&M Univ. Press.

Elster, Jon. 1979. *Ulysses and the Sirens: Studies in Rationality and Irrationality*. Cambridge, England: Cambridge Univ. Press.

Facts and Figures on Government Finance. 1979. Washington, D.C.: Tax Foundation.

Farnie, D.A. 1979. *The English Cotton Industry and the World Market 1815–1896*. Oxford: Clarendon Press.

Feenstra, Robert C., and Jagdish N. Bhagwati. 1982. "Tariff Seeking and the Efficient Tariff." In *Import Competition and Response*, edited by Jagdish N. Bhagwati, pp. 223–34. Chicago: Univ. of Chicago Press.

Findlay, Ronald, and Stanislaw Wellisz. 1982. "Endogenous Tariffs, The Political Economy of Trade Restrictions, and Welfare." In *Import Competition and Response*, edited by Jagdish N. Bhagwati, pp. 223–38. Chicago: Univ. of Chicago Press.

Findlay, Ronald, and Stanislaw Wellisz. 1983. "Some Aspects of the Political Economy of Trade Restrictions." 36 *Kyklos*, 469–81.

Fishlow, Albert. 1965. *American Railroads and the Transformation of the Ante-Bellum Economy*. Cambridge, Mass.: Harvard Univ. Press.

Foster, E. 1981. "The Treatment of Rents in Cost-Benefit Analysis." *American Economic Review* 71 (March): 151–54.

Fraser, W.H. 1970. "Trade Unionism." In *Popular Movements C. 1830–1850*, edited by J.T. Ward. New York: St Martin's Press.

Frey, B., and L.J. Lau. 1968. "Towards a Mathematical Model of Government Behavior." *Zeitschrift für Nationalokonomie* (December).

Frey, Bruno S., and Friedrich Schneider. 1982. "International Political Economy: An Emerging Field." Seminar Paper no. 227. Institute for International Economic Studies, University of Stockholm (November).

Friedman, Milton, and Anna Schwartz. 1963. *A Monetary History of The United States, 1867–1960.* Princteon, N.J.: Princeton Univ. Press.

Fries, Timothy. 1982. "Protection and Rent Seeking in a Stock Market Model of Trade under Uncertainty." Williams College. Mimeo (December).

Furubotn, Eirik G., and Svetozar Pejovich, eds. 1974. *The Economics of Property Rights.* Cambridge, Mass.: Ballinger.

Gaffney, Mason, and Warren J. Samuels. 1977. "Federal versus State Taxation of Energy Resources: Discussion." *National Tax Association Proceedings* 30: 252–58.

Gaskell, P. 1968. *Artisans and Machinery.* New York: Augustus M. Kelley.

Gintis, Herbert. 1976. "The Nature of Labor Exchange and the Theory of Capitalist Production." *Review of Radical Political Economics* 8 (Summer): 36–54.

Hahn, Frank. 1980. "General Equilibrium Theory." *The Public Interest* (Special Issue): 123–38.

Hale, Robert Lee. 1923. "Coercion and Distribution in a Supposedly Non-coercive State." *Political Science Quarterly* 38 (October): 470–94.

Halevy, Elie. 1950. *The Triumph of Reform, 1830–1841.* London: Ernest Benn.

Hall, Bowman N. 1980. "Joshua K. Ingalls, American Individualist." *American Journal of Economics and Sociology* 39 (October): 383–96.

Harberger, Arnold C. 1954. "Monopoly and Resource Allocation." *American Economic Review* 54 (May): 77–87.

Harberger, Arnold C. 1962. "The Incidence of the Corporation Income Tax." *Journal of Political Economy* 70 (June): 215–40.

Hardin, Russell. 1980. "Rationality, Irrationality and Functionalist Explanation." *Social Science Information* (August–October): 755–72.

Hayek, Friedrich. 1937. "Economics and Knowledge." *Economica* 4 (n.s) no. 13: 33–54.

Hayek, Friedrich. 1945. "The Uses of Knowledge in Society." *American Economic Review* 35, no. 4: 519–30.

Hewitt, Margaret. 1958. *Wives and Mothers in Victorian Industry.* London: Rockliff.

Hicks, John. 1974. *The Crisis in Keynesian Economics.* New York: Basic Books.

Hicks, John. 1983. "Structural Unemployment and Economic Growth: A 'Labor Theory of Value' Model." In *The Political Economy of Growth*, edited by Dennis C. Mueller. New Haven, Conn.: Yale Univ. Press.

Higgs, Henry, ed. 1925. *Palgrave's Dictionary of Political Economy*, vol. 2. London: MacMillan.

Hillhouse, Albert M. 1936. *Municipal Bonds: A Century of Experience.* New York: Prentice-Hall.

Hirschman, Albert O. 1968. "The Political Economy of Import-Substituting Industrialization in Latin America." *Quarterly Journal of Economics* 82 (1) (February): 89–99.

Hirschman, Albert O. 1981. "Morality and the Social Sciences: a Durable Tension." In *Essays in Trespassing: Economics to Politics and Beyond*, edited by A. O. Hirschman, pp. 294–306. New York: Cambridge Univ. Press.

Howell, George. 1981. "Liberty for Labour." [1891] In *A Plea for Liberty: an Argument against Socialism and Socialistic Legislation*, edited by Thomas Mackay. Indianapolis, Ind.: Liberty Classics.

Hutchins, B.A., and A. Harrison. 1966. *A History of Factory Legislation.* 3rd ed. New York: Augustus M. Kelley.

Hutt, William H. 1954. "The Factory System of the Early Nineteenth Century." In *Capitalism and the Historians*, edited by F.A. Hayek. Chicago: Univ. of Chicago Press, pp. 160–88.

Jensen, Michael, and W. Meckling. 1976. "Theory of the Firm: Managerial Behavior, Agency Costs and Ownership Structure." *Journal of Financial Economics* 3, no. 4: 305–60.

Johnson, Harry G. 1951. "Optimum Welfare and Maximum Revenue Tariffs." *Review of Economic Studies* 48: 28–35.

Johnson, Harry G. 1954. "Optimum Tariffs and Retaliation." *Review of Economic Studies* 55: 142–53.

Johnson, Harry G. 1960. "The Cost of Protection and the Scientific Tariff." *Journal of Political Economy* 68 (August): 327–45.

Johnson, Harry G. 1965. "A Theoretical Model of Nationalism in New and Developing States." *Political Science Quarterly* 80 (June): 169–85.

Johnson, Harry G. 1967. "The Possibility of Income Losses from Increased Efficiency or Factor Accumulation in the Presence of Tariffs." *Economic Journal* (March).

Jones, Ronald. 1971. "A Three-Factor Model in Theory, Trade and History." In *Trade, Balance of Payments and Growth: Papers in International Economics in Honor of Charles P. Kindleberger*, edited by Jagdish N. Bhagwati, Amsterdam: North Holland, pp. 3–21.

Kahn, Alfred E. 1982. Book Review. *New York Times Book Review.* December 12, p. 11.

Kindleberger, Charles P. 1951. "Group Behavior and International Trade." *Journal of Political Economy* 59 (February): 30–46.

Kirkland, Edward C. 1951. *A History of American Economic Life.* 3rd ed. New York: Appleton-Century-Crofts.

Knight, Frank H. 1947. *Freedom and Reform.* New York: Harper.

Knight, Frank H. 1950. Introduction. In *Principles of Economics* by Carl Menger, pp. 9–35. Glencoe, Ill.: Free Press.

Knight, Frank H. 1952. "Economic Freedom and Social Responsibility." In Studies in Business and Economics, no. 1. Emory University, Atlanta, pp. 3–24.

Koford, Kenneth. 1982a. "Centralized Vote Trading." *Public Choice* 39, no. 2: 245–68.

Koford, Kenneth. 1982b. "Optimal Voting Rules under Uncertainty." *Public Choice* 38, no. 2: 149–65.

Krueger, Anne Osborne. 1974. "The Political Economy of the Rent-seeking Society." *American Economic Review* 64 (June): 291–303.

Krueger, Anne Osborne. 1978. *Liberalization Attempts and Consequences.* New York: National Bureau of Economic Research.

Landes, Elizabeth M. 1980. "The Effect of State Maximum Hours Laws on the Employment of Women in 1920." *Journal of Political Economy* 88 (September): 476-94.

Lerner, Abba. 1960. "On Generalizing the General Theory." *American Economic Review* 50 (March): 121-43.

Lerner, Abba, and David C. Colander. 1983. "Guiding the Invisible Hand." *Journal of Transport Economics* 10, (April-August): 25-34.

Lindbeck, Assar. 1976. "Stabilization Policies in Open Economies with Endogenous Politicians." *American Economic Review* 66 (May): 1-19.

Lipset, Seymour Martin, and William Schneider. 1981. "Lower Taxes and More Welfare: A Reply to Arthur Seldon." In *Journal of Contemporary Studies* (Spring): 89-94.

Little, I.M.D.; Tibor Scitovsky; and C. Scott. 1970. *Industry and Trade in Some Developing Countries.* Oxford: Oxford Univ. Press.

Lyons, John Stephen. 1977. *The Lancashire Cotton Industry and the Introduction of the Powerloom, 1815-1850.* Ann Arbor, Mich.: Xerox University Microfilms.

Magee, Stephen P., and William A. Brock. 1983. "A Model of Politics, Tariffs and Rent Seeking in General Equilibrium." In *The Problems of Developed Countries and the International Economy: Human Resources, Employment and Development*, vol. 3, edited by Burton Weisbrod and Helen Hughes. Proceedings of the Sixth World Congress of Economists, August 1980, Mexico City. London: MacMillan: 497-523.

Magee, Stephen P.; William A. Brock; and Leslie Young. 1983. "Endogenous Tariff Theory: Black Hole Tariffs in a Special Interest Model of International Economic Policy with Endogenous Politics." University of Texas at Austin. Mimeo (November).

Malinvaud, Edmond. 1977. *The Theory of Unemployment Reconsidered.* Oxford: Basil Blackwell.

Marglin, Stephen. 1974. "What Do Bosses Do? Part I." *Review of Radical Political Economics* 6 (Summer): 33-60.

Marglin, Stephen. 1975. "What Do Bosses Do? Part II." *Review of Radical Political Economics* 7 (Spring): 20-37.

Marshall, Alfred. 1920. *Principles of Economics*, 8th ed. New York: MacMillan, book 6.

Marvel, Howard P. 1977. "Factory Regulation: A Reinterpretation of Early English Experience." *Journal of Law and Economics* 20 (October): 379-402.

Mayer, Wolfgang. 1983. "Endogenous Tariff Formation." University of Cincinatti. Mimeo (March).

McCormick, Robert E., and Robert D. Tollison. 1979. "Rent-Seeking Competition in Political Parties." *Public Choice* 34: 5-14.

McKean, Roland N. 1975. "Economics of Trust, Altruism, and Corporate Responsibility." In *Altruism, Morality and Economic Theory*, edited by Edmund Phelps, pp. 29-44. New York: Russell Sage Foundation.

McPherson, Michael. 1982a. "Mill's Moral Theory and the Problem of Preference Change." *Ethics* 92 (January): 252-73.

McPherson, Michael. 1982b. Review of Richard Posner's *The Economics of Justice. Law and Philosophy* 1 (Fall): 129–36.

McPherson, Michael. 1983. "Want Formation, Morality, and Some Interpretive Aspects of Economic Inquiry." In *Social Science as Moral Inquiry*, edited by Norma Haan and Robert Bellah. New York: Columbia Univ. Press, pp. 96–124.

Meade, James. 1952. *A Geometry of International Trade*. London: Allen and Unwin.

Meade, James. 1982. Wage Fixing. London: George Allen and Unwin.

Menger, Carl. 1950. *Principles of Economics*. Glencoe, Ill.: Free Press.

Messerlin, Patrick A. 1981. "The Political Economy of Protectionism: The Bureaucratic Case." *Weltwirtschaftliches Archiv* 117, no. 3: 469–95.

Mill, John Stuart. 1965. *Principles of Political Economy with Some of Their Applications to Social Philosophy*, vol. 2. Toronto: Univ. of Toronto Press.

Mises, Ludwig von. 1966. *Human Action*. New York: Henry Regnery.

Mishan, Ezra. 1981. *Economic Efficiency and Social Welfare*. London: Allen Unwin.

Moak, Lennox L., and Albert M. Hillhouse. 1975. *Concepts and Practices in Local Government Finance*. Chicago: Municipal Finance Officers Association.

Moore, Thomas Gale. 1978. "The Beneficiaries of Trucking Regulation." *Journal of Law and Economics* 21 (October): 327–43.

Morris, C. Robert. 1958. "Evading Debt Limitations with Public Building Authorities: The Costly Subversion of State Constitutions." *Yale Law Journal* 68 (December): 234–45.

Mueller, Dennis C., ed. 1983. *The Political Economy of Growth*. New Haven, Conn.: Yale Univ. Press.

Mundell, Robert. 1962. "Review of Janssen, Free Trade, Protection and Customs Union." *American Economic Review* 52 (June): 622.

Murrell, Peter. 1983. "A Comparison of German and U.K. Growth." In *The Political Economy of Growth*, edited by Dennis C. Mueller, pp. 109–31. New Haven, Conn.: Yale Univ. Press.

Myrdal, Gunnar. 1968. *Asian Drama*. New York: Pantheon.

Naqvi, S.N.H. 1964. "Import Licensing in Pakistan." *Pakistan Development Review* (Spring). Reprinted in *Studies in Commercial Policy and Economic Growth*, edited by N. Islam. Karachi. The Pakistan Institute of Development Economics, (1970): 89–105.

Nardinelli, Clark. 1980. "Child Labor and the Factory Acts." *Journal of Economic History* 15 (December): 739–55.

Neff, W.F. 1929. *Victorian Working Women*. New York: Columbia Univ. Press.

Niskanen, William A. 1968. "The Peculiar Economics of Bureaucracy." *American Economic Review* 58 (May): 293–305.

Niskanen, William A. 1971. *Bureaucracy and Representative Government*. Hawthorne, N.Y.: Aldine.

North, Douglass C. 1981. *Structure and Change in Economic History*. New York: W.W. Norton.

North, Douglass C., and Robert Paul Thomas. 1973. *The Rise of the Western World*. Cambridge, England: Cambridge Univ. Press.

Nozick, Robert. 1974. *Anarchy, State and Utopia*. New York: Basic Books.

Okun, Arthur. 1981. *Prices and Quantities: A Macroeconomic Analysis.* Washington, D.C.: Brookings Institution.

Olson, Mancur. 1965. *The Logic of Collective Action.* Cambridge, Mass.: Harvard Univ. Press.

Olson, Mancur. 1982. *The Rise and Decline of Nations.* New Haven, Conn.: Yale Univ. Press.

Olson, Mancur. 1983a. "The Political Economy of Comparative Growth Rates." In *The Political Economy of Growth*, edited by Dennis C. Mueller, New Haven, Conn.: Yale Univ. Press.

Olson, Mancur. 1983b. "The South Will Fall Again: The South as Leader and Laggard in Economic Growth. *Southern Economic Journal* 49, no. 4 (April): 917–32.

Otani, Yoshihika. 1980. "Strategic Equilibrium of Tariffs in General Equilibrium." *Econometrica* 48 (April): 643–62.

Parfit, Derek. 1980. "Prudence, Morality, and the Prisoner's Dilemma." *Proceedings of the British Academy.*

Pelling, Henry. 1963. *A History of British Trade Unionism.* London: MacMillan.

Peltzman, S. 1976. "Toward a More General Theory of Regulation." *Journal of Law and Economics* 19 (August): 211–40.

Pinchbeck, Ivy. 1969. *Women Workers and the Industrial Revolution 1750–1850.* New York. Augustus M. Kelley.

Pollard, Sidney. 1963. "Factory Discipline in the Industrial Revolution." *Economic History Review*, 2nd series, 16, no. 2: 254–71.

Posner, Richard. 1970. *Economic Analysis of Law.* Boston: Little Brown.

Posner, Richard. 1975. "The Social Costs of Monopoly and Regulation." *Journal of Political Economy* 83 (August): 807–27.

Posner, Richard. 1981. *The Economics of Justice.* Cambridge, Mass.: Harvard Univ. Press.

Pryor, Frederic L. 1983a. "A Quasi-Test of Mancur Olson's Theory." In *The Political Economy of Growth*, edited by Dennis C. Mueller. New Haven, Conn.: Yale Univ. Press, pp. 90–105.

Pryor, Frederic L. 1983b. "Growth and Fluctuations of Production in O.E.C.D. and East European Nations." Swarthmore College. Mimeo.

Ratchford, B.U. 1941. *American State Debts.* Durham, N.C.: Duke Univ. Press.

Rawls, John. 1971. *A Theory of Justice.* Cambridge, Mass.: Harvard Univ. Press.

Reder, Melvin. 1979. "The Place of Ethics in the Theory of Production." In *Economics and Human Welfare: Essays in Honor of Tibor Scitovsky*, pp. 133–46. New York: Academic Press.

Redford, Arthur. 1968. *Labour Migration in England 1800-1850.* New York: Augustus M. Kelley.

Reich, Michael, and James Devine. 1981. "The Microeconomics of Conflict and Hierarchy in Capitalistic Production." *Review of Radical Political Economics* 12 (Winter): 27–45.

Riker, William H. 1962. *The Theory of Political Coalition.* New Haven, Conn.: Yale Univ. Press.

Riker, William H. 1982. *Liberalism against Populism.* San Francisco: Freeman.

Robertson, Wyndham. 1975. "Going Broke the New York Way." *Fortune* (August): 144–49; 212–14.

Robinson, Joan. 1933. *The Economics of Imperfect Competition.* London: MacMillan.

Samuels, Warren J. 1966. *The Classical Theory of Economic Policy.* Cleveland: World.

Samuels, Warren J. 1980. "Economics as a Science and Its Relation to Policy: The Example of Free Trade." *Journal of Economic Issues* 14 (March): 163–85.

Samuels, Warren J. 1981. "Maximization of Wealth as Justice: An Essay on Posnerian Law and Economics as Policy Analysis." *Texas Law Review* 60 (December): 147–72.

Sapir, Andre. 1983. "Foreign Competition, Immigration and Structural Adjustment." *Journal of International Economics* 14 (May): 381–94.

Scherer, F.M. 1983. "Research and Development and Declining Productivity Growth." *American Economic Review* 73 (2) (May): 215–18.

Schlosser, D.; C. Hoffman; A. Bauer; and G. Coleman. 1977. *Municipal Authorities in Pennsylvania.* Harrisburg, Pa.: State of Pennsylvania Department of Community Affairs.

Sen, Amartya. 1967. "Isolation, Assurance, and the Social Rate of Discount." *Quarterly Journal of Economics* 81: 112–24.

Sen, Amartya. 1977. "Rational Fools: A Critique of the Behavioral Foundations of Economic Theory." *Philosophy and Public Affairs* 6 (Summer): 317–44.

Siegan, Bernard H., ed. 1977. *The Interaction of Economics and the Law.* Lexington, Mass.: Lexington Books.

Siegan, Bernard H. 1980. *Economic Liberties and the Constitution.* Chicago: Univ. of Chicago Press.

Singer, Peter. 1973. "Attruism and Commerce: A Defense of Titmuss against Arrow." *Philosophy and Public Affairs* 2 (Spring): 312–20.

Small, Albion W. 1924. *Origins of Sociology.* Chicago: Univ. of Chicago Press.

Smith, Adam. 1776. *An Inquiry into the Nature and Causes of the Wealth of Nations.*

Sombard, Werner. 1904. "The Industrial Group." In *Economics, Politics, Jurisprudence, Social Science,* vol. 7. New York: Houghton Mifflin.

Sraffa, Pierro. 1926. "The Laws of Return Under Competitive Conditions." *Economic Journal* 36: 535–50.

Stigler, George J. 1957. "Perfect Competition, Historically Contemplated." *Journal of Political Economy* 65, no. 1 (February): 1–17.

Stigler, George J. 1961. "The Economics of Information." *Journal of Political Economy* 69, no. 3: 213–25.

Stigler, George J. 1982a. "The Economists and the Problem of Monopoly." *American Economic Review* 72 (May): 1–11.

Stigler, George J. 1982b. "Economics and Public Policy." *Regulation* (May–June): 13–17.

Stigler, George J. 1983. "The Economist as Preacher." In *The Economist as Preacher and Other Essays*. Chicago: Univ. of Chicago Press.

Taylor, George Rogers. 1951. *The Transportation Revolution, 1815–1860*. White Plains, N.Y.: M.E. Sharpe.

Temin, Peter. 1969. *The Jacksonian Economy*. New York: W.W. Norton.

Titmuss, Richard M. 1971. *The Gift Relationship: From Human Blood to Social Policy*. New York: Vintage Books.

Tollison, Robert D. 1982. "Rent Seeking: A Survey." *Kyklos* 35 (Fasc 4): 575–602.

Tullock, Gordon. 1967a. "The Welfare Costs of Tariffs, Monopolies and Theft." *Western Economic Journal* 5 (June): 224–32.

Tullock, Gordon. 1967b. *Toward a Mathematics of Politics*. Ann Arbor: Univ. of Michigan Press.

Tullock, Gordon. 1975. "The Transitional Gains Trap." *Bell Journal of Economics*. (Autumn): 671–75.

Tullock, Gordon. 1978. "The Backward Society: Static Inefficiency, Rent-Seeking and the Rule of Law." Working Paper no. CE 78–7–1. Blacksburg, Va.: Center for Study of Public Choice.

Tullock, Gordon. 1980. "Rent-Seeking as a Negative Sum Game." In *Toward a Theory of the Rent-Seeking Society*, edited by James M. Buchanan, Robert Tollison, and Gordon Tullock, pp. 16–36. College Station: Texas A&M Univ. Press.

Tunzelman, G.N. von. 1978. *Steam Power and British Industrialization to 1860*. Oxford: Clarendon Press.

Urban Areas: Housing, vol. 2. 1970. Shannon, Ireland: Irish Univ. Press.

Ure, Andrew. 1967. *The Philosophy of Manufactures: An Exposition of the Scientific, Moral, and Commercial Economy of the Factory System of Great Britain*. New York: Augustus M. Kelley.

U.S. Department of Commerce, Bureau of the Census, *Census of Governments*, various issues.

Vanek, Jaroslav. 1970. *The General Theory of Labor-Managed Market Economies*. Ithaca: Cornell Univ. Press.

Viner, Jacob. 1931. "Cost Curves and Supply Curves." *Zeitschrift für Nationalokonomie*: 23–46.

Ward, J.T. 1962. *The Factory Movement 1830–1855*. London. MacMillan.

Webb, Beatrice, and Sidney Webb. 1920. *The History of Trade Unionism*. London: Printed by the authors.

Williamson, Oliver E. 1980. "The Organization of Work: A Comparative Institutional Assessment." *Journal of Economic Behavior and Organization* 1 (March): 5–38.

Williamson, Oliver E.; Michael Z. Wachter; and Jeffery E. Harris. 1975. "Understanding the Employment Relation: The Analysis of Idiosyncratic Exchange." *Bell Journal of Economics* 6, no. 1 (Spring): 250–80.

Wing, Charles. 1967. *Evils of the Factory System Demonstrated by Parliamentary Evidence*. New York: Augustus M. Kelley.

Wood, L.S., and A. Wilmore. 1927. *The Romance of the Cotton Industry in England*. London: Oxford Univ. Press.

Young, Leslie. 1982. "Comment on Findlay and Wellisz." *Import Competition and Response*, edited by Jagdish Bhagwati, pp. 238–43. Chicago: Univ. of Chicago Press

Young, Leslie, and Stephen P. Magee. 1982. "A Prisoner's Dilemma Theory of Endogenous Tariffs." University of Texas at Austin. Mimeo (April).

Young, Leslie, and Stephen P. Magee. 1983. "Black Hole Tariffs with Politics, Rent Seeking and Uncertainty." University of Texas at Austin. Mimeo (March).

INDEX

255

LIST OF CONTRIBUTORS

Gary Anderson is currently a doctoral candidate at the Center for Study of Public Choice at George Mason University. His publications include articles on industrial organization, law and economics, economic history, and the history of economic thought. His current research focuses on empirical applications of the theory of the rent-seeking society.

James T. Bennett is Professor of Political Economy and Public Policy at George Mason University. His primary research interests include public policy issues, the economics of government and bureaucracy, and labor unions. He is author of four books, including *Underground Government: The Off-Budget Public Sector* (with Thomas DiLorenzo), more than a dozen monographs, and sixty journal articles. He is editor of the *Journal of Labor Research*.

Jagdish N. Bhagwati is probably the foremost international trade theorist today. Formerly at M.I.T., he is currently the Arthur Lehman Professor of Economics at Columbia University. He has written on trade theory, development theory and policy, internal and international migration, and educational models. He is an editor of the *Journal of International Economics* and author of the two-volume *Essays in International Theory* and (with T.N. Srinivasan) of *Lectures on International Trade*.

Richard A. Brecher is Professor of Economics at Carleton University in Ottawa, Canada. His research in the theory of international trade has been published in such journals as the *American Economic Review*, the *Journal of Political Economy*, and the *Quarterly Journal of Economics*. He is editor of the *Journal of International Economics*.

261

William A. Brock is currently the F. P. Ramsey Professor of Economics at the University of Wisconsin. He is a general economic theorist and has published over fifty articles and several books, and has given over 100 invited lectures around the world. He was a Sherman Fairchild Distinguished Scholar at Cal Tech in 1978 and was elected a Rumms Faculty Fellow at the University of Wisconsin at Madison in 1981.

Harold Demsetz is currently Professor of Economics at the University of California at Los Angeles. One of the founders of the "property rights" school of economics and the "new economics of institutions," he is known as one of the most interesting and provocative thinkers in economics. He is the author of a variety of articles and is a leader in the conservative economic rivival. His book *Economic, Legal and Political Dimensions of Competition* deals with many of these rent-seeking ideas.

Thomas J. DiLorenzo is Assistant Professor of Economics at George Mason University. He is coauthor of *Underground Government: The Off-Budget Public Sector* (1983) and *Labor Unions and the State* (1984). He has published numerous articles in such journals as the *American Economic Review, Public Finance Quarterly*, and the *International Review of Law and Economics.* He is an Adjunct Scholar of the Cato Institute.

Elias Dinopoulos has taught at Brown University and is presently Assistant Professor of Economics at Michigan State University. His research interests include the areas of imperfect competition and international trade, international factor mobility, and political economy of international trade restrictions.

Ronald Findlay is the Ragnar Nurkse Professor of Economics at Columbia University. He has written widely on economic subjects, including international trade theory, capital theory, and welfare economics, and is the author of the books, *Trade and Specialization* and *International Trade and Development Theory.*

Kenneth J. Koford is an Assistant Professor of Economics at the University of Delaware. His degrees are from Yale and U.C.L.A. He has done research on efficient vote-trading in legislatures, on the market for advertising and entertainment in cable television, and on incentive policies to reduce inflation.

Stephen P. Magee is the Fred H. Moore Professor, Department of Finance, at the University of Texas. Formerly of the University of California, Berkeley, and the University of Chicago, he is the author of *International Trade and Distortions in Factor Markets* (1976), *International Trade* (1980), and coauthor of

Endogenous Tariff Theory (1983). He bridges three schools: international trade theory, public choice theory, and international finance.

Michael S. McPherson is Professor of Economics at Williams College. He has written on ethical foundations of economics and on economics of education. He is coeditor of a new journal, *Economics and Philosophy.*

Nicholas Mercuro has been on the faculty of the University of New Orleans since 1976, where he is currently Associate Professor of Economics. He is the author of several articles in the area of law and economics and has undertaken studies on energy and environmental issues. He is presently coauthoring a book entitled *Law, Economics, and Public Policy.*

Douglass C. North is Luce Professor of Law and Liberty and Professor of Economics at Washington University (St. Louis). One of this country's leading economic historians, he has been a pioneer in theorizing about the development of economic institutions and is the author of *The Rise of the Western World* (with R.P. Thomas) and *Structure and Change in Economic History.*

Mancur Olson is the Distinguished Professor of Economics at the University of Maryland. He is past president of the Public Choice Society and the Southern Economic Association. He has published a number of books and articles, including, *The Rise and Decline of Nations* and *The Logic of Collective Action.*

Frederic L. Pryor is one of the leading specialists in the field of comparative economic systems. His books include: *The Communist Foreign Trade System; Public Expenditures in Communist and Capitalist Nations; The Origins of the Economy;* and *A Guidebook to the Comparative Study of Economic Systems.* Currently he is Professor of Economics at Swarthmore College.

Warren J. Samuels is Professor of Economics at Michigan State University. His principal areas of research include the history of economic thought; law and economics, including the theory of property, regulation, and the compensation principle; and public utility economics. He has been president of the History of Economics Society, editor of the *Journal of Economic Issues*, and a member of the editorial boards of *Southern Economic Journal*, and *Policy Studies Journal.* He also is editor of the research annual, *Research in the History of Economic Thought and Methodology*, and of the series, *Recent Economic Thought.* His books include *Law and Economics* (with A.A. Schmid), *The Classical Theory of Economic Policy*, and *Pareto on Policy.*

T. N. Srinivasan is the Samuel C. Park, Jr., Professor of Economics at Yale University and has written extensively on international trade theory. His most recent book is *Lectures on the Theory of International Trade* with J.N. Bhagwati.

Robert D. Tollison is Associate General Director of the Center for the Study of Public Choice and Professor of Economics at George Mason University. He was formerly director of the Bureau of Economics at the Federal Trade Commission. His publications cover a wide variety of subjects in virtually all areas of modern economics. He is President-Elect of the Southern Economics Association, and his most recent publication is *The Theory of Public Choice II*, coedited with James Buchanan.

Gordon Tullock was formerly University Distinguished Professor at Virginia Polytechnic Institute and is currently Professor of Economics at George Mason University. Besides being one of the founders of the public choice school of economics, he has written a wide variety of books, including *Politics of Bureaucracy* and *Toward a Mathematics of Politics*. Regardless of the subject he is always willing to take controversial and strongly conservative stands. He is currently editor of the *Journal of Public Choice*.

Stanislaw Wellisz is a Professor of Economics at Columbia University. He is one of the leading theorists in economic development and the theory of organization of the firm and is an expert on Eastern Europe. His publications include the book, *The Economics of the Soviet Bloc*, and articles in numerous journals on development and growth.

ABOUT THE EDITOR

David Colander is currently the Christian A. Johnson Professor of Economics at Middlebury College. He is a specialist in alternative approaches to macroeconomic stabilization policy and is the author of *MAP: A Market Anti-Inflation Plan* (together with Abba Lerner).